LEARN THE LANGUAGE OF THE HOLY QURAN

LEARN THE LANGUAGE OF THE HOLY QUR'ÃN

Dr. Abdullah Abbas Nadwi

KITAB BHAVAN
NEW DELHI-110002

Kitab Bhavan
Publishers, Distributors, Exporters & Importers
1784, Kalan Mahal, Darya Ganj
New Delhi-1100 02 (India)

Phone : (91-11) 23277392/93, 23274686, 30906494
Website : www.kitabhavan.com
Fax : (91-11) 23263383
Email : nasri@vsnl.com
Email : nusrat@bol.net.in

Edition 2007

ISBN : 81-7151-331-X

Published in India by:
Nusrat Ali Nasri for Kitab Bhavan
1784, Kalan Mahal, Darya Ganj
New Delhi-1100 02 (India)

Printed in India at :-
Nice Printing Press
Khureji Khas, Delhi-110051

CONTENTS

Chapter

PREFACE

Arabic, as the famous linguist A.L. Schlozer (d. 1781) has pointed out, belongs to the Semitic group of languages. more specifically, it is an off-shoot of the languages of south-west Arabia. While its origins lie buried in remote antiquity, by the third century (C.E.), Arabic had developed into a full-fledged language.

In our time most of the Semitic languages have disappeared. In addition to Arabic, the only living semitic languages are modern Hebrew, Amheric and a dialect of Aramaic. As for Arabic, it remains not only a fully alive language but also enjoys a unique importance. It alone can serve as the source of knowledge of all Semitic languages. whenever the grammarians of these languages are faced with intracate grammatical problems, they are forced to have recourse to consulting parallel grammatical rules in Arabic, particularly as they are exemplified in the Qur'an.* Moreover enormous change has taken place in the vocabulary of all semitic languages let alone change in word-meaning-that the present versions of these languages have little resemblance with their original versions. The only exception is Arabic, the language of the Qur'an which retains its old grammar, syntax and vocabulary, making it the archetype of the entire family of Semitic languages.

Since the language of the Qur'an is Arabic, it is the main source of knowledge about Islam. About 800 million Muslims of the world recite the Qur'an in its original language regardless of whether they understand it or not, and a good number of them do cherish the desire to comprehend the Qur'an without the medium of translation. Moreover, there are a large number of people around the globe who wish to learn this language because of its political importance, for it is official language of no less than the twenty-one member states of the Arab league. gradually the importance of Arabic has also been enhanced because of the

---

* Sabatino Moscati, **An Introduction to the Comparative Grammar of Semitic Studies**, amply illustrates this.

overwhelming importance of the Arab countires in international commerce and finance. Thanks to these, a number of text books and grammars for learning Arabic have been appearing in the western countires and the volume of these publications is on the increase. The authors of these works have taken pains to make the learning of the language easy for beginners. The process of learning that on encounters in these works appears some what mechanical for many of these authors because they had little appreciation for the literary beauty of Arabic. In the case of some one might even suspect that their instinctive prejudice against Arabic had led them to the conviction that it could not be presented in an interesting, systematic and simple manner. This being the state of affairs, it is the duty of Muslim scholars to make concerted efforts to prouduce good readers that would facilitate and speed up the process of learning Arabic for native speakers of English and other International languages. Unfortunately, this challenging task has not been taken up by many scholars, and mine is thus one of the very effort which have been to fill up the gap.

Professor Abdussalam Kidwai[✲] of india pioneered a method for teaching Arabic in 1942. His main idea was to make the Qur'an the prime source of teaching Arabiclanguage. He compiled a book consisting of ten primary lessons for this purpose and it proved very useful. the present work is an adaptation of the idea originated by professor Kidwai.[✲✲] His work was designated for Urdu-speaking adults of the Subcontinent who were acquainted with the Arabic alphabets, and with some Arabic vocabulary while attempting to present this language to English-speaking people, the present aouthor was in a far less advantagous position since the potential readership will presumably have no or very meager knowledge of Arabic alphabets and vocabulary. This made my task an exceedingly difficult one.

The lessons of this book have been arranged in simple grammatic classifications supported by verses of the Holy Qur'an as illustrations of the postulated rules in Phonology, Morphology and Syntax. It is an attempt to assist those who whish to acquire proficiency in this language for the sake of understanding the Qur'an. It is hoped that they will get used to the Qur'anci style

---

✲ Incharge of Education, Nadwatul Olma, Lucknow, India and Academic Secretary of Darul Musannifeen, (Shibli Academy), India.

✲✲ His way of explanation is also adopted in the first three chapters.

and language and in the process also be able to develop a degree of familarity with Arabic idiom as such.

This is an experimental attempt which, hopefully, will conduce to a speedier and easier learning of Arabic. The author has made efforts to cover all the essential elements for learning the language. It goes without saying that there will always be scope for improvement. Any suggestions or advice that would enable me to imporve this work will be more than welcome and will be greatly appreciated.

The author is greatly indebted to Mr. Sayyid Muhsin Ba-Roum* for publishing the first edition of this book through the famous publishing hose of Dar Al Shorouq, and also for writing its Foreward.

A. A. NADWI

---

* A well known educationist in Saudi Arabia.

FOREWORD
BY
SAYYID MUHSIN A. BA-ROUM

The Holy Qur'an was revealed to theHoly Prophet Muhammed (Peace be on him) so as to become an immortal source of guidance and inspiration for man's conduct, both individual and collective; an indispensable guide for man in his quest for a way of life based on justice, truth, righteousness, benevolence and moral excellence. This Book has been an inexhaustible spring which has quenched the thirst of knowledge of different classes of scholars and thinkers who have been trying down the ages to grasp the miraculous nature of the Qur'an form the grammatical and literary points of view, and have been struggling to fathom the rich meaning and the profound truths about the universe and life that this book embodies. The Qur'an has oberwhelmed people of different intellectual levels, and of diverse attitudes and temperaments who have lived in different ages and times and has truck them for its profound earnestness, its literary flourish and its unmistakably miraculous nature.

Arabic literature is full of works in the field of Qur'anic studies which have treated the above-mentioned subject. One of the subjects which has been a constant theme of our scholars is a study of theHoly Qur'an in order to deduce there form the correct grammatical rules for the Qur'an was revealed in clear Arabicspeech. This has guaranteed immortality for the Arabic language. History witnesses that Muslims have never ceased to relish reciting the verses of the Qur'an and reflecting upon their meaning.

My friend, Dr. Abdullah Abbas Nadwi, Assistant Professor of Arabicat King Abdul Aziz University (Mecca branch) undertook to write the present book in order to facilitate the learning of Arabic language for those who are not the native speakers of this language. In attempting to do so, he has drawn upon Qur'anic verses and Qur'anic passages in order to illustrate the rules of Arabic grammar. I hope the readers will agree with me that he has eminently succeeded in this task. In his exposition and explanation of grammatical rules, the author has followed the arrangement found in the books written for teaching Arabic to the native speakers of the language. This should help the non-Arabic-speaking students to practice Arabic grammar in the most adequate manner, to become familiar with its difficulties, and to develop command over the language for purposes of reading and writing.

I have no doubt that recourse to the berses of the Qur'an in trying to explain grammatical rules will be highly useful for the non-Arabic Muslim learners of Arabic language. Having been born in an Islamic environment, or having embraced it as a result of the attraction they found in it, they look upon Islam as the guiding principle of their life. It is this which developed in them the longing to learn the language of the Qur'an and to enjoy the lustrous beauty of the Qur'anic rhetoric, the candour and sharpness of its style and to grasp the profound wisdom of the Qur'anic teachings.

The work of Dr. Nadwi accomplishes remarkably well the numerous spiritual, intellectual and educational purposes which he had set out to accomplish. He has also taken care to avoid verbal extravagance and dilettantism and has attempted to make the book as easy and simple as possible. He indeed deserves the gratitude of the world of learning for the great contribution he has made to the Arabic language.

THE ALPHABETS

The Arabic Alphabets (حُرُوفُ الهِجَاءِ huruful hejaa) consist of 28 letters (29 if hamza is counted as a separate letter). Three of them: وَاو waw, أَلِفْ 'alif and ى ya are used as long vowels or dipthongs and also as weak consonants.

The following table shows the various forms of these letters according to whether the letter is isolated ,initial, medial or final.

Care shall be taken to distinguish letters which are similar to each other in form and differ in districal points or dots.

Name of the Letter and Transcription	Isolated Form	Preceding Letter	Medial Letter	Succeeding Letter
ألف 'alif a	أ	أ	ـأ	أ
باء baa b	ب	ـب	ـبـ	بـ
تاء taa t	ت	ـت	ـتـ	تـ
ثاء thaa th	ث	ـث	ـثـ	ثـ
جيم jeem j	ج	ـج	ـجـ	جـ
حاء haa h	ح	ـح	ـحـ	حـ
خاء **khaa kh**	خ	ـخ	ـخـ	خـ
دال daal d	د	ـد	ـد	د
ذال **dhaal dh**	ذ	ـذ	ـذ	ذ
راء raa r	ر	ـر	ـر	ر

Name of the Letter and Transcription	Isolated Form	Preceding Letter	Medial Letter	Succeeding Letter
زاى zaa z	ز	ـز	ـز	ز
سين seen s	س	ـس	ـسـ	سـ
شين sheen sh	ش	ـش	ـشـ	شـ
صاد saad s	ص	ـص	ـصـ	صـ
ضاد daad d	ض	ـض	ـضـ	ضـ
طاء taa t	ط	ـط	ـطـ	طـ
ظاء zaa z	ظ	ـظ	ـظـ	ظـ
عين ain	ع	ـع	ـعـ	عـ
غين ghain gh	غ	ـغ	ـغـ	غـ
فاء faa f	ف	ـف	ـفـ	فـ

Name of the Letter and Transcription		Isolated Form	Preceding Letter	Medial Letter	Succeeding Letter
قاف	qaaf q	ق	ـق	ـقـ	قـ
كاف	kaaf k	ك	ـك	ـكـ	كـ
لام	laam l	ل	ـل	ـلـ	لـ
ميم	meem m	م	ـم . ـم	ـمـ	مـ
نون	nun n	ن	ـن	ـنـ	نـ
هاء	haa h	ه	ـه	ـهـ . ـهـ	هـ
واو	waw w	و	ـو	ـو	و
ياء	yaa y	ى	ـى	ـيـ	يـ

VOWELS

Arabic has four short vowels:

fatha	signed as ــَــ on the top of a letter and pronounced as **a** in " **a**bove ".
kasra	signed as ــِــ on the beneath of a letter and pronounced as **e** in " **e**nergy ".
ḍamma	signed as ــُــ on the top of a letter and pronounced as ' **o** ' in " **o**pera ".
sukun	signed as ــْــ or ــۡــ on the top of a letter is a stop or closed letter vowellen

For the transcription (a) stands for fatha (i) for kasra and (u) for ḍamma.

Long vowels or dipthongs are three:

ألف	' alif
واو	wow
ياء	yaa

Examples:

عَالِمٌ	aalimun , learned man.
كَاتِبٌ	kaatibun , writer.
نَائِمٌ	naa ء imun , sleeping one.
بَعِيدٌ	baعidun far
سَعِيدٌ	saعidun proper name
يَعُودُ	yaعud (3rd Pers. Imperfect) , he returns or will return.
مَمْنُونٌ	mamnun (Part Passive) an obliged one.
يَكُونُ	yakunu (Imperfect , 3rd Pers.) he is or will be.

Students should carefully note all the signs on the following letters.

ثْ	ثُ	ثِ	ثَ
جْ	جُ	جِ	جَ
دْ	دُ	دِ	دَ
رْ	رُ	رِ	رَ
شْ	شُ	شِ	شَ

EXERCISE

أَ	أَخ	أَب	أَرض
إِ	إِذا	إِلى	إِله
أُ	أُم	أُخت	أُسرة
أْ	اِبدأْ	اِملأْ	اِهدأْ

بَ	بَدأَ	بَاب	كتبَ
بِ	أَبِى	كتابِى	بِسم
بُ	أَبُوك	بُشرىٰ	كتبُوا
بْ	اركبْ	اكتبْ	اذهبْ

تَ	تَرك	تَعب	نبتَ
تِ	بيتي	بنتِي	تِمساح
تُ	أكلتُ	فهمتُ	تُفاح
تْ	ذهبتْ	قالتْ	رجعتْ

HAMZAH

1.Hamzah is a separate letter that should not be mixed up with alif. For alif is always vowelless i.e. it has sukun only, e.g.:

ما maa - لا laa - حا ḥaa- خا **kh**aa etc.

While Hamzah joins its following letter with a short vowel ,e.g. أُخْتٌ **ukh**tun , sister, إِبْنٌ ibnun, son, أَرْضٌ ardun, earth.

2.There are four types of the writing a hamzah:

I.Initial hamzah is always written **on** or **under** alif, e.g.:

إِعْلَمْ	iعalam, know! or make known (kasra vowelled)
أَصْغَرُ	as**gh**ar, smaller than ...(fatha vowelled)
أُنْصُرْ	unsur, help! (damma vowelled)

II.The final Hamzah is written at the end of a dipthong e.g.:

بَــدَأَ	badaء**a** to start.
لُــؤْلُؤ	luءlu ء a pearl.
شَاطِئٌ	**sh**ati ء shore.

III.Hamzah occurring after a long alif will be written on the line as a separate letter as:

هَوَاء	hawae ء , air.
حَوَّاء	ḥawwa ء , eve.
بَطْحَاء	baṭhaa ء , sandy land.

IV.The medial hamzah is written on (ا) **alif** if the preceding letter is vowelled with fatha, on و **waw** if it is preceded by a ḍamma vowelled letter, and on ى **ya** if the preceding letter has kasra, e.g.

قَرَأَ	qara ء a, to read.
بَطُؤَ	batu ء a, to become lazy.
قُرِئَ	quri ء a, it is read (Passive).

3.The initial Hamzah of the definite article أَل **al** is termed as هَمْزَةُ الوَصْلِ hamzatul wasl, Hamzah of connection, written and pronounced when occurs at the begining of a sentence e.g.:

اَلْقرآن يَهدِى إِلَى الخَيْرِ	The Qur`an guides to the good.

but it is omitted when a word having an article ال **al** is preceded by another, e.g. (From the Holy Qur'an)

هُوَ اللهُ الخَالِقُ الْبَارِئُ المُصَوِّرُ لَهُ الأَسْمَاءُ الْحُسْنَى يُسَبِّحُ لَهُ مَا فِي السَّمَوَاتِ وَالأَرْضِ وَهُوَ العَزِيزُ الحَكِيمُ	**59-24** He is Allah, the Creator, the Shaper out of naught, the Fashioner His are the most beautiful names. All that is in the heavens and the earth glorifieth Him and He is the Mighty, the Wise.

It is opposed to the ordinary Hamza cailed همزة القطع Hamzatulqatع It is always written and pronounced, e.g.

إبْنِ لِي صَرْحًا
أُدعُ إِلَى سَبِيل رَبِّكَ بِالْحِكْمَةِ والمَوْعِظَةِ الْحَسَنَةِ
أَبْشِرُوا بِالْجَنَّةِ .

EXERCISE

The Nunation (Tanween)

See Chapter 1

أ

أٌ	إٍ	أً
مبـدأٌ	مبـدإٍ	مبـدأً

ب

بٌ	بٍ	بـاً
بابٌ	بابٍ	باباً

ج

جٌ	جٍ	جاً
زجاجٌ	زجاجٍ	زجاجاً

SHADDAH

Shaddah is a sound of double consonant, e.g. in English a words such as irregular or innocent etc. but in Arabic one letter is not written twice, it is written single with a mark of Shaddah, above the letter, that means this letter should be pronounced twice. e.g. مَرَّ marra, instead of writing مَرْرَ or قَلَّ instead of writing قَلْلَ This type of verbs have appearance of being biliteral, e.g. Hajja, حجَّ jarra, جرَّ marra, مرَّ etc.

The following table should be carefully exercised by the students:

بُّ	بِّ	بَّ	بَ
ربُّه	ربِّى	ربَّك	

لُّ	لِّ	لَّ	لَ
يقلُّ	معلِّم	علَّم	

نُّ	نِّ	نَّ	نَ
يرنُّ	إنِّى	إنَّه	

MADDA

آ

If a Hamza, vowelled with fatha, is followed by the long vowel; alif (the hamzated fatha) is dropped in writing and the long vowel alif is written over the alif horizontally as آ **aa**, this sign is called Madda and occurs chiefly at the begining of a sentence such as: قُرآن , instead of writing قُرْاان or رآه instead of راَاه

SOME IMPORTANT RULES OF ARABIC CHARACTERS

1.In the Arabic characters ,the third letter تاْء Taa is written in its preceding form as ـت and ـة (ة). The former is called تاء المفتوحة Taa al Maftuha that is used in writing Pronouns as you will learn latter. The latter ـة or ة is called تاء المربوطة which occurs as feminine ending and turns to **haa** sound (26th letter) when is put at the end of a sentence , for example :

The تاء taa in الجنة is المربوطة of feminine ending , and it is to be vocalized clearly with its vowel . But if this word happens to occur at the end of a sentence it will be read جَنَّهْ jannah instead of جَنَّةٌ or الجَنَّةُ

2.When the ال **al** of the article is prefixed to a word , in certain letters its **lam** (ل) is pronounced clearly , they are :

ق ، ب ، ج ، ح ، خ ، م ، و ، ه ، ى

This group of letters is called حروف القمرية huruful qamariyatu as in the word القمر (q) belongs to this group .

Letters in which the **lam** (ل) of the article is not pronounced and the preceding letter is assimilated to the letter which occurs after **lam** (ل) of the article with a **shadda**, is called حروف الشَّمْسِيَّة as the letter ش belongs to the group of these letters . They are :

ن ، ل ، ط ، ظ ، ص ، ض ، ش ، س ، ر ، ز ، ذ ، د ، ث ، ت

Vocalize the follwoing words and compare each to the other.

الرَّجُلُ arrajulu	الإِنسَانُ alinsaanu
الذَّهَبُ **adh dh**ahabu	البُرَادُ alburaadu
الشَّمْسُ **ash sh**amsu	القرآن al Qur'anu

3.The first letter ألف is written as illustrated in the table. Besides there is another form of writing it i.e. a small sign (ٰ) put on Yaa the final letter as هُدٰى hudaa, instead of writing هُدًا it is called ألف المقصورة alif maqsuratu. In the modern printing this sign (ىٰ) is omitted, only **Fatḥa** sign on the succeding letter indicates the type of pronunciation.

Thus هُدَى (i.e. the **yaa** without vowelling) is enough.

CHAPTER 1

THE NOUN AND THE ARTICLE

1. The Noun:

مُحَمَّد Mohammad , حَامِد Hamid , مَحْمُود Mahmood , بَشِير Bashir , نَاصِر Nasir and خَالِد Khalid are the names of persons. They are called Proper Nouns.

In a formal Language this type of name is pronounced with a suffix of a **nun** sound. Thus: The word 'Mohammad' will be pronounced as مُحَمَّدٌ Mohammad**un** and

حَامِد	Hamid	as	حَامِدٌ	Hamid**un**.
محمود	Mahmood	as	مَحْمُودٌ	Mahmood**un**
بَشِير	Bashir	as	بَشِيرٌ	Bashir**un**.
نَاصِر	Nasir	as	نَاصِرٌ	Nasir**un**.
خَالِد	Khalid	as	خَالِدٌ	Khalid**un**.

The **nun** sound , say "Nunization " is marked here as "un " ; it may be changed to "in " or "an " according to the noun in the construction of a sentence as will be explained Later.

Common nouns such as شَجَر **Shajar** : tree , حَجَر **Hajar** stone , تُفَّاح **tuffah** : an apple , بَيْت **bait**: house , رَب **Rabb**: Lord , رَسُول **Rasool**: messenger , are also subject to the nunization , unless an article أَل is prefixed. In case a word is made preoper noun through prefixing أَل (al), The nunization will be removed. Compare:

شَجَرٌ	shajarun	as	الشَّجَرُ	ashshajaru
حَجَرٌ	Hajarun	as	الحَجَرُ	alhajaru
تُفَّاحٌ	tuffahun	as	أَلتُّفَّاحُ	attuffahu
بيتٌ	baitun	as	اَلْبيتُ	albaitu
كِتابٌ	Kitabun	as	ألكِتابُ	alkitabu

2. The Article:

Arabic has only one definite article to turn a common noun into a proper one , i. e. أَل **al** as it is illustrated above. The indefiniteness of a common noun is indicated by **nunization.** Thus تُفَّاحٌ tuffah**un** means any apple , while التُّفَّاحُ **attuffahu** means a particular apple. The informal usage of noun is free from nunization. Also it occurs only on a singular and a word of Arabic origin. Thus a non - Arabic word or dual or plural will not be suffixed with nun sound.

3. Gender:

Arabic has two genders i. e. masculine and feminine. There is no common gender in this Language as in English.

A common sign of a feminine noun is " ة ta " that is to be suffixed to the final letter of a noun , e.g.

عَاقِلٌ	ع aaqilun	a wise man	Masc.
عاقِلَةٌ	ع aaqilatun	a wise woman	Fem.
نَافِعٌ	nafe ع un	useful person or thing.	Masc.
نَافِعَةٌ	nafe ع atun	a usueful woman or thing.	Fem.
عَالِمٌ	ع aalimun	a man of Knowledge	Masc.
عَالِمَةٌ	ع aalimatun	a woman of Knowledge	Fem.
مَحْمُودٌ	mahmoodun	a praised person.	Masc.
مَحْمُودَةٌ	mahmoodatun	a praised person.	Fem.

This " ة ta " of feminine gender is changed into a " ه ha " sound in speech ; also in formal language when it occurs at the end of a sentence e.g.:

كَانَتْ ضَرْبَةً قَاضِيَهْ the stroke was decisive.

Example From The Holy Qur'an

ادْخُلوا فِى السِّلْمِ كَافَّهْ	2-208 (People !) Enter in peace together.

The feminine gender nouns كَافَّهْ and قَاضِيَهْ were كَافَّةً and قَاضِيَةً respectively but their ة ta ' has been changed to ه ha because they occurd at end of the sentence.

4. Numbers:

Apart from singular and plural numbers which is common to

all Languages , Arabic has an additional number , between singular and plural that is " the dual " for two. e.g.:

Singular	Dual	Plural
مُسْلِمٌ muslimun	مُسْلِمَانِ muslimaane	مُسْلِمُونَ muslimuna
كَاتِبٌ Katibun	كَاتِبَانِ Katibaane	كَاتِبُونَ Katiboona
قَادِمٌ Qadimun	قَادِمَانِ Quadimane	قَادِمُونَ Qadimoona

In case of a feminine gender the additional infixed vowel shows the number i. e. " **aane** " or " **una** ". This takes place after ة 'ta' of feminine gender , thus:

Masculine	Feminine
مُسْلِمٌ Muslimun	مُسْلِمَةٌ Muslimatun
مُسْلِمَانِ Muslimaane	مُسْلِمَتَانِ Muslimataane

But the plural مُسْلِمُونَ ' muslimoona ' will be turned to ' مُسْلِمَاتٌ muslimatun ' e.g.

	Singular	Dual	Plural
Masc.	قَادِمٌ Qadimun	قادِمانِ Qadimane	قَادِمُونَ Qadimoona
Fem.	قَادِمَةٌ Qadimatun	قادمَتان Qadimatane	قادماتٌ Qadimatun
Masc.	كَاتِبٌ Katibun	كَاتبانِ Katibaane	كَاتبونَ Katiboona
Fem	كَاتِبَةٌ Katibatun	كَاتِبَتَان Katibataane	كَاتباتٌ Katibaatun

EXERCISE

1. Write in Arabic and put ' nunization ' accordingly:
   Khalid , Sharif , Nasar , Habib , Rashid , Ali , Fatimah , Obaid , Rashidah , Karim , ع aliah , Hussain.

2. Write the following names with and without article أل al:

بيتٌ	House	دار	House	حُجْرَةٌ	Room
سَقْفٌ	Roof	جِدَارٌ	Wall	أرضٌ	Earth
سَماءٌ	Heaven	فردوسٌ	Paradise	نارٌ	Fire
رسولٌ	Messenger	قرآنٌ	Qur'an	نافِعٌ	useful one
رافِعٌ	Rafe ع un	رَحِيمٌ	Merciful	فَضْلٌ	Kind

3. State the dual number of the following nouns with genders:

كاتِبٌ ، شَاعِرٌ ، طَبِيبٌ ، طَبَّاخٌ ، نَجَّارٌ ، حكيمٌ

4. Mention the plural form of these

مُسْلِمٌ ، مُؤمِنٌ ، عاقِلٌ ، حكيمٌ ، شهيدٌ ، سائقٌ ، شاعِرٌ ، خطيبٌ ،كاتبٌ

CHAPTER 2.

THE SIMPLE NOMINATIVE SENTENCES

رَسُولٌ	Rassoolun	Messenger
واسِعٌ	Waaseعun	Wide
رَبٌّ	Rubbun	Lord
خَلِيْفَةٌ	Khalifatun	Caliph
ناضِجٌ	Naadijun	Ripe
حكِيْمٌ	Hakeemun	A wise man
كريمٌ	Karimun	A kind man
صادِقٌ	Saadiqun	A true man
دِينٌ	Dinun	Religion
لذيذٌ	Ladhidhun	Delicious
شاعِرٌ	Shaaعirun	A poet

خالِدٌ حكيمٌ	Khalid is a wise man.
بَشِيرٌ شاعِرٌ	Bashir is a poet.

مَحْمُودٌ عالمٌ	Mahmood is a learned man.
حامِدٌ كريمٌ	Hamid is a kind man.
مُحَمَّدٌ رَسُولٌ	Mohammad is the Messenger.

1. This type of sentences are formed by two nouns. The first word of each sentence is a proper name (marked with " un " Nunization) that needs no article أل. The second word which qualifies the predicate , is a common noun. To form such sentences you have only to 'nunize' the last letters of both words and remove 'is , a , an , ' of English construction. Thus if you want to translate:

Hafiz is a poet. & Ali is a writer,

1. Put the Arabic word شَاعِرٌ for poet, (the common noun) and كَاتِبٌ for writer (the common noun).
2. Nunize the endings of each word so that will be :

حافظٌ شاعِرٌ	Hafizun Shaa ع erun
علىٌ كاتِبٌ	ع aliun katibun.

2. In case the first word (the subject of the sentences) is not a proper noun, the article أل will be prefixed while the second word will remain 'nunized' , thus :

أَلقُرآنُ كتابٌ	al Qur`anu kitabun	Qur`an is a book.
أَلإسلامُ دينٌ	al-Islamu deenun	Islam is a religion.
الرَّسُول صادقٌ	ar-rasoolu sadiqun	The messenger is a true man.

There should be an agreement in number and gender between subject and predicate i - e.

If a subject is a feminine , dual or plural , the predicate should be same accordingly.

EXAMPLES

Sing.Masce.

سعيدٌ عالِمٌ	Saعeedun عaalimun	saeed (A proper name) is a learned man.

Sing.Masc.

الطَّالِبُ مُجتَهِدٌ	Attaalibu mujtahidun	The student is a hard worker.

Sing.Fem.

سَعِيدَةٌ عالِمَةٌ	Saعeedatun عaalimatun	Saeeda (A proper name) is a learned woman.

Sing.Fem.

الطَّالبَةُ مُجتَهِدَةٌ	Attalibatu mujtahidatun	The student (F) is a hard worker.

Dual Masc.

الرَّجلانِ مُؤمِنَانِ	arrajulaane mominane.	The (two) men are believers.

Dual Fem.

الطَّالِبَتَانِ مُجتَهِدتَانِ	attalibatane mujtahidatane	The(Two-F)students are hard workers.

Plur.Masc.

الرِّجالُ مؤمنونَ	arrijaalu mominoona	(All) men are believers.

Plur.Fem.

الطَّالباتُ مجتهداتٌ	attalibatu mujtahidatun	The students (F) are hard workers.

RULES

1. A complete sentence formed by nouns i.e. a simple Nominal sentence is called in Arabic جملة إسمية 'Jumlatun Ismiyatun'. or al Jumlatul Ismiyatu اَلْجُملَةُ الاسْمِيةُ

   It has مُبتَدا Mubtada (Subject) and خَبَّرٌ 'khabarun' (Predicate).

2. Predicate should agree with the subject in number and gender.

EXERCISE

1. Translate into Englis:

اللهُ رَبٌّ ، مُحَمَّدٌ رَسُولٌ ، اَلْقُرْآنُ كِتَابٌ ، اَلْجَنَّةُ حَقٌّ ، اَلنَّارُ حَقٌّ ،
اَلدِّينُ حَقٌّ ، الدُّنْيَا فَانِيَةٌ ، الآخِرَةُ بَاقِيَةٌ ، الخُلَفَاء صَادِقُونَ ، اَلنِّسَاءُ
مُؤْمِنَاتٌ ، اَلْمَرْأَةُ تَقِيَّةٌ ، البِنْتُ مُؤَدَّبَةٌ ، الرِّسَالَة سَمَاوِيَّةٌ ، اَلْكَعْبَة قِبْلَةٌ ،
اَلْعِلْم نُورٌ ، اَلْجَهْلُ ظَلَامٌ ، اَلْحَدِيثُ صَحِيحٌ ، اَلْجَواب كَامِلٌ ،
الخَطِيبُ وَاعِظٌ ، العَبْدُ مُطِيعٌ ، اَلْحُكُومَةُ إِسْلَامِيَّةٌ ، اَلشَّرِيعَةُ نَافِعَةٌ ،
الرِّجَالُ قَوَّامُونَ ، اَلْجَنَّتَانِ عَالِيَتَانِ ، اَلْبَابَانِ وَاسِعَانِ ، اَلْكَلِمَتَانِ
خَفِيفَتَانِ ، اَلْمُؤْمِنَاتُ قَانِتَاتٌ ، اَلْبَنَاتُ حَافِظَاتٌ

2. Translate into Arabic:

Hamid is a wise man.
The physician is clever.
The translation is excellent.
Fatima is a learned (woman)
The boy is tall.
Both of two boys are successful.
Both of the two travellers are coming.
The wealth is gone (ذاهِبَةٌ)
Houses are large.

The believer women are fortunate.

Hafiz is a poet.

Both of the two friends are

Close (to each other) use: (قَرِيْبَانِ)

Rashid is a traveller.

The surgeon is an expert (one)

The work is useful.

The house is wide.

The girl is small.

Habib is a surgeon.

The faith is firm. (ثابِت)

Both of the two (female) students are hard workers.

Streets are narrow.

The way is clean.

Both of the two sisters are God-fearing (تَقِيَّتَانِ)

3. (*a*) Form dual forms of the following words :

الجَنَّةُ ، الخَلِيفَةُ ، أَلْمَرأَةُ ، مُؤَدَّبَةٌ ، سَماوِيَّةٌ ، الحديثُ ، الجَوابُ ، الخَطِيْبُ

(*b*) Write the singular of the following words :

الرِّجَال ، المؤمِنَاتُ ، البابانِ، أَلنِّسَاءُ ، أَلْخُلَفَاءُ ، أَلْعِبَادُ ، الْخطَبَاء ، الجَنَّاتُ ، الرَّاشِدُون ، القَانِتَاتُ

(c) Write the plurals of the following words :

الكتابُ ، صَادِقٌ ، ثَابتٌ ، ألجِدَارُ ، ألدَّارُ ، ألبَيْتُ ، ألقَلَمُ

4. Make ten sentences from the following:-

احمد .. صَادِقَةٌ .. الصَّباحُ .. اللَيلُ .. شاعر .. ألأُخت .. المَسَاءُ .. النَّهَارُ ..

VOCABULARY

الجَنَّةُ	Heaven
حَقٌّ	Fact, True
الآخِرَة	The hereafter
فانِيَةٌ/فانى	Going, Gone
الخُلَفَاءُ	Caliphs
النِّسَاءُ	Women
سَمَاوِيَّةٌ/سماوى	Heavenly
العِلْمُ	Wisdom, knowledge
ظَلامٌ	Darkeness
الوَلَدُ	The boy
صَحِيحٌ	Right

كَامِلٌ	Complete
وَاعِظٌ	Advisor of good things preacher
مُطِيْعٌ	Obedient
الشَّرِيْعَةُ	The Islamic law
اَلنَّارُ	The Hell
الدُّنيَا	The world
باقٍ/بَاقِيَةٌ	Remaining
الرِّسَالَةُ	The message
خَلِيفَةٌ	Caliph
المَرأَةُ	Woman :
القبلة	Direction of prayers
نُورٌ	Light
البِنْتُ	The girl
الحَدِيثُ	The talk
الجوّاب	Answer
الخَطِيْبُ	The Speaker
العبد	The slave of Allah
الحُكُومَةُ	The government

CHAPTER 3

THE POSSESSIVE CASE OR GENETIVE

God's messenger. Prophets's order. Girl's school. Hamid's House. Khalid's book. Men's souls. In English this kind of sentences are formed with nouns by adding a simple apostrophe (s) (---'s) to the singular and the irregular plurals (e. g. men's souls). to form this kind of sentences in Arabic we have to follow the rules below:.

1.A. Replace the English words by the Arabic words ; e.g.
God=Allah أَللهُ Messenge r = رَسُولٌ rasul
Prophet=Nabi نبيٌّ Girl = بِنْتٌ bint
Men=Bashar or nass بَشَرٌ bashar نَاسٌ naas

B. Interchange the place of words i.e the word which occrus first in English, put it latter and vice versa ,thus God's messenger in Arabic will be: رسول/اللهِ

C. Omit the apostrophe ('s)
Thus God's messenger will become in Arabic " messenger God " e. g. رسولُ اللهِ rasulullahi and Prophet's order will be read: order prophet أَمرُ النَّبِي, amrunnabi.

D. Put a short 'u' vowel sign (ـُ) on the final letter of the first vowel e.g. in above sentences:

Rasulullah رسولُ اللهِ. The Lam of رسول is the point of damma (ضمه).°°

E. Put a short 'i' vowel sign (ِ) on the final letter of the second name , that is "ha" in the word " Allah " of this sentence. Thus Rasulullahi رسولُ اللهِ would be exact translation of God's messenger.

The second sentence is Prophet 's order, after applying the above process, it would be in Arabic أمْرُ النَّبِي

Note

The first noun is called مُضَافٌ "mudaf". It will remain always as a common noun and in no case will take an article. but the second noun that is مُضَافٌ إِلَيْهِ "mudaf elaih" should be proper noun or be particularized by ال as shown above in نبي which is read النّبي

2. The another form of genitive in English is formed by using a particle 'of' between two nouns e.g. House of Lords. Land of Peace, fieldof actaivity etc .In Arabic there is no particle of this kind. The rule mentioned above will be applied here too, but you need not to interchange the places of nouns. Thus House of Lords will be rendered in Arabic.

دار = house, الأمراء lords:

°° The final letter of each word is the point where vowel is changed according to the formation of a sentence it is called اعراب i ع raab (declension) that will be dealt in chapter 22.

House of Lords	دارُ الأُمَرَاءِ	daarulomara-i
Land of Peace	أَرْضُ السلام	ardussealaami
Field of Activity	مَيدَانُ النِّشَاطِ	maidaanunnishati

Examples From The Holy Qur'an

رَسُولُ اللهِ	Allah 's messenger.
نَاقَةُ اللهِ	Allah 's she- camel.
حَدِيثُ الجُنودِ	the story of the hosts.
عذابُ الحَرِيقِ	The Chastisement of burning
حِزْبُ الشَّيْطَانِ	The group of satan.
عذَابُ النَّارِ	The chastisement of the Fire.
صَاحِبُ الحُوتِ	The companion of fish.
يومُ الفَصْلِ	The day of decision.
نَصْرُ اللهِ	Allah's help.
لَيْلَةُ القَدْرِ	The night of power.
حَبُّ الحَصِيدِ	The grain of crops.
أَصْحَابُ السَّعيرِ	The people of the Hell.

EXERCISE

1. Translate into Arabic:

A. The teacher's son.
The girl 's dress.
The house of Allah.
The door of house.
Ahmad 's pen.
The eyes of the bird.
The wood of the chair.
The merchant's shop.
The boy's school.
The book of Islam.
The pen of the writer.
Hamid's watch.
Bird's eye.
President's chair.

B. with the combination of chapter 11.
The teacher's son is a student.
(The) merchant's shop is (a) big (one).

Note **words in brackets are not to be followed in Arabic.**

The girl's dress is fine.
The boy's school is (a) famous (one).
The pen of the writer is known.
Allah's book is Qur 'an
the messenger's tradition is Sunnah.
The King's order is to be obeyed.
Ramadan 's fasting is prescribed.
The morining pryaer is a must .
Mohammad is Allah's Messenger.
Qur 'an is Allah 's book.

2. Translate into English:

A. حَدِيثُ الرَّسُولِ ، يَوْمُ الدِّينِ ، أَصْحَابُ الْيَمِينِ ، اَصْحَابُ الْأُخْدُودِ ، اَصْحَابُ الْكَهْفِ ، سَوط عَذَابٍ ، شَرُّ الْبَرِيَّةِ ، اَصْحَابُ الْفِيل ، مِثْقَالُ ذَرَّةٍ ، حَدِيثُ الغَاشِيَةِ ، عِمَارَةُ الْمَسْجِدِ ، نضْرَةَ النَّعِيمِ ، كِتَاب الفُجَّار ، نكَال الآخرَةِ ، فَكُّ رَقَبَةٍ ، سقَايَةُ الحَاجِ ، وَادِ النَّمْلِ ،

B. حَدِيثُ الرَّسُولِ مَعْلُومٌ ، يَومُ الدِّين شَدِيدٌ ، أَصْحَابُ الْيُمينِ مُسْلِمُونَ ، أَصْحَابُ الأُخْدُودِ مَيِّتُونَ ، أَصْحَابُ الْكَهْفِ شَبَابٌ ، أَصْحَابُ الفِيلِ خَاسِرُونَ

3. Compare between two sentences and mention difference between them

فَكُّ رَقَبَةٍ ، فَكُّ الرَّقَبَةِ ، عِمَارَةُ مَسْجِدٍ ، عِمَارَةُ الْمَسْجِدِ ، كِتَابُ الفُجَّارِ ، كِتَابُ فَاجِرٍ ، سَوْطُ عَذَابٍ ، سَوْطُ العَذَابِ

4. Correct the following sentences if there is any mistake

حَدِيثُ الرَّسُول مَعْلُومٌ ، حَدِيث الآخرَةِ مَعْلُومَةٌ ، سَوطُ العَذَابِ شَدِيدٌ ، أَصْحَابُ الفِيلِ رِجَالٌ ، شَمْسُ النَّهَارِ طَالِعٌ ، ضَوْءُ الْقَمَرِ مَطْلُوبٌ ، خَالَةُ حَمِيدٍ قَادِمٌ ، عَمَّ مَحْمُودٍ ذَاهِبَةٌ

VOCABULARY

Teacher	مُعَلِّمٌ	Mu ع allimun			
Merchant	تَاجِرٌ	Tajirun	Pl.	Tujjaarun	تُجَّارٌ
Girl	بِنْتٌ	Bintun	Pl.	Banatun	بَنَاتٌ
Boy	وَلَدٌ	Waladun	Pl.	Aulaadun	أَوْلَادٌ
House	دَارٌ	Daarun	Pl.	Diarun-Doorun	دُورٌ- دِيَارٌ
House	بَيتٌ	Baitun	Pl.	Buyootun	بُيُوتٌ
Book	كتابٌ	Kitaabun	Pl.	Kutubun	كُتُبٌ
Door	بَابٌ	Baabun	Pl.	Abwaabun	أَبْوابٌ
Pen	قَلَمٌ	Qalamun	Pl.	Aqlamun	أَقْلَامٌ
Writer	كَاتِبٌ	Kaatibun	Pl.	Kuttabun	كُتَّابٌ
Watch	سَاعَةٌ	Saaعatun	Pl.	Saaعaatun	سَاعَاتٌ
Eye	عَيْنٌ	Eainun	Pl.	عeyoonun	عُيُونٌ
Wood	خَشَبٌ	Khashabun	Pl.	Akhshaabun	أَخْشَابٌ
Chair	كُرْسِيٌّ	Kursiun	Fl.	Karaasiun	كَرَاسِيٌّ
President	الرَّئِيسُ	Raieesun	Pl.	Ru'asaaun	رُؤَسَاءٌ
Student	الطَّالِبُ	Tallibun	Pl.	Tullabun	طُلَّابٌ
Shop	دُكَّانٌ	Dukkanun	Pl.	Dakaakeenun	دَكَاكِينٌ

King	مَلِكٌ	Malikun	Pl.	Mulookun	مُلُوكٌ
Order	أمْرٌ	Amrun	Pl.	Awaamirun	أوَامِرٌ
Prescribed	فَرْضٌ	Fardun	Pl.	Furoodun	فُرُوضٌ
Obligatory	واجب	Waajibun	Pl.	Waajibaatun	وَاجِبَاتٌ
Son	ابن				

أصْحَابٌ	(Pl) صَاحِبٌ Companion		
الدِّينُ	Judgement	يَوْمٌ	The day
الأخْدَودُ	The trench	سَوطٌ	A protion
عَذَابٌ	The Chastisement	شَرٌّ	Worst
خَيرٌ	Best	البَرِيَّةُ	Creature
الفِيلُ	Elephant	مِثْقَالُ	Atom's weight
الغَاشِيَةُ	Overwhelming	عِمَارَةٌ	Building
المَسْجِدُ	The Mosque	نَضْرَةٌ	Brightness
النَّعِيمُ	Bliss	كِتَابٌ	The Devine write, a record, a book
فُجَّارٌ	Wickeds	فاجِرٌ	sing:
نَكَالٌ	(An example of punished one) punishment		

فَكٌّ	To make free
سَقَايَةُ	To give drink
وادٌ	Valley
التَّلاقُ	Meeting

رَقَبَةُ	Neck
الحَاجُّ	Pilgrim
نَمْلٌ	Aunt
حَدِيثٌ	Talk , Story

CHAPTER 4

THE VERB

1. The Root Form

Arabic verbs are mostly tri-literal, that is, they are based on roots of three consonants. Thus the basic meaning of verb فتح which means opening, is given by three consonants ف ت ح **Fth**. The basic meaning of writing is given by three consonants ك ت ب **ktb.** The basic meaning of نصر helping is expressed by three consonats ن ص ر **nsr.** Thus **kataba** means he wrote or has written. كَتَبَ زَيْدٌ Zaid has written or Zaid wrote. كَاتِبٌ **kaatibun,** writer مَكْتُوبٌ **Maktoobun,** the letter, مكتب **Maktabun** an office or writing table. similarly نَصَرَ **Nasara** he helped نَصَرَ رَاشِدٌ **Nasara Rashidun,** rashid helped نَصَرَتْ فَاطِمَةٌ **Nasarat Fatimatun,** Fatima helped نَاصِرٌ **Nasirun,** Helper, مَنْصُورٌ **Mansoorun,** one who has been helped and so on. In an Arabic dictionary all words are derived from a root from (in English : finite verb and in Persian and Urdu : مصدر **Masdar**), Thus you will find مِفْتَاحٌ **Miftaahun** (a key or an opener), under the part of verb the basic meaning of which is opening.

2. The Morpheme

(*a*) To indicate patterns of verbs, the grammarians use the three consonants of the verb فَعَلَ fa ع ala "to do". The ف of which represents the first radical, the ع of which represents the second radical and the ل the third. Thus in the verb كَتَبَ **Ktb** ك is ف radical, ت is ع radical and ب is the ل radical; in نَصَرَ Nsr ن is ف radical, ص is ع radical and ر is ل radical. You can also refer to these radicals by numbers as initial middle and final radicals.

(b) In a simple tri-literal verb the first and third radicals are vowelled with **fatha** (a short "**a**" vowel sign : َ but the second radical may be vowelled with **fatha** or **kasra** (a short'i' vowel sign ِ) or with **damma** (a short 'u' vowel sign ُ Thus a verb كتب kataba نَصَرَ nasara or فَتَحَ fataha may be symbolized as :

I . فَعَلَ fa ع ala (i.e CaCaCa)* as كَتَبَ **Kataba** "he wrote" نَصَرَ **Nasara,** "he helped," فَتَحَ **Fataha,** "he opened".

II . fa ع ila type (Ca Ci Ca) as فَرِحَ **Fareha** he became glad, سَمِعَ sami ع a be heard, عَلِمَ ع alima be knew.

III. فَعَلَ fa ع ula, type (Ca Cu Ca) as شَرُفَ sharufa, he was or been honoured, نَبُلَ nabula he was or become noble عَظُمَ ع zuma, he was or became great.

---

* c:consonant. a : a short vowel 'a'.'i' a short vowel 'i' 'u' a short vowel "u" In Arabic fatha, kasra and damma, respectively.

3. Tenses

The main tenses of the Arabic verb are the perfect and the imperfect. The perfect denotes a completed action, often referring to the past while the imperfect denotes an incomplete action, most often referring to the present or the future.
The conjugation of verb begins in Arabic whth the third person, and the order for the persons in the conjugation is third, second, first.

The Arabic verb also has a dual- form for the second and third persons, (see chapter1) . As to the first person, it has no dual form.

4. Added - Forms

There are also derived froms in which additions to the triliteral root give differnet shades of meaning , these will be dealt with in chapter 16 - 18. Each root form - maks certain stock patterns and produces its own particular modifications of the basic meaning of the root.

5. Modifications of the verb

The modified morphemes of the verb are prouduced by prefixing, suffixing, or infixing of the vowels or fixed pronouns in perfect tense suffixes denote the number and the gender. No consonant or vowel is prefixed in the perfect tense.

Masculine **3 rd person**

Singular	I فَعَلَ	fa ع ala	He did
Dual	II فَعَلا	fa ع alaa	They (two) did
Plural	III فَعَلوا	fa ع alu	They (all) did

Feminine

Singular	IV فَعَلَتْ	fa ع alat	She did
Dual	V فَعَلَتا	fa ع alataa	They (two Fem.) did
Plural	VI فَعَلْنَ	fa ع alna	They (all Fem.) did

Masculine **2nd person**

Singular	VII فَعَلْتَ	fa ع alta	You (one) did
Dual	VIII & XI فَعَلْتُما	fa ع altuma	You (two) did for both Masc. & Fem.
Plural	IX فَعَلْتُمْ	fa ع altum	You (all) did

Feminine

Singular	X فَعَلْتِ	fa ع alti	You (one Fem.) did
Plural	XII فَعَلْتُنَّ	fa ع altunna	You (all Fem.) did

Dual case is shown above.

Ist Person

Singular	XIII فَعَلْتُ	fa ع altu	I did	There is no dual in First Person.
Plural	XIV فَعَلْنا	fa ع alnaa	We did	

on the same pattern any root of the tri-ilteral consonants can be formed. e.g. from NSR: nasara, nasaraa, nasaru, nasarat, nasarataa, nasarna, nasrarta nasartuma, nasartum, nasarti, nasartunna, nasartu, nasarnaa.

LMS: Lamasa, Lamasaa, lamasu, lamasat, lamasataa, lamasna, lamasta, lamastuma, lamastum, lamasti, lamastunna, lamastu, lamasnaa

and so on. These verbal morphems of the Past perfect tense are fromed by suffixing the vowels and fixed pronouns. They are: t, in IV taa,in V na, in VI ta, in VII tuma, in VIII & XI tum, in IX ti, in X tunna, in XII tu, in XIII and naa, in XIV.

Examples From The Holy Qur'an

Form I فَعَلَ

مَنْ فَعَلَ هذا بآلهتنا	**21-59** who **has done** this to our gods?
كيف فَعَلَ رَبُّكَ	**105-1**. How thy Lord **did.**
واذ أَخَذَ الله مِيثَاقَ النَّبِيِّينَ	**3-81 Recall the time when** (إِذ) alah **took** (أَخَذَ) the convenant of the Prophets
وقَتَلَ داوودُ جالُوتَ	**2-251** And David Killed Goliath.

Form II فَعَلَا

فَأَكَلَا مِنْهَا فَبَدَتْ لَهُمَا سَوْءاتُهُمَا	**20-121** And **they both ate** from the tree, so that their nakedness dawned upon them

فَلَمَّا بَلَغَا مَجْمَعَ بَيْنِهِمَا	18-61 When both of them reached the confluence.

Form III فَعَلُوا

خَرَجُوا مِنْ دِيَارِهِمْ	2-243 They (people) came out of their land.
رِجَالٌ صَدَقُوا مَا عَاهَدُوا اللهَ عَلَيْهِ	33-23 They are men among the believers **who have been true** to the convenant, they made with allah.
الَّذِينَ قَتَلُوا أَوْلَادَهُمْ	6-140 Those who killed their children.

Form IV فَعَلَتْ

كُلَّمَا دَخَلَتْ أُمَّةٌ لَعَنَتْ أُخْتَهَا	7 - 38 As often as (كلما kullama) a nation enters hell it curses its sister nation.
Note : The word أُمَّه "ummah" nation is feminine in arabic.	

فَلَمَّا تَغَشَّاهَا حَمَلَتْ	7-189 When he covered her, she conceived.
فَلَمَّا سَمِعَتْ بِمَكْرِهِنَّ	12-31 When **she heard** of their back biting ....

Form V فَعَلَتَا

كَانَتَا رَتْقًا فَفَتَقْنَاهُمَا	21-30 The heavens and earth were one mass and we rent them apart.

Note: The word كَانَتَا kaanataa does not belong to the triliteral consonantal verb; it represents a weak verb but in H. Q. this form has not occured with consonants.

Form VI فَعَلْنَ

وَأَخذْنَ مِنكُم مِيثَاقًا غَلِيظًا	**4-21** And they (women) have taken from you a strong covenant.
فَإنْ خَرَجْنَ فَلَا جُنَاحَ عَلَيْكُمْ فِيمَا فَعَلْنَ فِى أَنْفُسِهِنَّ مِنْ مَعْرُوف	**2-240** Then if (فَإنْ) (these ladies) **go away** there is no blame on you for what **they did** of lawful deeds.

Form VII فَعَلْتَ

ومن حَيْثُ خَرَجْتَ فَوَلِّ وَجْهَكَ شَطْرَ الْمَسْجِدِ الحَرَامِ	**2-149** And from whatsoecer place, **thou came** from, turn thy face towards the sacred Mosque.
وَإِنْ حَكَمْتَ فَاحْكُمْ بَيْنَهُمْ بِالْقِسْطِ	**5-42** And if **thou judge**, Judge between them with equity.
قالوا : أَأَنْتَ فَعَلْتَ هٰذا بِآلِهَتِنَا يا إبراهيم	**21-62** They said: Hast thou done this to our gods, O abraham?

Form VIII & XI فَعَلْتُمَا

Not accord in the H. Quaran.

Form IX فَعَلْتُمْ

وَإِذَا حَكَمْتُمْ بَيْنَ النَّاسِ أَنْ تَحْكُمُوا بِالعَدْلِ	**4-58** And when **you Judge** between people, you Judge with Justice.
قَالَ هَلْ عَلِمْتُمْ مَا فَعَلْتُمْ بِيُوسُفَ وَأَخِيهِ وَإِذْ قَتَلْتُمْ نَفْساً فَادَّارَءْتُمْ فِيهَا	**12-89** He said: **Do you Know.** How you **treated** (but, did) Joseph and his brother? **2-72** And when you killed a man, then you disagreed about it.

Form X فَعَلْتِ

إِنَّكِ كُنْتِ مِنَ الخَاطِئِين	**12-29** Surely thou were (a lady is addressed) one of the sinful.

Note : Not accord in the H. Q. from the consonantal verb. There fore, an example is given from a weak verb as in case of form V.

Form XI فَعَلْتُمَا

(2 P.Fem.) see form VIII 2 P Masc.

Form XII فَعَلْتُنَّ

Not accord in the triliteral consonants, but with the weak and added patterns. There are some examples in the H.Q.

يَا نِسَاءَ النَّبِيِّ ! **لَسْتُنَّ** كَأَحَدٍ مِنَ النِّسَاءِ إِنِ اتَّقَيْتُنَّ .	**33-32** O! Wives of the Prophet , **you are not** like any other woman if you keep your duty (to Allah)
وَإِن **كُنْتُنَّ** تُرِدْنَ اللَّهَ وَرَسُولَهُ وَالدَّارَ الآخِرَةَ فَإِنَّ اللَّهَ أَعَدَّ لِلْمُحْسِنَاتِ مِنْكُنَّ أَجْرًا عَظِيمًا .	**33-29** And if you are desiring Allah and his Messenger and the abode of the Hereafter , when surely allah has prepared for the doers of good among you a mighty reward.

Form XIII فَعَلْتُ

قالت : رَبِّ إِنِّي **ظَلَمْتُ** نَفْسِي	**27-44** She said: My Lord! Surely **I have wronged** myself.
قال **بَصُرْتُ** بِمَا لَمْ يَبْصُرُوا بِهِ **فَقَبَضْتُ** قَبْضَةً مِنْ أَثَرِ الرَّسُولِ **فَنَبَذْتُهَا**	**20-96** He said: **I perceived** what they perceived not, so **I took** a handful from the foot prints of the messenger , then **I cast** it away
قال رَبِّ إِنِّي **قَتَلْتُ** مِنْهُم نَفْسًا	**28-33** He said My Lord , I killed one of them.

Form XIV فَعَلْنَا

قالا : رَبَّنَا **ظَلَمْنَا** أَنْفُسَنَا	**7-23** They said : Our Lord , we have wronged ourselves ;

ما عَلِمْنَا عَلَيْهِ مِن سُوءٍ	**12-51** Those ladies said: We knew of no evil on his part.

Note 1. The particle قَدْ "**qad**" which often occurs before Perfect, expresses the completion or certainty of the action and may sometimes be translated as "already", but is generally omitted in translation.

Example from The Holy Qur'an

قد جَاءَكُمْ بَصَائِرُ مِن رَبِّكُمْ	**6-104** Indeed come to you clear proofs from your Lord.
قَدْ خَسِرَ الَّذِينَ كَذَّبوا بِلِقَاءِ اللهِ	**6-31** They are losers in-deed, who rejected the meeting with allah.
قد سَمِعَ اللهُ	**58-1** Indeed Allah has heard.
قَدْ عَلِمْنَا ما تَنْقُصُ الأَرْضُ مِنْهُم	**50-4** Indeed we Knew what earth diminishes of them.

Note 2. Often an additional ل is prefixed to قد **qad** which becomes لَقَدْ **laqad** to emphasise in the meaning of the Verb.

Examples from H.Q.

لَقَدْ أخَذْنَا مِيثَاقَ بَنِى إِسْرَائِيلَ	**5-70** Certainly We made a convenant with the children of Israel.
لَقَدْ خَلَقْنَا الإِنْسَانَ فِى أَحْسَنِ تقويمٍ	**95-4** Certainly We made man in the best make.

Note 3. The negative of the Perfect is formed by placing "**maa**" before the verb e.g. مَا كَتَبَ maa kataba, he did not write.

Example from the Holy Qur'an

مَا أَنْزَلْنَا عَلَيْكَ الْقرآن لِتَشْقَى	**20-2** We have not revealed upon thee the Quran that thou mayst be in hardship.
مَا جَعَلَ اللهُ لِرَجُلٍ مِنْ قَلْبَيْنِ فِى جَوْفِه	**33-4** Allah has not made for anyone two hearts within him.
ما قَدَرُوا اللهَ حَقَّ قَدْرِهِ	**22-74** they estimate not allah with His due estmation.

EXCERCISE

A. Conjugate the following verbs : قَتَلَ ، فَتَحَ ، جَمَعَ ، ذَهَبَ

Name the patterns , giving their numbers and the standard form (fa ع ala)e.g. بَلَغَتْ 3 pers. Sing. Fem. IV

نَصَرَ ، نَصَرْنا ، نَصَرَتَا ، نَصَرْنَ ، دَخَلُوا ، دَخَلْتُمْ ، دَخَلْتُنَّ . دَخَلْتُ ،
بَرَزَتْ ، بَرَزْتُمَا ، بَرَزْتِ ، بَرَزَتَا ، جَمَعَا ، جَمَعْتُمَا

B. Translate into English :

قَتَلَ داوود جَالُوتَ ، ذَهَبَ موسٰى إِلَى الجَبَلِ ، ذَهَبَ راشدٌ إِلَى الحَدِيقَةِ ، قالتا لا نَسْقِى حَتَّى يُصْدِرَ الرِّعَاءُ ، قَالَا إِنَّا رَسُولَا رَبِّكَ ، سمِعَا نِدَاءَ الحَقِّ ، رَحِمَ اللهُ عَبْدًا قَال آمِيْنا ، قُلْتُم مَا أَردْنَا إلا الْخَير ، قُلْتُنَّ ذَهَبْنَا إلى أَقْرَبَائِنَا ، تَلَوْتُ جُزءًا مِن الْقُرآنِ الْكَرِيمِ ، سَمِعْتُ الأذَانَ فَقُمْتُ لِلصَّلَاةِ ، دَخَلْنا الْمَسْجِدَ مَعَ وَالِدِى وَأخِي ، خَرَجْتُ مِنَ الْمَدْرَسَةِ ظُهراً ، يَا هَارُون وَيَا رَاشِد لِمَا ذَهَبْتُمَا إِلَى السُّوق ؟ النِّسَاءُ سَمِعْنَ النَّصِيحةَ ، البَنَاتُ ذَهَبْنَ إلى الْمَدْرَسَةِ

C. Translate into Arabic :

1. Have you written (هل كتبتُ) Your article on Arabic language ? Yes. نَعَمْ I did and put it on that big table.
2. The maid opened the door of the house.
3. The beggar sought food from me.
4. Have you been (هل كنت) out today?
5. I went to the mosque to pray.
6. My uncle performed Haj this year. My sister visited me at home.
7. I received the guests at my house.
8. I used to stay with Hasan. (كُنْتُ أَسْكُنُ)
9. She used to write on long papers.(كانت تَكْتُبُ)
10. She was a good girl in her manners.

D. Distinguish the following patterns putting their number from the stable verb (fعl)

كنَّ ، قُلْنَ ، كانَتَا ، قُلتَ ، قلتُ ، كانَتْ ، قَالَتْ

VOCABULARY

قتَلَ	(3rd Pers. Masc.) to Kill
دَاوُود	David (Proper name)
جالوتَ	Jaloot (Proper name)
الحَدِيقَةُ	garden.

لا نَسْقِي	we do not give water (to our flocks)
يَصْدِرُ	(Imperfect , from صدر) to come out.
الرِّعَاءُ	shepherds
رسُولا + رسولَانِ	two messengers
سَمِعْنَا	(1st Pers. Plur.) we heard.
نِدَاءً	call.
اَلْحَقُّ	the truth
رَحِمَ	(3rd Pers. Sing. Masc.) May be merciful
آمينَ	May God accept the prayer.
ما أرَدْنا	we do not intend
أقْرِبَاءُ	(plural of قريب) relatives
تَلوتُ	(1st Pers. Sing.) I recited.
جُزْءاً	one part.
السُّوقُ	market.
نَصِيْحَةُ	good advice
Article مقال maqaal	

CHAPTER 5

DOUBLED AND WEAK VERBS

Arabic verbs are mostly tri - literal but some of them have the appearance of being bi - literal. It happens in the following cases:

1. Some verbs have the same letters as the second and third radical.

   In this case the second radical has " Shaddah " (that is a sound of a doubled consonant e. g. in English the words such as ir - regular , in - nocent etc. but in Arabic one letter is not written twice , it is written single with a mark on the head that means this letter should be pronounced twice e. g. مَرَّ **marra** , instead of writing مَرَرَ

   This type of the verbs have appearance of being bi - literal , e.g. حَجَّ hajja - to perform Hajj.

Example From The Holy Qur'an

فَمَنْ حَجَّ الْبَيْتَ	**2-158** who is on pilgrimage to the House (of God).

جَرَّ	Jarra - to drag , to draw.
مَرَّ	Marra - to pass.

Example from The Holy Qur'an

وَهِيَ تَمُرُّ مَرَّ السَّحَابِ .	**27-88** (and it) flying with the flight of clouds.

Note When the third radical is not followed by any vowel sign, it is marked with sukun (ْ).

Shadda will be removed and both radical will be written and pronounced separately as in cases of pattern VI and onward.

I	Marra	مَرَّ	He passed
II	Marraa	مَرَّا	They (2 M) passed
III	Marru	مَرُّوا	They (Plu M) passed
IV	Marrat	مَرَّتْ	She (sin. fem) passed
V	Marrataa	مَرَّتَا	They (2 fem) passed
VI	Mararna	مَرَرْنَ	They(Plu.Fem.)passed
VII	Mararta	مَرَرْتَ	You (sing. m) passed
VIII	Marartuma	مَرَرْتُمَا	You(2MorFem)passed
IX	Marartum	مَرَرْتُم	You (Plu. M) passed
X	Mararti	مَرَرْتِ	You(Sing. Fem)passed
XI	Marartunna	مَرَرْتُنَّ	You(Plu. Fem)passed

XII	Marartu مررتُ	I (Sing) passed
XIII	Mararnaa مَرَرْنا	We (Plu) passed

2. When on the three radicals is a semi - vowel : a , w , i , ی ، أ ، و such as in the verb كَانَ to be , it will be dropped in certain places.

Notice the following table carefully.

I	كَانَ	Kaana
II	كَانَا	Kaanaa
III	كَانُوا	Kaanu
IV	كَانَتْ	Kaanat
V	كَانَتَا	Kaanata
VI	كُنَّ	Kunna
VII	كُنتَ	Kunta
VIII - XI	كُنتُمَا	Kuntuma
IX	كُنتُم	Kuntum
X	كُنْتِ	Kunti
XII	كُنتُنَّ	Kuntunna

XIII	كُنتُ	Kuntu
XIV	كُنَّا	Kunna

(see chapters 9 and 30)

This is the most frequently used stem in the Holy Qur'an as well as in all Arabic literature. The modified forms are to be adjusted with the verbs such as قال qaal to say (literal he said) خاضَ khadda , to think , to discuss (lit. he thought , he discussed).

The modification of these type of verbs are based on the second radical of the verbal noun or more exactly on the roots. (not on the pattern of 3rd person singular masculine as observed in case of consonant verbs). Thus كانَ —— قالَ qaala is 3rd pers sing masc. of the root كَوْنٌ kon and قَولٌ qol. When the second radical is ya ى e. g. بَيْعٌ to sell , the patterns from I to V will be same as in كانَ and قالَ but from VI onward will be vocalized with kasra as بِعْنَ be ع na , be ع ta , be ع tu and so on.

Examples from The Holu Qur'an :

I قالَ **qaala**, he said.	
قَالَ نُوحٌ رَبِّ إِنَّهُم عَصَوْنِي	**71 - 21** Noha said : My Lord , surely they disobey me.

كان **kaana,** he was. he is.	
وَكَانَ اللهُ غفورًا رحيمًا	**4- 152** And Allah is (it was) forgiving , Merciful.

طال **Taala,** he perolonged.	
حتى طالَ عَليهُمُ الْعُمُرُ	**21- 44** Until life was prolonged.

II. قالا **qaalaa,** they (two-Masc). said	
قَالَا : رَبَّنَا إِنَّنَا نَخَافُ أَنْ يَفْرُطَ عَلَيْنَا	**20- 45** They (two) said: Our Lord , we fear lest he hasten to do evil to us.

كَانَا **kaanaa,** they (two-Masc), were	
كَانَا يَأْكُلَانِ الطَّعَامَ	**5- 75** They (two) used to have food.

III. قَالُوا **qaalu,** they (plur Masc), said	
قَالُوا رَبُّنَا اللهُ ثُمَّ اسْتَقَامُوا	**41 - 30** They said: Our Lord is Allah then continued in the right way.

كانوا **kaanu,** they (plur Masc). were.	
كَانُوا لَا يَتَنَاهَوْنَ عَنْ مُنْكَرٍ فَعَلُوهُ	**5- 79** They forbade not one another the hateful thing they did.

IV. قَالَتْ	qaalat, she (Sing Fem). said.
قالت : رَبِّ أَنَّىٰ يَكُونُ لِى وَلَدٌ وَلَم يَمْسَسْنِى بَشَرٌ	**3 - 47** She said : My Lord how I can have a son and man has not yet touched me.

كَانَتْ	kaanat, she (Sing Fem), was.
كَانَتْ مِنَ الغَابِرِينَ	**7 - 83** She was of those who remained behind

V. قَالَتَا	qaalata, they (dual Fem), told
قَالَتَا لَا نَسْقِى حَتَّى يُصْدِرَ الرِّعَاءُ	**28-23** They said (two girls) we can not water until shephered takes away (their sheeps)

كَانَتَا	**kaanata**, they (dual Fem), were.
كانتا تَحْتَ عَبْدَيْنِ مِنْ عِبَادِنَا صَالِحَيْنِ	**66 - 10** They were both under two of our righteous servants.

VI. قُلْنَ	Qulna, they (Plur).
قُلْنَ حَاشَ لله مَا عَلِمْنَا عَلَيْهِ مِنْ سُوءٍ	**12-51** They (Plur. Fem). said : Holy Allah We knew of no evil on his part.
فَإِن كُنَّ نِسَاءً فَوْقَ اثْنَتَيْنِ	**4 - 11** If thore be more than two female.

VII. قُلْتَ	**qulta,** you told

كُنْتَ	**kunta,** you were
أَأَنْتَ قُلْتَ لِلنَّاسِ	**5 - 116** Didst thou say to men.
وَمَا كُنْتَ بِجَانِبِ الْغَرْبِيِّ إِذْ قَضَيْنَا إِلَىٰ مُوسَى الْأَمْرَ وَمَا كُنْتَ مِنَ الشَّاهِدِينَ	**28 - 44** And thou wast not on the western side when we revealed to Moses the commandment not wast thou among those present.

VIII & IX. قُلْتُمَا	**qultuma**	you (dual Masc. & Fem) told or
كُنْتُمَا	**kuntuma,**	You (dual Masc. & Fem) were

(Not occured in the Holy Qur'an but very often used in Arabic)

X. قُلْتُمْ	**qultum,** You (plu. Masc.) told.
وَإِذْ قُلْتُمْ يَا مُوسَىٰ لَنْ نَصْبِرَ عَلَىٰ طَعَامٍ وَاحِدٍ.	**2- 61** And when you told O'Moses , we cannot endure one food.

كُنْتُمْ	**kuntum,** You (plu. Masc.) were
وَكُنْتُمْ عَلَىٰ شَفَا حُفْرَةٍ مِنَ النَّارِ فَأَنْقَذَكُمْ مِنْهَا	**3-103** And you were onthe brink of the pit then He saved you from it.

XI. قُلْتِ	qulti You (Sing. Fem) told.

(Not occured in The Holy Qur'an but from the verb جَاءَ Jaa, (coming):

لَقَدْ جِئْتِ شَيْئًا فَرِيًّا	**19 - 27** May ! thou hast indeed brought a strange thing.

كُنْتِ	**kunti** You (Sing. Fem.) were.
إِنَّكِ كُنْتِ مِنَ الْخَاطِئِينَ	**12 - 29** Surely, thou art one of the sinfuls.

XII. قُلْتُنَّ	**qultunna,** You (Plur. Fem.) told.
لَسْتُنَّ كَأَحَدٍ مِنَ النِّسَاءِ	**33 - 32** You are not like other women.

كُنْتُنَّ	**kuntunna,** You (Plur. Fem.) were.
وَإِنْ كُنْتُنَّ تُرِدنَ الله وَرَسُولَهُ	**33 - 29** And if you desire Allah and His Messenger.

XIII. قُلْتُ	**qultu,** I told (Common to Masc. & Fem.)

كُنْتُ	**kuntu,** I was.
إن كنتُ قلتُه فقَدْ عَلِمتَه	**5 - 116** If I had said it thou wouldst indeed have known it.

XIV. قُلْنَا qulnaa,	we (Plu. Masc. & Fem.) told
وَقُلْنَا يَا آدَمُ اسْكُنْ أَنْتَ وَزَوْجُكَ الْجَنَّةَ	2- 35 And We said: O'Adam dwell thou and thy wife in the garden.

كُنَّا kunnaa , we were	
وَأَنَّا كُنَّا نَقْعُدُ مِنْهَا مَقَاعِدَ لِلسَّمْعِ	72-9 And that: we used to sit in some of the sitting place thereof to steal hearing.

Note : Patterns VI faعalna and XIV faعalnaa = qulnaa , kunna , have very slight difference , as the former has a short ending vowel while the latter has a long one. Compare qulna , qulnaa , kunna , kunnaa.

EXERCISE.

A. Translate into Arabic:

Ali said: There were many fine fruits in my garden. Your father was a true Muslim. My sister was a Teacheress. All of you (Masc) were present over there. Both of them were good players. There were two girls going to the school early in the morning. You were successful in the examination.

She was learning the Qur'an. They (Fem) were good in their manners. I was very happy to see you here.

Did you write (هل كتبتَ) your article on Arabic language ? yes (نَعَم) I did , and put it on that big table. The begger sought food from me. The maid opened the door of the house. Have you been (هل كنت) out to - day ? I went to mosque to pray. My uncle performed Haj this year. My sister visited me at home. I received the guests at my house.

I used to stay with Hasan. She used to write on long papers.

She was a good girl in her manners.

B. Translate into English :

جَحَدُوا بِآيَاتِ رَبِّهِم ، ما سَمِعُوا نِدَاءَ ضَمِيرِهِمْ وَأَعْرَضُوا عَنْ أَدَاءِ الْوَاجِبِ ، لَقَدْ تَابَ اللهُ عَلَى النَّبِيِّ وَالْمُهَاجِرِينَ وَالأَنْصَارِ ، يَا أَيُّهَا الَّذِينَ آمَنُوا تُوبُوا إِلَى اللهِ ، وَقَالَ الَّذِينَ كَفَرُوا لِلَّذِينَ آمَنُوا لَوْ كَانَ خَيْراً مَا سَبَقُونَا إِلَيْهِ ، كُنْتُم خَيْرَ أُمَّةٍ أُخرِجَتْ لِلنَّاسِ . كَانَ اللهُ غَفُوراً رَحِيمًا ، قُولُوا حُسْناً ، قُولُوا قَوْلاً مَعْرُوفًا ، قَالَتِ النَّصَارَى لَيْسَتِ الْيَهُود عَلَى شَيْءٍ ، وَقَالَتِ الْيَهُودُ لَيْسَتِ النَّصَارَى عَلَى شَيْءٍ ، الإِسْلَامُ دِينٌ كَامِلٌ لِكُلِّ زَمَانٍ وَمَكَانٍ ، القُرآنُ ثَرْوَةٌ لِلْبَشَرِ جَمِيعًا ، هِدَايَةٌ لِلْعَالَمِينَ ، كَانَ النَّاسُ أُمَّةً وَاحِدَةً .

C. Distinguish the following patterns putting their number and the stable verb (i. e. فَعَلَ)

كُنَّ ، قُلْنَ ، كَانَتَا ، كُنْتَ ، قُلْتَ ، قُلْتِ ، كُنْتَ ، قُلْتِ ،كُنْتَ ، كَانَتْ ، قَالَتْ ،

D. Conjugate the following verbs.

Thob ثَوَّبَ bsr بَصَّرَ jrr. جَرَّ

VOCABULARY

مَرّوا	P. masc plu to pass (by)
آمَنوا	P. masc plu to believe
إتَّقُوا	P. masc plu to fear God
قَالُوا	P. masc plu to say , to speak , to tell
سَدِيدٌ	accurate , right , correct
اسْكُنْ	(command) live , dwel
زَوْجُكَ	thy wife ,, thy couple , couple thy
الْجَنَّة	The paradise
جَحَدُوا	p. masc. plu. They denied
آياتٍ	signs sign. آية aayat
تَابَ	as قال : to return , to forgive
النَّبِيّ	the Prophet
المُهَاجِرِينَ	plu. Masc. immigrants مهاجر sing
نَصُوحاً	unreturnable
كَفَرُوا	P. Masc. Plu rejected
لا تَسمَعُوا	do not listen

الْغَوا فِيه	take it as false
لَو كانَ	if it was
خير	good
سَبَقُو + نَا	.P. Masc Plu a pronoun = do not: they could get (it) before
قومى =قوم + ى	qom + I = mine , qomi = my people
اِتَّخَذُوا	they put , adopted
مَهْجُورٌ	forsaken thing
نَسَوا	P. M Plu they forgot
ألذِكر	The Holy Qur'an , lit reminder
بُورٌ	doomed to perish

Article	مَقَالٌ	maqaal
Arabic language	اللغة العربية	
Big	كَبِير	
uncle	أَلعَمَّ + my = عمى my uncle	
visited	زَارَتْ as قَالَت	
I used to	كُنْتَ	
She was	كَانَتْ	

table	الطَّاوِلَةُ
maid	الخَادِمَة
out	الخَارِج
sister	الأُخْتُ
received	المُسْتَقْبِل
She used to	كَانَتْ

CHAPTER 6

THE VERBAL SENTENCES

In Arabic the sentences are of two kinds:

1. The Nominal sentences الْجُمَلُ الاسْمِيةُ in which the subject appears first, e.g. اللهُ رَبٌّ Allah is the Lord مُحَمَّدٌ رَسُولٌ Mohammad is the Messenger. اللهُ بَسَطَ الرِّزْقَ Allah has amplified the Provision.This type of sentence are already dealt with in chapter 2.

2. Verbal sentences الْجُمَلُ الفِعْلِيَّةُ in which the verb appears before the subject e.g أتى أمْرُ اللهِ Allah's commandment has come, خَلَقَ اللهُ السَّمٰوَاتِ وَالأَرْضَ Allah has created the heavens and the earth.
أَرْسَلْنَا مُوسَىٰ We have sent Musaa. بَعَثَ اللهُ رَسُولا Allah has sent a messenger and بَسَطَ اللهُ الرِّزْقَ Allah has amplified the provision.

3. In verbal sentences the verb always appears in the singular even in cases where the subject following the verb is dual or plural, e.g فَعَصَىٰ فِرْعَوْنُ الرَّسُولَ (But) Pharaoh disobeyed the Messenger سَأَلَ سَائِلٌ a questioner asked دَخَلَ (مَعَهُ السِّجْنَ) فَتَيَانِ and two

youths entered the prison with him سَجَدَ المَلاَئِكَةُ كُلُّهُمْ أَجْمَعُونَ So the Angels bowed down one and all, جَاءَ إِخْوَةُ يُوسُفَ Joseph's brothers came قَالَتْ امْرَأَةُ الْعَزِيزِ The Chief's wife said سَجَدَتِ الْبِنْتَانِ The two girls bowed down and سَجَدَتِ النِّسَاءُ The women bowed down.

4. The verb appears in singular, masculine even when the subject is plural fem. e.g. قَال نِسْوَةٌ the ladies said. It appears, sometimes in singular, feminine though the subject is plural masculine e. g. قَالَتِ الْأَعْرَابُ آمَنَّا the bedouins said: We have believed. but it should be noted that this rule applies when the plural from is broken, in case the plural is solid e.g. المسلمون only singular masculine verb will work.

5. Declension of the verbal sentence.

A perfect verb has an established mark as observed in the chapters 1 & 3.

The following nouns, if they are the subject of a sentnece, take **damma** mark

the object of the sentences vocalized with **fatha** e.g.

دَخَلَ خَادِمٌ بَابًا　　دَخَلَ الخَادِمُ الْبابَ　　جَمَعَ اللهُ الرُّسُلَ

Compar the nominal and verbal sentences

الجُمْلَةُ الإِسْمِيَّةُ Nominal Sentences	الجُمْلَةُ الفِعْلِيَّةُ Verbal Sentences	
المسلِمُ فَتَحَ البَابَ	فَتَحَ المسلمُ البابَ	the Muslims opened the door
المُسْلِمَانِ فَتَحا الْبَابَ	فَتَحَ المُسْلِمَانِ البابَ	Two Muslims opened the door.
المُسْلِمُونَ فتحوا البابَ	فَتَحَ المُسْلِمون البابَ	Muslims opened the door
المُسْلِمَةُ فَتَحَتِ البَابَ	فَتَحَتْ المُسْلِمَةُ البَابَ	The Muslim woman opened the door.
المُسْلِمَتَانِ فَتَحَتَا البَابَ	فَتَحَتِ المُسْلِمَتَانِ البَابَ	Two Muslim women opened the door.
المُسْلِمَاتُ فتحنَ البابَ	فتحتِ المُسْلِمَاتُ البابَ	The Muslim women opened the door .

When the plural form is broken such as العلماء (sing. عالم) you can say قالَتِ العُلَمَاءُ ƹolama said and vice versa. قال نِسْوَةٌ women told.

6. When a subject is broken plural, the verb will be singular feminine, unless they refer to the male human beings. e.g. ظَهَرَتِ النَّجومُ the stars appeared but ظَهَرَ الرِّجَالُ the men appeared though ظَهَرَتِ الرِّجَالُ is also endorsed by the grammarians.

The word order in a verbal sentence :

The normal order in an English verbal sentence is : subject, verb, object e.g. A girl has broken the glass. But in Arabic the order is : verb, subject, direct object. Thus the above sentence (A girl has broken the glass) will be placed as : Broke a girl the glass.

The place of the adverbs and others is often a direct object, e.g. حَضَرَ المُسْلِمُونَ الصَّلَاةَ Muslims joined the prayer (Lit : arrived) .

Examples from the Holy Qur'an:

قَدْ فَرَضَ اللهُ لَكُمْ تَحِلَّةَ أَيْمَانِكُم	**66-2** Allah indeed has sanctioned ✲ for you the expiation of your oath.

(يَا مَرْيَمُ) لَقَدْ جِئْتِ شَيْئًا فَرِيًّا	**19-27** O' Mary thou has indeed brought a strange thing.

وَنَهَى النَّفسَ عَنِ الْهَوَىٰ	**79-40** And (one who) restrained himself from low desires.

كَذَّبَتْ قَوْمُ نُوحٍ الْمُرْسَلِينَ	**26-105** The people of Noh have rejected the Messengers.

✲ The verb فرض signifies to prescribe ; impose sanction.

حَتَّى زُرْتُمُ المَقَابِرَ	**102-2** Until you came to the graves.

إِنَّا أَعْطَيْنَاكَ الْكَوْثَرَ	**108-1** Surely , we have given thee the kothar.

أَخَذَ عَلَيكم موثِقاً مِنَ اللهِ	**12-80** (Your father) took from you a convent in Allah,s name.

أَمَّا مَنْ خافَ مَقَامَ رَبِّه	**79-40** And as for him who fears his Lord.

ولَقَد أَضَلَّ مِنْكُم جِبِلاً كَثِيراً	**36-62** And certainly he led stray numerous from amog you.

ولقَد رآه نَزْلَةً أخرىٰ	**53 -13** And certainly he saw Him in another descent.

أَكْثَروا فيها الفسادَ	**89-12** And (they) made great mischief herein

فَسَجَدَ الْمَلَائِكَةُ كُلُّهُمْ أَجْمَعُونَ	**15-30** So the angels made obeisance of them together.

قَالَتِ الأَعْرَابُ آمَنَّا	**49-14** The dwellers of the desert said we believe.

قَالَ نِسْوَةٌ فِى الْمَدِينَةِ	**12-30** the women of the town said

مَا كَانَ مُحَمَّدٌ أَبَا أَحَدٍ مِن رِجَالِكُمْ	**33-40** Mohammad is not father of any of your men.

EXERCISE

A. Translate into English :

لَيْلَةُ الْقَدْرِ خَيْرٌ مِنْ أَلْفِ شَهْرٍ — أَسَّسَ بُنْيَانَهُ عَلَىٰ التَّقْوَىٰ

فَعَصَىٰ آدَمُ رَبَّه فَغَوَىٰ — نَاجَيْتُم الرَّسُولَ

عَمِلُوا الصَّالِحَاتِ — أَهْلَكْتُ مَالاً لُبَدًا

نَهَىٰ النَّفْسَ عَنِ الْهَوَىٰ — حَتَّىٰ إِذَا بَلَغَتِ الْحُلْقُومَ

أَكْثَرُوا فِيهَا الْفَسَادَ — أَرْسَلَ عَلَيْهِمْ طَيْرًا أَبَابِيلَ

أَذْهَبَ عَنَّا الْحَزَنَ — ظَلَمْتُمْ أَنْفُسَكُمْ

B. Translate into Arabic :

Man has passed from a space of tim

We have created man of mixed semen.

We put him to the proof.

We show him the right path.

Allah saved them from the evil of that day.

I have come to give you plain warning.

We burdened no soul beyond its capacity.

He created men from nothing.

He is Merciful, Forgiver

VOCABULARY

لَيلةُ القَدرِ The night of Majesty (or Power)	
خيرٌ best	ألفٌ one thousand
شَهرٌ month	عَصَى disobeyed
غَوَى he misguided	عَملوا they did (Masc)
نَهَى he Restrained	النَّفْسَ soul, person (himself)
هَوَى he desired	الفَسَادَ micshief
أكثَرُوا they made great (overdoing)	
أرْسَلَ he sent	طَيرٌ bird
أبَابِيل name of certain birds (Put as such)	

أَذهَبَ	removed	الحَزَنَ	sorrow
ظَلَمتُمْ	you did wrong	أسس	established
نَاجيتُمْ	whispered	أهلكتُ	distroyed
مَالٌ	wealth	لُبَدَا	adj . a big sum
بَلَغَتْ	reached	الْحلقُوم	throat

The prepositions and pronouns will be dealt latter here are some of them to help you in the translation.

Preposition

مِنْ	from , than
عَنْ	from
فى	in

Pronouns

ه	His	ربه	His Lord
ها	Her	فيها	In her
نا	Us, our	عنا	From us

دَهْر	The space of time
خَلَقَ	To create (use xiv from)
هَدَى	(hada)to show the path
إنقاذ	Delivered
أَنْذَرَ	Warning
وُسْعٌ	Capacity
الرَّحِيم	The Mercyful
دَلِيلٌ	(n) proof
الصِّراطُ	Right path
شَرٌّ	Evil
فَوقُ	Beyond; up
لا شَيء	Nothing
الغَفَّارُ	The Forgiver

CHAPTER 7

THE IMPERFECT TENSE

اَلمُضَارِع Almudareع

1. This tense is formed by prefixing one of the four letters: الف (a) ن (n) ت (t) ى (y) to the root-form as الف (a) and ن (n) for 1st. person, ت (t) for 2nd and third persons as will be illustrated in the conjugation. These pronominal prefixes are termed "sign of the imperfect". It also has suffixes to denote number of the person; they are آن aane , ـون una, ـن na, ـن una, ين eena.

2. The imperfect tense expresses an action still incompleted at the time to which reference is being made. It refers to the present or future as generally is assumed.

The conjugation of imperfect indicative of فَعَلَ the standard root-form is as below:

3 rd person

Imperfect I	sing. masc.	يَفْعَلُ	yafعalu	he does or will do

Imperfect II dual masc.	يَفْعَلانِ	yafعlaane	they do, will do
Imperfect III plu masc.	يَفْعَلُونَ	yafعloona	they do, will do
Imperfect IV sing. fem.	تَفْعَلُ	tafعalu	she does, will do
Imperfect V dual fem.	تَفْعَلانِ	tafعalane	they (two) do or will do
Imperfect VI plu fem.	يَفْعَلْنَ	yafع alna	they (all) do or will do

2 nd person

Imperfect VII sing. masc.	تَفْعَلُ	tafعalu	you do, will do
Imperfect VIIIdual masc.	تَفْعَلانِ	tafعalaane	you (two) do or will do (as 3 P dual. fem)
Imperfect IX plu masc.	تَفْعَلُونَ	tafعaluna	you (all) do or will do

Imperfect X sing. fem	تَفْعَلِيْنَ	tafɛaleena	you do or will do

Imperfect XI dual as	dual 3 P fem. and dual 2 P. Masc

Imperfect XII plu. fem	تَفْعَلْنَ	tafɛalna	you all (F) do or will do

First person

Imperfect XIII	sing	أَفْعَلُ	aafɛalu	I do, will do
Imperfect XIV	dual and plu	نَفْعَلُ	nafɛalu	We do, will do.

3. Groups of the trilateral verbs :

There are five groups or famelies of the triliteral verbs.

A. The vowel of the second radical of the Perfect is 'a' i-e. fatha and the same radical in the Imperfect has" u " i-e. damma e.g.

نَصَرَ يَنْصُرُ	Nasara, Yansuru	to help
بَلَغَ يَبْلُغُ	Balagha, Yablughu	to reach
كَتَبَ يَكْتُبُ	Kataba, Yaktubu	to write

B. The 2nd radical in Perfect has (a ـَ) vowel and (i ـِ) in the Imperfect e.g. daraba , Yadribu يَضْرِبُ ضَرَبَ to beat.

C. The 2nd radical in the Perfect has (i ـِ) vowel and the Imperfect has (a ـَ) vowel as سَمِعَ يَسْمَعُ samie ع a , Yasma ع u.

D. The 2nd radical in both Perfect and Imperfect has vowel (a ـَ) eg. فَتَحَ ، يَفْتَحُ fataha , Yaftahu.

E. Both have (u ـُ) vowel as كَرُمَ ، يَكْرُمُ Karuma , Yakrumu.

The Knowledge of these groups is useful for the consulting an Arabic dictionary as well as it assists in forming an idea about the nature of a word and the shade of the meaning.

4. The Imperfect itself denotes only unfininshed action but it may be made to indicate the future by putting a particle سَوفَ before it, or prefixing a letter س (s), e.g. (from the holy Qur'an) :

سَيَقُولُ السُّفَهَاءُ من النَّاس ..	**2-142** the fools among the people will say...
سَوْفَ يُحَاسَبُ حِسَابًا يَسِيرا	**84-8** His account will be taken by an easy reckoning.

5. When used with Present singnificance the imperfect most often gives the meaning of the habitual present especially in the Holy Qur'an, e.g.

يَفْعَلُ اللهُ ما يَشَاءُ	**14-27** Allah does what He pleases.

يُخْرِجُ الحَىَّ مِنَ المَيِّتِ ، ويُخْرِجُ المَيِّتَ مِنَ الحَىِّ . ويُحْىِ الأرضَ بَعدَ مَوْتِها	**30-19** He brings forth the living from the dead and brings forth the dead from the living and gives life to the earth after its death.

يَا أَهْلَ الْكِتَابِ لِمَ تَلْبِسُونَ الْحَقَّ بِالبَاطِلِ وَتَكْتُمُونَ الحقَّ وَأَنْتُمْ تَعْلَمُون	**3-71** O' people of the book! Why do you counfound the truth with falsehood, and hide the truth while you know.

The Imperfect may give the meaning of the continuous Present, e.g. (from the Holy Qur'an):

أَتَقْتُلُونَ رَجلاً أَن يَقُولَ : رَبِّى اللهُ !	**40-28** Are you killing a man because he says: My Lord is Allah.

Or may indicate the future, e.g. (from the Holy Qur'an) :

يَلْبَسُونَ مِن سُنْدُسٍ وَإِسْتَبْرَقٍ مُتَقَابِلِينَ	**44 - 53** They will wear fine and thick silk facing one another.

Examples from The holy Qur'an:

Imerfect Form	I	يَفْعَلُ

ويَفْعَلُ اللهُ ما يَشَاءُ	**14-27** And Allah does what He pleases.
يَخْلُقُ اللهُ ما يَشاءُ	**24-45** And Allah creates what He pleases.

Imperfect Form	II	يَفْعَلانِ

كانا يَأْكُلانِ الطَّعَامَ	**5-75** They both used to eat food
وَدَاوودَ وَسُلَيْمَانَ إِذْ يَحْكُمَانِ فى الْحَرْثِ	**21-78** And David & Solomon, when they were giving judgement concerning the field.

Imperfect Form	III	يَفْعَلُونَ

يَقولُونَ مَالا يَفْعَلُون	**26-226** They say what they do not.
فَالْيَومَ الَّذِينَ آمَنُوا مِنَ الْكُفَّارِ يَضْحَكُونَ	**83-34** so this day those who believe laugh at the dis-believers.

فَوَيْلٌ لِلَّذِينَ يَكْتُبُونَ الْكِتَابَ بِأَيْدِيهِمْ ثُمَّ يَقُولُونَ هٰذَا مِنْ عِنْدِ اللهِ	**2-79** Woe! then to those who write the book with their hands then say, this is from Allah.

Imperfect Form	IV	تَفْعَلُ

وَيَدْرَؤُا عَنْهَا الْعَذَابَ أَنْ تَشْهَدَ أَرْبَعَ شَهَادَاتٍ بِاللهِ إِنَّهُ لَمِنَ الْكَاذِبِينَ	**24-8** And it shall avert the chastisement from her, if she testifies four times bearing Allah to witness, that he is of those who lie.
يَوْمَ تَشْهَدُ عَلَيْهِمْ أَلْسِنَتُهُمْ وَأَيْدِيهِمْ وَأَرْجُلُهُم بِمَا كَانُوا يَعْمَلُونَ	**24-24** On the day when their tongues and their hands and their feet bear witness against them as to what they used to do.

Note:

Almost all plurals especially of broken type (see chapter 13) are taken as feminine and the verb for such predicate will be a feminine singular.

Imperfect Form V تَفْعَلَانِ

وَوَجَدَ مِنْ دُوْنِهِم امرَأتين تذودان	**28 - 23** And he found besides them two women keeping back their (flocks)

Imperfect Form VI يَفْعَلْنَ

وَلَا يَحِلُّ لَهُنَّ أَن **يَكْتُمْنَ** مَا خَلَقَ اللهُ فِى أَرْحَامِهِنَّ .	**2-228** And it is not lawful for them (women) to conceal what Allah has created in their wombs.
وَاللَّائِى **يَئِسْنَ** مِن الْمَحِيضِ	**65-4** And those of your women who **despair** of mensturation.

Imperfect Form VII تَفْعَلُ

وَإِذْ **تخلق** من الطِّين كَهَيْئة الطير بِإِذْنِى **فَتَنْفُخُ** فِيهَا فَتَكُون طيراً بِإِذْنِى **وَتُبْرِئُ** الأَكْمَهَ وَالأَبْرَصَ بِإِذْنِى	**5- 110** When thou created, out of clay, a thing like the form of a bird by My permission then thou did breath into it and it became a bird by My permission and thou didst heal the blind and the leprous by My permission.

Imperfect Form VIII تَفْعَلاَنِ

فَبِأَيِّ آلاَءِ رَبِّكُمَا تُكَذِّبَانِ .	**55-13** (O' jinn and Human beings!) Which of the bounties of your Lord will you deny?

Note

The verb تُكَذِّبَانِ though represents Form VIII but not from triliteral type. It is from one of an added verbs , which will be dealt with latter.

Imperfect Form IX تَفْعَلُونَ

وَإِذْ أَخَذْنَا مِيثَاقَكُم لاَ تَسْفِكُونَ دِمَاءَكُمْ وَلاَ تُخْرِجُونَ أَنْفُسَكُمْ مِنْ دِيَارِكُمْ ثُمَّ أَقْرَرْتُمْ وَأَنْتُمْ تَشْهَدُونَ ثُمَّ أَنْتُمْ هٰؤُلاَءِ تَقْتُلُونَ أَنْفُسَكُمْ .	**2-84** And when we made a convenant with you: you **shall not** shed your blood not turn your people out of your cities; then you promised and you bear withness; yet ,you it is who would slay your people'.
أَفَتُؤْمِنُونَ بِبَعْضِ الْكِتَابِ وَتَكْفُرُونَ بِبَعْضٍ .	**2-85** Do you then believe in part of the book and deny the other?.

Imperfect Form X تَفْعَلِين

قَالُوا أَتَعْجَبِينَ مِنْ أَمْرِ ٱللهِ	**11-73** They said: Wonderest thou at Allah's commandment.

Imperfect Form XI تَفْعَلَانِ

Not occured in triliteral indicative imperfect. An example may be driven from subjunctive imperfect (which will be dealt with in next chapter) of a weak verb :

إِنْ تَتُوبَا إِلَى اللهِ ..	**66-4** If you both turn to Allah

Imperfect Form XII تَفْعَلْنَ

إِنْ كُنْتُنَّ تُرِدْنَ ٱلْحَيَاةَ ٱلدُّنْيَا	**33-28** if you (ladies) wish the worldly life. (again this form has not occurred in tri-literal) .

Imperfect Form XIII أَفْعَلُ

إِنَّنِى مَعَكُمَا أَسْمَعُ وَأَرَىٰ	**20-46** Surely, I am with you both .I hear and I see .

Imperfect Form XIV نَفْعَلُ

يَوْمَ نَحْشُرُهُمْ جَمِيعاً	**6-22** When we shall gather, them all together.
وَنَطْمَعُ أَنْ يُدْخِلَنَا رَبُّنَا مَعَ ٱلْقَوْمِ ٱلصَّالِحِينَ .	**5-84** And we desire that our Lord may cause us enter with the righteouse people.

EXERCISE

A. Conjugate the Imperfect tense from the following verbs

كَرُمَ ، حَفِظَ ، جَمَعَ ، ضَرَبَ ، قَال ، قَتَلَ

B. Distinguish the following forms by their numbers and stable forms from

تأكلون ، نَبْعَثُ ، تَعْبثُونَ ، تَسْجُدُونَ ، تَسجُدِينَ ، تَقْتُلونَ ،
يَقْتُلنَ ، تَحفَظنَ ، نَأكُلُ ، أَنْصر ، يَنْصُرُونَ ، تَحْمَدَانِ

C. Translate into English :

١ – وَإذ قُلنَا للملائكة اسْجُدُوا لآدَمَ فَسَجَدُوا إلَّا إبليسَ أَبى وَاستكبر وَكَانَ مِنَ الكافرين

٢ – وإذ قال موسٰى لِقومه إنَّ الله يَأْمُرُكم أنْ تذبحوا بَقَرَة قالوا أَتَتَّخِذُنَا هُزُواً قال أعوذ بالله أن أكون مِنَ الجاهلينَ

٣ - وإذْ أَخَذْنَا مِيثاقَ بَنِى إسْرَائِيلَ لَا تَعْبُدُونَ إِلَّا اللهَ

٤ - وَإذْ أخَذْنَا مِيْثاقَكُم لا تَسفِكُونَ دِماءَكُم وَلا تُخْرِجُونَ أَنْفُسَكُمْ مِن دِيَارِكُم ثُمَّ أقْرَرْتُم وأَنْتُم تَشْهَدُونَ

D. Translate into Arabic:

For the first three years, or rather less, of his mission, the Prophet preached only to his family and his intimate friends, while (use بَيْنَمَا) the people of Mecca as a whole regarded him as one who had become (أُصبَحَ) a little made. The first of all his converts was his wife Khadija , the second his cousin Ali whom he adopted , the third his servant Zayd his old friend Abu Bakr also was among those early converts with some of his dependents.

If you are in doubt concerning that which we revealed to Mohammad, produce a Sura of this like and call your witnesses beside Allah if you are truthful.

VOCUBULARY

إِذْ	when , remember that time when
اَلْمَلَائِكَة	Angels
سَجَدُوا	they bow their head in respect (Perf 3 P. M)
أَبَىٰ	he refused (Perf 3 P. M. sing)

إِسْتَكْبَرَ	he was proud (Perf 3 P.M. sing)
ذَبَحَ	to sacrifice (Perf 3 P.M. sing)
أَعُوذُ	I seek refuge (Imper I P)
مِيْثَاقٌ	convenant
سَفَكَ	to shed blood
يَخْرُجُ	to turn out , cause to get out
أَقْرَرْتُمْ	You promised
تَشْهَدُونَ	You bear witness

People	الْقَوْمُ	The first of all	أَوَّلُهُمْ
Convert	الَّذِى أَسْلَمَ	Servant	اَلْخَادِمُ
Dependence	تَحْتَ الْكِفَالَةِ	Doubt	اَلشَّكُّ
Concerning with	عَمَّا/ عَنْهُ	(preposition)	
To produce	يَنْتِجُ/ إِنْتَاجٌ	Call witness	تَشْهَدُ
Truthful	الصَّادِقُ		

CHAPTER 8

MOODS OF IMPERFECT

Arabic has three kinds of moods :

1.	Indicative	اَلْمُضَارِعُ الْمَرْفُوعُ
2.	Subjunctive	اَلْمُضَارِعُ الْمَنْصُوبُ
3.	Jussive	اَلْمُضَارِعُ الْمَجْزُومُ

The Imperfect indicative has already been dealt with in chapter 7, which makes a plain statement, whether applicable to the present or the futrue. But the Imperfect, by slight changes may be in subjunctive or jussive omoods. Arab grammarians take the indicative case as an absolute unit that is influenced and shaped according to the prefixed nouns or particles that are called in arabic العوامل ع awamil (elements) e.g. The simple Imperfect tens such as يَفْعَلُ he does or will do is vowelled with "damma" in its final letter and gives the meaning of a plain statement but when it is preceded by a particle such as لَنْ or لَمْ its vowel of the final letter will be changed and the meaning will differ from what has its absolute case. However, the Indicative mood of the Imperfect could be introduced as فعل المضارع . The Imperfect Tens, i.e, its simple case

Without an element. These عوامِل elements that turn the indicative mood to the subjunctive one, are :

I.	أن	an
e.g.	أَمَرتُه أنْ يَذْهَبَ	, I ordered him to go .

II.	ألّا (أن + لا = ألا)	may not
e.g.	أَلّا يَقُول إِنّي لَا أَعْلَم	so he may not say I do not know.

III.	لن	will never
e.g.	لنَ يذْهَبَ محمود	Mahmood will never go.

IV	لِأن	in order to
e.g	لِأن يَفْعَلَ ما يَشَاءُ	sc he may do what he pleases.

V.	حتى	until
e.g.	حَتى يَعُودَ إِلَى الحَقِّ	until (or so that) he may return to the truth .

These particles or noun which we may call العَوامِلُ bring two-fold changes in the simple indicative forms of the Imperfect:

1. They change the vowel of the final letter from damma to fatha,

thus يفعلُ becomes يَفْعَلَ and omit "nuns" of duals and plurals except those of feminine plurals:
يَفْعَلْنَ (3rd Pers.,Plur.Fem) تَفْعَلْنَ (2nd Pers.Plur.Fem.)

2. give the meaning of subjunctive mood. The conjugation with لن will never'is as following:

	Singular
3Rd Person, Masc	لَن يذهَبَ
3rd Person, Fem.	لن تَذْهَبَ
2nd Person, Masc.	لن تذهَبَ
2nd Person, Fem.	لَن تَذْهَبِى
1st Persom, Masc. &Fem.	لَنْ أذْهَبَ

	Daul
3rd Person, Masc.	لن يذهبا
3rd Person, Fem.	لن تذهبا
2nd Person, Masc.	لن تذهبا
2nd Person, Fem.	لن تذهبا

	Plural
3rd Person, Masc.	لن يَذْهبوا
3rd Person, Fem.	لن يَذْهَبْنَ
2nd Person, Masc.	لن تَذهبُوا
2nd Person, Fem.	لن تَذْهَبْنَ
1st Person, Masc.& Fem.	لَن نَذْهَبَ

The Nun of Fem.Plural is not omitted.The subjunitive is also made by placing one of the following elements before the indicative (mudaare ع مضارع)

كى ، لِ ، أن

Here are some examples from the Holy Qur'an :

أن "an" = lest, to ...

أنْ تقولَ نَفسٌ يَا حَسْرَتى ..	**39-56** Lest a soul should say o woe is me.

أوَ لَمْ يَرَوا أنَّ الله الذى خَلَقَ السَّموات والأرضَ قادِرٌ على أن يَخْلُقَ مِثْلَهُمْ	**17-99** See thy not that Allah created the heavens and the earth, is able to create the like of them.

أَلَّا (أن + لا = أَلَّا)	alla	so may not
حَقِيقٌ عَلَىٰ أَن لَّا أَقُولَ عَلَى اللهِ إِلَّا الْحَقَّ		**7-105** worthy of not saying about Allah except the truth.

لَنْ	lan	will never
فَلَنْ يَغْفِرَ اللهُ لَهُمْ		**9-80** Allah will nver forgive them

لِ	le	for, that
لِيَعْلَمَ أَنِّى لَم أَخُنْهُ بِالْغَيْبِ		**12-52** This is that he might know that I have not been unfaithful to him in secret.

لِإِنْ	lean	for, that
وَأُمِرتُ لِأَنْ أَكُونَ أَوَّلَ الْمُسْلِمِينِ		**39-12** And I am commanded to be the first of those who submit.

حَتَّى	hatta	untill
حَتَّى يَمِيزَ الْخَبِيثَ مِنَ الطَّيِّبِ		**3-179** untill He separates the evil from the good'

كيلا	Kayla	so that, so that not.

كَيْلاَ يَكُونَ دُولَةَ بَيْنَ الأَغْنِيَاءِ	**59- 7** So that it be not taken by turns by the rich among you
لَنْ تَنَالوا الْبِرَّ حَتَّى تُنْفِقُوا مِمَّا تُحِبُّونَ	**3-92** You can not attain to righteousness unless you spend out ot what you love.
قُلْتُم لَن يَبْعَثَ اللهُ من بَعْدِهِ رَسُولا	**40-34** You said Allh wil nver raise after him a messenger.
وَأَنَّا ظَنَنَّا أن لَنْ تقولَ الإِنْسُ والجِنُّ عَلَى الله كَذِبا	**72-5** And we thought that men and jinn will not utter a lie against Allah
لِيَغْفِرَ لَكَ اللهُ ما تَقَدَّمَ مِن ذَنْبِكَ وما تَأَخَّرَ	**48-2** That allah may cover for thee thy shortcomings in the past and those to come
وَكَفَّ أَيْدِيَ النَّاسِ عَنْكُمْ وَلِتَكُونَ آيَةً لِلْمؤمِنِينَ	**48-20** And He held back the hands of men from you and that it may be a sign for the believers.
لِيَقْطَعَ طَرَفاً مِنَ الَّذينَ كَفَروا	**3-127** That He may cut off a part of those who disbelieve.

لِيَجْزِى اللهُ الصَّادِقِينَ بِصِدقِهِم وَيُعَذِّبَ المنافقينَ إن شاءَ أو يتوبَ عليهم	**33-24** That Allah may reward the truthful for their truth chastise the hypocrites if He pleases, or turn to them (mercifully)
لَمَسْجِدٌ أُسِّسَ على التقوىٰ من أوَّل يوم أَحَقُّ أن تَقُومَ فيه	**9-108** A Mosque founded on observance of duty from the first day is more deserving that then shouldst stand in it.
يُرِيدُونَ أن يُبَدِّلوا كلامَ اللهِ	**48-15** they desire to change the words of Allah.
أَلَّا تَخَافُوا وَلا تَحْزَنوا	**41-30** Fear not, nor be grieved.
حتى يَلِجَ الجمَل فى سمِّ الخِيَاطِ	**7-40** Untill the camel passes through the eye of the needle.
لا تَدخُلوا بُيُوتاً غير بُيُوتِكُم حَتى تَستَأنِسوا	**24-27** Enter not houses other than your own houses, until you have asked permission.

لِكَى لَا تَحْزَنُوا عَلَىٰ ما فَاتَكُم	**3-153** that you not grieve what escaped you.

EXERCISE

A Translate into Arabic:

I will never go over there. (use لَنْ)

He came to me in order that we might go to school today together

My uncle came here this afternoon to recite the Holy Qur'an.

I can not enter my brother's room because he locked the door of his room and took the key with him.

Why did they (Fem.) take this book?

She took this to read it.

Boys who played football in front of my house came again today to play there.

Does they (Fem.) know that his teacher wants to go to Mecca,this year to perform Hajj?

My brother made mistake in his calculation but he was afraid to say so lest his neighbour laugh at him (in order that his neighbour might not laugh at him).

He came here to be present at this session.

We went up the mountain this morning to play there with the boys and our neighbours.

Who took the key of my car?

Thy brother's knif is very sharp.

Thy father will never accept to go somewhere at the time of prayers.

B. Translate into English:

أمَرَ اللهُ المسلمينَ أن يتَبِعُوا أوامِرَه وأن يَجتَنِبوا المُنْكَرَاتِ وأَنْ يَفْعَلوا الخَيْر ويأمروا بِهِ وَألَّا يَقُولوا على اللهِ إلَّا الحَقَّ ، وأنْ يَعدِلوا بَيْنَ النَّاسِ ، وَألَّا يَجْعَلُوا الدِّينَ لَهْواً . إنَّ اللهَ يَغْفِرُ الذُّنوبَ جَميعاً ولَنْ يَغْفِرَ لِلْمُشْرِكِينَ لِأنَّ الشِّركَ ظُلْمٌ عَظِيمٌ . لَا تَتْرُكِ الطَّعَامَ مَكْشُوفاً حَتَى يَقَعَ الذُبابَ فِيهِ ، حافِظْ على صحتكَ كي لا تَمْرَضَ . لأن يهدىَ اللهُ انساناً عَلى يَدِكَ فَهُوَ خيرٌ لَكَ مِنَ الأموال الطَائِلَةِ وَاعْمَل لِدِينِكَ وَوَطَنِكَ قَبْلَ فَوَاتِ الأَوانِ.. أن تقولَ لو كُنْت قَوِيًا شَابًا فعلتُ كَذا وَكَذا .

VOCABULARY

In order to, that	لِأَن
To recite	تَلَا ـ يَتْلُو
He locked	قَفَل ، يَقفلُ
To perform	أدَّىٰ ، يُؤَدِّى
Calculation	حاسبَ ، يُحاسبُ

Neighbour	جِيرَان PL الجَارُ
Session	الدَّورَة
Knif	السكين
To follow	اتبع ، يتبعُ
To avoid	أَعْرَضَ ، يُعرِض
Forbidden things	المُحرَّماتُ
The Truth	الصِّدقُ
To do just	عَدَل ، يعدِل
Leasure	اللَّهْو
Forgives	العَفْوُ
Sins	الذُّنوبُ
Wrong	الظُّلم
Open	فَتَحَ ، يَفْتَحُ المَفْتُوحُ
Uncounted	لَا يُحصَىٰ
Passing away	مَضَىٰ ، يَمْضى
Youthful	الفتُوَّة
Flys	الذُبَاب
Scribing	الشِّرْكُ

CHAPTER 9

MOODS OF THE IMPERFECT-II

The Jussive

1. The mood of negative (or jussive) does not vary from the subjunctive (Mood of statement) except that the final radical takes "Sukun" ـْـ i.e. the final letter is cloased and had no vowel e.g.

Conjugation			
3 rd. P. sing Masc	يَكْتُبْ	2 nd P. Sing Masc	تَكْتُبْ
Dual	يَكْتُبَا	Dual	تَكْتُبَا
Plu	يَكْتُبُوا	Plu	تَكْتُبُوا
sing. Fem	تَكْتُبْ	sing Fem	تَكْتُبِى
Dual	تكتبا	Dual	تَكْتُبَا
Plu	يَكْتُبْنَ	Plu	تَكْتُبْنَ
Ist p. Sing	أَكْتُبْ	Ist p. Dual & Plu	نَكْتُبْ

2. the verb كان "to be" in this mood loses its " و " when the last radical is vowelless.e.g.

3 rd P sing Masc	يَكُنْ	2 nd P. sing Masc	تَكُنْ
Dual	يَكُونَا	Dual	تَكُونَا
Plu	يَكُونُوا	Plu	تَكُونُوا
Sing Fem	تَكُنْ	Sing Fem	تَكُونِى
Dual	تَكُونَا	Dual	تَكُونَا
Plu	يَكُنَّ	Plu	تَكُنَّ
Ist P. Sing	نَكُنْ	Ist P. Dual & Plu	أَكُنْ

3· This mood is used after the following particles:

I. لا "do not" i.e. with prohibition e.g.

لاَ تكتُبْ do not write	لا تَكُنْ كَذَّابًا don't be liar

H.Q.

لا تَدْخُلوا مِنْ بَابٍ وَاحِدٍ	**12-67** Do not enter by one gate.
لا تكُنْ لِلخَائِنِينَ خَصِيماً	**3-104** And be not one pleading the cause of dishonest.

II. لم to deny a statement when so used it gives the meaning of the past perfect e.g.

Perfect ما كَتَبَ he did not write

Imperfect (Jussive) لم يَكْتُبْ he did not write.

H.Q.

مَا جَعَلَ اللهُ لِرَجُلٍ مِنْ قَلْبَيْنِ فِى جَوفِهِ	**33-4** Allah has not made for any man two hearts within him.
لَمْ نَجْعَلْ لَهُ مِنْ قَبْلُ سَمِيًّا	**19-7** We have not made before any one his equal.

III. لمّا "not yet" e.g. لمّا يَكْتُبْ he has not yet written

H.Q.

وَلَمَّا يَدْخُلِ الإِيمَانُ فِى قُلُوبِكُمْ	**49-14** And faith has not yet entered into your hearts.

Note : A vowelless letter is changed to kasra —— when followed by a definite article as in لَمْ يَدْخُلِ الإِيمَانُ

IV. After the "Lam of command" لاَمِ الأَمْرْ which expresses a command, e.g.

لِيَكْتُبْ رِسَالَةً إلى أخيه let him write a letter to his brother.

H.Q.

لِيُنْفِقْ ذُو سَعَةٍ مِن سَعَتِهِ	**65-7** Let him who has abundance spend out of his abundance.

V. In the Protesis and Apodosis correlative conditional sentences* which are introduced by the particles مَنْ "إِنْ" "if" he who, if anyone e.g. إِنْ تَجْلِس أَجْلِسْ if thou shall sit I shall sit.

مَنْ يَعْمَلْ سُوءاً يَنْدَم he who does evil will regret,

H.Q.

إِنْ يَشَأْ يُذْهِبْكُم أَيُّهَا النَّاسُ	**4-133** If He please will take you O people.
مَنْ يَعْمَلْ سُوءاً يُجزَ بِهِ	**4-123** Whoever does evil will be requited for it.

VI. After particles أَيْنَ where أَيَّ which, attached to "to" ما e.g. from

H.Q.

أَيْنَمَا تَكُونُوا يُدْرِككُّمْ المَوتُ	**4-78** Werver you are death will overtake you.
أَيًّا مَّا تَدْعُوا فَلَهُ الأَسْمَاءُ الْحسنَىٰ	**17-110** By whatever(name) you call on Him, He has the best names.

4. The Jussive may be rendered more exphatic by adding a vowelless"nun" نون خفيفه or a duplicated nun نونٌ مُشَدَّدَة this form Energetic forms (Modus energicus).

---

* conditional sentenees will be dealt in chapter 26

Modus energicus I	Modus energicus II
يكتُبَنْ	يكتُبَنَّ

This is often strengthened by prefixing the particle ل e.g. لَيَكْتُبَنَّ

H.Q.	
وَلَتَعْلَمُنَّ أَيُّنَا أَشَدُّ عَذَابًا وَأَبْقَى	**20 - 71** surely thou shalt know who among us will have severer chistisement and lasting one.

with negative particle لا may give the meaning of "thou shalt not" e.g. لا تَقْتُلُنَّ thou shalt not kill.

H.Q.	
ولا تقُولوا لِمَن يُقْتَلُ فِي سَبِيلِ اللهِ أَمْوَاتٌ	**2-154** Thou shalt not say dead for these who are killed in the path of Allah.

Examples From The Holy Qur'an	
فَلَا تَقُلْ لَهُمَا أُفٍّ وَلَا تَنْهَرْهُمَا	**17-23** Do not say "Fie" to them (parents) nor chidthem.
وَأَمَّا السَّائِلَ فَلَا تَنْهَرْ	**93-10** And him who asks, do not chide.
وَلَا تَقْرَبُوا الفَوَاحِشَ	**6-15** Do not get nigh to indecen cies

لا تَجْعَل مَعَ اللهِ إلٰهًا آخَرَ	**17-22** Associate not any other god with Allah.
(خُذْهَا وَ) لاَ تَخَفْ	**20-21** Seize it and fear not.
أَوَلَمْ يَنظُرُوا فِى مَلَكُوتِ السَّموَاتِ وَالأَرْضِ	**7-185** Do they not consider the kingdom of heavens and the earth.
لَمْ نَجْعَل لَهُ مِنْ قَبلُ سَمِيًّا	**19-7** We have not made before any on his equal
أَلَمْ أَقُل لَّكَ إِنَّكَ لن تَسْتَطِيعَ مَعِىَ صَبْرًا	**18-75** Did I not say to thee that thou couldst not have patience with me
لِيَعْلَم أَنِّى لَمْ أَخُنْهُ بِالْغَيْبِ	**12-52** This is that he might learn that I have not been unfaithful to him.
لاَ يَنْفَعُ نَفْسًا إِيمَانُهَا لَمْ تَكُنْ آمَنَتْ مِنْ قَبْلُ	**6-158** Its faith will not profit a soul which believed not before.
لَمْ يَكُنِ الَّذِينَ كَفَرُوا مِنْ أَهْلِ الْكِتَابِ وَالْمُشْرِكِينَ مُنفكِّينَ حَتّٰى تَأْتِيَهُمُ الْبَيِّنَةُ	**98-1** Those who disbeliveve from among the people of the book and the idolaters could not have been freed till clear evidence came to them.

وَلَمَّا يَدْخُلِ الْإِيمَانُ فِى قُلُوبِكُمْ	**49-14** .. and faith has not yet entered in Your hearts.
ولمَّا يَعْلَمِ اللهُ الَّذِينَ جاهَدُوا مِنْكُمْ	**3-142** And Allah has not yet knows those from among you who strive hard.
بَل لَمَّا يَذُوقُوا عَذَابِ	**38-8** Nay, they have not yet tested my chistisement.
لِيَقْضِىَ عَلَينا رَبُّكَ	**43-77** Let thy Lord make an end of us.
مَا نَنْسَخْ مِنْ آيَةٍ أو نُنْسِهَا نَأْتِ بِخَيْرٍ مِنْهَا	**2-106** Whatever versese abrogate or cause to be forgotten, we bring one better than it.
وَإِنْ يَمْسَسْكَ بِخَيْرٍ فَهُوَ عَلَى كُلِّ شَىْءٍ قَدِير	**6-17** And if he touch thee with good, He is Possessor of power over all things.
وَإِنْ تُصِبْهُمْ سَيِّئَةٌ بِمَا قَدَّمَتْ أَيْدِيهِم إِذَا هُمْ يَقْنَطُونَ	**30-36** And if an evil befall them for what their hands have already wrongth Lo they despair .

EXERCISE

Translate into Arabic

Let Macca be the most beautiful city under the sun, students! He did not know (use لَمْ) any news from his home. O girl do not go market this time, O boy don't open the window. I did not understand (use لَمْ) this orgument. Boys are lazy, they did not memorize conjugations. Do not leave your friends in the anxiety. Do not prevent me from praying. Let us drink the Zamzam. The sister and mother were not able to go out. Let me be at your side among these groups. O Ali I asked Bakr to com in, but some one else entered. Next month a visiting professor will come to the university. If Hasan goes home I will go with him. Whatever my father decides I will obey him. My brother could not carry this heavy chair yesterday evening because he was very tired. Thy friend Habib drank a cup of tea this morning. Do not open these two windows.

Translate into English :

١ – فَمَنْ يَعْمَلْ مِنَ الصَّالِحَاتِ وَهُوَ مُؤْمِنٌ فَلا كُفْرانَ لِسَعْيِه وإنَّا لَه كَاتِبُونَ

٢ – قُل لَنْ يُصِيبَنَا إلا مَا كَتَبَ اللهُ لَنَا هُوَ مولانَا وَعَلَى اللهِ فَلْيَتَوَكَّلِ المُؤمِنُون

٣ – وتاللهِ لأَكِيدَنَّ أصنامكم

٤ – بِسْمِ اللهِ الرَّحْمٰنِ الرَّحِيمِ الٓر كِتَابٌ أَنْزَلْنَاهُ إِلَيْكَ لِتُخرِجَ النَّاسَ مِنَ الظُّلُمَاتِ إلى النُّور بِإِذْنِ رَبِّهِم إلى صِراطِ العَزِيزِ الحَمِيد

٥ – قَالَ قَائِل مِنهم لا تَقْتُلوا يُوسُفَ وألقُوه في غَيْبتِ الْجُبِّ يَلْتَقِطه بَعْضُ السَّيارَةِ إِنْ كُنُتم فَاعِلِينَ . قَالُوا يَا أَبَانَا مَا لَكَ لا تأمنّا على يُوسُفَ وإِنَّا لَهُ لناصِحُون إرْسله مَعَنَا غداً يرتع ويَلعبْ وَإِنَّا لَهُ لَحَافِظُونَ

VOCABULARY

أَجْمَلُ الْمُدُنِ	Most beautiful city	دَلِيلٌ	arguement
كَسْلَانُ ، كَسَالَى	lazy	حَفِظَ	to memorize
التَّصْرِيفِ	conjugation	قَلَقٌ	anxiety
مَنَعَ	to prevent	جَانِبٌ	side
زَائِر	visit or he visted (3pm)		
قَرَّرَ	to decide	أَطَاعَ	to obey
حَمَلَ	to carry	ثَقِيلٌ	heavy
لِأَنْ	because	متعب/تَعْبَانٌ	tired
الصَّالِحَةُ	Plu. الصَّالِحَاتِ good	دَخَلَ	to enter
سَعَى	effort	كُفْرَانَ	rijection
تَاللهِ	by Allah	مَوْلَى	Lord
يُصِيبُ	(imper.3P.singM) befall of evil		
كَيْدَ	to plan لَأَكِيدَنَّ I shall plan certainly		
أَصْنَام	idols	صَنَم	sing
الظُّلُمَاتِ	The Darkness	تَوَكَّلَ	to trust
إذن	permission	تَوَلَّى	to turn
العَزِيز	The powerful one	Allah's name of tributes.	
الحَمِيد	The preaised one		
غَيَبَتِ الجُبِّ	The bottom of the well		

يَلْتَقِطْهُ	Imper. perfe اِلْتَقَطَ to pick up		
(خَوفٌ) أخافُ	To gear	مُدْبِرِين	showing back
غافِلون	Headless	النُّور	(The) Light
الصَّمَدُ	One on whom all depend		
يُولَدُ	Begotten		
ناصِحُون	well - wishers	صِرَاطٌ	path
يَرْتَعُ ، رَتَعَ	enjoy	السَّيَّارَةُ	travellers
يَحْزُنُ . حَزِنَ	to grieve	الذِّئْبُ	Wolf
ذَهَبَ بِهِ	to tke some one with		
يَلِدُ وَلَدَ	begets	أَحَدٌ	One
كُفُوءً	Simllar	غَدًا	tomorrow
		يَلعبُ . لَعِبَ	play

CHAPTER 10

THE PASSIVE VOICE

1. The Active voice of the verb is called مَعْلُومٌ **'Known'** while the Passive is termed as مَجْهُولٌ , **'unkonow'**. The passive is formed by changing the vowels of the active. It is characterised by h"damma" ـُ on the first letter of the active following "kasra" ـِ in the perfect and Fatha ـَ in the imperfect, e.g.

Active	Passive
Perfect:	
فَتَحَ he opened.	فُتِحَ it was opened.
فَتَحَ بَابًا he opened a door.	فُتِحَ بَابٌ a door was opened.
كَتَبَ رِسَالَةً he wrote a letter.	كُتِبَتْ رِسَالَةٌ a letter was written.
نَصَرَنِى he helped me.	نُصِرْتُ I was helped.
Imperfect:	
يَفْتَحُ he opens	يُفْتَحُ It is (being) opened.
يَكْتُبُ he writes.	يُكْتَبُ It is (being) written.
يَنْصُرُكَ he helps you.	تُنْصَرُ You are (will be) helped.

The following conjugation will show you the places of vowels:

Perfect

Sing. 3rd Pers. Masc.	نُصِرَ nusira	he was helped.
Sing. 3rd Pers. Fem.	نُصِرَتْ nusirat	She was helped.
Sing. 2nd Pers. Masc.	نُصِرْتَ nusirta	thou wert helped.
Sing. 2 nd Pers. Fem.	نُصِرْتِ nusirti	Thou (f) were helped.
Sing. 1st Pers. Masc & Fem.	نُصِرْتُ unusirtu	I was helped.

Imperfect

Sing. 3rd Pers. Masc.	يُنْصَرُ yunsaru	he is helped.
Sing. 3rd Pers. Fem.	تُنْصَرُ tunsaru	she is helped.
Sing. 2nd Pers. Masc.	تُنْصَرُ tunsaru	thou art helped.
Sing. 2nd Pers. Fem.	تُنْصَرِين tunsareena	thou art helped.
Sing. 1st Pers. Masc. & Fem.	أُنْصَرُ ansaru	I was helped.

2. In case of the imperfect subjunctive and jussive the conjugation will be as below:

Subjunctive

يُكْتَبَ	yuktaba
تُكْتَبَ	tuktaba
تُكْتَبِي	tuktabi
أُكْتَبَ	uktaba

Jussive

يُكْتَبْ	yuktab
تُكْتَبْ	tuktab
تُكْتَبِي	tuktabi
أُكْتَبْ	uktab

3. The passive voice of perfect from weak verbs is given below:

Perfect

Active

قال qaala	he said.
دَعَا daعa	he called.
باع baعa	he sold

Passive

قِيلَ qeela	it was said.
دُعِيَ duعiya	he was called.
بِيعَ beeعa	it was sold.

The passive of imperfect from weak verbs will be as following:

Imperfect

Active

يَقُولُ yaqoolo	he says
يَدعو yadعu	he calls
يَبِيعُ yabeeعu	he sells

Passive

يُقَالُ yoqaalu	it is said.
يُدعىٰ yudعa	he is called.
يُبَاعُ yubaaعu	it is sold.

4. The subject of a passive verb is called نَائِبُ الْفَاعِلِ i.e 'representative of the doers'. The Arabic passive is not like English in which the doer is mentioned with particle

'by' e.g. the glass was broken by the maid. In Arabic for this purpose, an active voice will be used e.g. كَسَرتِ الخَادِمَةُ كَأساً This is the reason why this form in Arabic is termed by المجهول i.e. the doer of that act is unknown.

5. **The Participle** (Active and Passive)

The Active participle (from the triliteral verb) is formed by adding an 'alif after first radical and vowelling the second radical with kasra, thus:

فاعِلٌ fa ع ilun	a doer,	Masc. Sing.
فاعِلانِ fa ع ilanne	two doers,	Masc. Dual.
فاعِلُون fa ع iloona	doers,	Masc. Plur.
فاعِلَةٌ fa ع ilatun	a doer,	Fem. Sing.
فاعِلَتانِ fa ع ilataane	two doers,	Fem. Dual.
فاعِلاتٌ fa ع ilaatun	doers,	Fem. Plur.

The Passive Participle (that is not English Past Participle) is formed on the measure مَفْعُولٌ for the simple triliteral verb. The following conjugation will illustrate the prefixed letters and vowelling:

maf ع oolun 'which is done', one on whom an action is befallen.

مكتوبٌ Maktoobun	written.
مَفْتُوحٌ Maftoohun	opened.
مَضْرُوبٌ Madroobun	struck.

Dual. Masc.	مفعولان مفعولَيْنِ	Maf ع ulaane. Maf ع ulaine.	(Nomanatire)
Sing: Fem.	مَفْعُولَةٌ	Maf ع ulatun.	(Accasative & Genative)
Dual. Fem.	مفعولتان	Maf ع ulataane.	Also مَفْعُولَتَيْنِ Maf ع ulataine in Acc. and Gen
Plur. Masc.	مَفْعُولُون	Maf ع uloona.	Also مَفْعُولِين Maf ع ulena in Acc. and Gen
Plur. Fem.	مَفْعُولاتٌ	Maf ع ulaatun.	

Examples from They Holy Qur'an:

3rd Pers. Sing. Masc. فُعِلَ

يَا أَيُّهَا الَّذِينَ آمَنُوا كُتِبَ عَلَيْكُمْ الصِّيَامُ كَمَا كُتِبَ عَلَى الَّذِينَ مِن قَبْلِكُمْ .	**2-183** O' you who believe, fasting is prescribed for you (lit. written upon you) as it was prescribed (was written) for those before you.
وحُشِرَ لِسُلَيْمَانَ جُنُودُه	**27-17** And there were gathered together into solomon his armies.
وَجُمِعَ الشَّمْسُ والْقَمَرُ	**75-9** And the sun and moon are brought together.
أفَإنْ مَاتَ أو قُتِلَ	**3-144** If then he dies or is killed.

3rd Pers. Plural. Masc. فُعِلُوا

مَا مَاتُوا وَمَا قُتِلُوا	**3-156** They did not die and have not been killed.
أَمْ خُلِقُوا من غَيرِ شَیءٍ	**52-35** Or were they created without a (creative) thing?
أُذِنَ للذين يقاتِلُون بِأَنَّهم ظُلِمُوا	**22-39** Permission (to fight) is given to those who are fought because they have been wronged.

3rd Pers. Sing. Fem. فُعِلَتْ

أَفَلَا يَنْظُرُونَ إِلَى الإِبِلِ كيفَ خُلِقَتْ	**88-17** will they not regard the camels how they are created?
بِأَیِّ ذَنْبٍ قُتِلَتْ	**81-9** For what sin she was killed.
وَإِذَا الصُّحُفُ نُشِرَتْ	**81-10** And when the books are spread.

2nd Person. Plur. Masc. فُعِلْتُمْ

وَلَئِنْ قُتِلْتُمْ فی سبيل الله أو مُتُّمْ	**3-157** And what though you be slain in Allah's way or die
وَلَئِن مُتُّمْ أَو قُتِلْتُمْ لَإِلَى الله تُحْشَرُونَ	**3-158** And what though you be slain or die, when into Allah you are gathered.

1st Person. Sing. Masc. & Fem. فُعِلْتُ

وَلَئِن رُجِعْتُ إِلَىٰ رَبِّى إِنَّ لِى عِنْدَهُ لَلْحُسْنَىٰ	**41-50** And if I am sent back to my Lord I shall have sure good with Him.
وَلَئِنْ رُدِدْتُ إِلَىٰ رَبِّى لَأَجِدَنَّ خَيْراً مِنْهَا مُنْقَلَباً	**18-36** If I am returned to my Lord I will certainly find a returning place better than this.

1st Person, Plur. Masc. & Fem. فُعِلْنَا

يَقُولُونَ لَو كَانَ لَنَا مِنَ الأَمْرِ شَىْءٌ مَا **قُتِلْنَا** هٰهُنَا	**3-154** They say: Had we any hand in the affairs, we sould not have been slain here.

From Weak Verbs

3rd Pers. Sing. Masc:	جِيىءَ geeya (active: جاء jaa ء a)
	قُضِيَ qudiya (active: قَضَىٰ qada)

وَجِيىءَ بِالنَّبِيِّينَ وَالشُّهَدَاءِ **وَقُضِيَ** بَيْنَهُمْ بِالْحَقِّ	**39-69** ... and the prophets and witnesses **are brought** up and **judgement is given** between them with justice.

قِيلَ qeela (active: قال qaala)

وَقِيلَ بُعْدًا لِلْقَومِ الظَّالِمِينَ	**11-44** and **it was said**, away with the inquitous people.

3rd Pers. Plur. Masc. سُقُوا suqoo (Active: سَقَىٰ saqaa)

وَسُقُوا مَاءً حَمِيمًا	**47-15** and (who) **are given** boiling water to drink.

1st Pers. Sing. Masc. نُهِيتُ nuheeto (Active: نَهَىٰ naha)

قُلْ : إِنِّى نُهِيتُ أَنْ أَعْبُدَ الَّذِينَ تَدْعُونَ مِنْ دُونِ اللهِ	**6-56** say (O'Mohammad) I **am forbidden** to serve those whom you call upon besides Allah.

Imperfect

3rd Pers. Sing. Masc. يُفْعَلُ

وَمَا أَدْرِى مَا يُفْعَلُ بِى	**46-9** and I know not what **will be done** with me.
لم يُخْلَقْ مِثْلُها فى البلادِ	**89- 8** The like of which **was not created** in the lands.
يُعْرَفُ المُجْرِمُونَ بِسِيمَاهُمْ	**55-41** The guilty **will be known** by their marks.

3rd Pers. Plur. Masc. يُفْعَلُون

أَيُشْرِكُون مالا يَخْلُقُ شَيْئاً وَهُم يُخْلَقُون	**7-191** Attribute they as partners to Allah those who created naught, but are **themselves created**
ثُمَّ إليه يُرْجَعُونَ	**6-36** Then to Him they **will be returned.**
يُقَاتِلُونَ فى سَبِيلِ الله فَيَقْتُلُونَ وَيُقْتَلُونَ	**9-111** They fight in the way of Allah and slay and **be slain.**

3rd Pers. Sing Fem. تُفْعَلُ

وإلى الله تُرْجَعُ الأمُور	**2-210** And all cases are returned to Allah.
ستُكْتَبُ شَهَادَتُهم وَيُسْئَلُونَ	**43-19** Their testimony will be recorded and they be questioned.

3rd Pers. Plur. Fem. يُفْعَلْنَ

ذَلِكَ أَدْنَى أَن يُعْرَفنَ فَلاَ يُؤْذَيْنَ	**33-59** That will be better, so that they may be recognized and not annoyed.

2nd Pers. Sing. Masc. تُفْعَلُ

وَلَا تُسْئَلُ عَنْ أَصْحَابِ الْجَحِيمِ	**2-119** And thou **will not be asked** about owners of the hellfire.

2nd Pers. Dual. Masc. تُفْعَلانِ

قَالَ : لَا يَأْتِيكُمَا طَعَامٌ تُرْزَقَانِهِ إِلَّا نَبَّأْتُكُمَا بِتَأْوِيلِهِ	**12-37** He said : The food which you (two) are given, shall not come unto you but I shall tell you interpretation.

2nd Pers. Plur. Masc. تُفْعَلُونَ

اُدْخُلُوا الْجَنَّةَ أَنْتُمْ وَأَزْوَاجُكُمْ تُحْبَرُونَ	**43-70** Enter the garden, you and your wives, to be made glad.
إِنْ تَجْتَنِبُوا كَبَائِرَ مَا تُنْهَوْنَ عَنْهُ	**4-31** If you avoid the great things which you are forbidden, we will remit from you your evil deeds.

اسم الفاعل Active Participle

Sing. Masc.

إِنِّي لَا أُضِيعُ عَمَلَ عَامِلٍ مِنْكُمْ	**3-195** Lo ! I suffer not the work of any worker.
بَلْ هُوَ شَاعِرٌ	**21-5** Nay, He is but a poet.

فَلَعَلَّكَ بَاخِعٌ نَفْسَكَ	**18-6** Yet it may be, (that) thou will torment thy soul.

Dual. Masc.	
قَالُوا : إِنْ هٰذَانِ لَسَاحِرَانِ	**20-63** They said: These are two wizards.

Plural. Mase.	
وَالَّذِينَ هُمْ لِلزَّكَاةِ فَاعِلُونَ	**23-4** And who are paers of Zakat (poordue).

Sing. Fem.	
وُجُوهٌ يَوْمَئِذٍ نَاعِمَةٌ لِسَعْيِهَا رَاضِيَةٌ فِى جَنَّةٍ عَالِيَةٍ لَا تَسْمَعُ فِيهَا لَاغِيَةً .	**88-8/11** In that day other faces will be **calm, Glad** for their effort past. In a high garden, where they hear no idle speech.

Plur. Fem.	
إِنَّ الْمُسْلِمِينَ و الْمُسْلِمَاتِ و الْمُؤْمِنِينَ و الْمُؤْمِنَاتِ و الْقَانِتِينَ و الْقَانِتَاتِ	**33-35** Lo! Men **who surrender** unto Allah and women **who surrender** and men **who believe,** and women **who believe,** and men **who obey** and women **who obey.**

اسم المفعول Passive Participle

Sing. Masc.	
أُولَئِكَ لَهُمْ رِزْقٌ مَعْلُومٌ	**37-41** For them there is a **known** provision.
كِتَابٌ مَرْقُومٌ	**83-20** A written record (book)

Sing. Fem.	
فِيهَا سُرُرٌ مَرْفوعَةٌ وَأَكْوابٌ مَوْضُوعَةٌ وَنَمَارِقُ مَصْفُوفَةٌ وَزَرَابِيُّ مَبْثُوثَةٌ	**88-13/16** Wherein are couches raised, and goblets set at hand, and cushions ranged, and silken carpets spread.

EXERCISE

A. Translate into Arabic:

The doors of the mosque were opened, and the prayers were offered with (خُشُوعٌ) humility. She did not know that her brother was given a prize. Yesterday. I know that the Arabs are conquerors and the enemies the conquered. The men mentioned are (some) of (بَعْضَ) my friends. His courage has been mentioned in the his tory books. He was killed with (ب) the sword because the mad men were angry with him. You have been (كنتَ) here for a long time, (period), perhaps you will go now. The prince attended the first session of the Islamic solidarity conference. It was inaugurated by the royal ṣpeech. King Faisal entered the history through (خلال) its widest gate. The Qur'an. is the widely read book in the world. It is recited in the morning and evening. Muslim is he who discharges his duties and obey his Lord and benifits to the humanbeing.

B. Translate into English :

بِسْمِ ٱللهِ الرَّحْمَنِ الرَّحِيمِ . قَدْ أَفْلَحَ الْمُؤْمِنُونَ . الَّذِينَ هُمْ فِى صَلَاتِهِم خَاشِعُونَ .
وَالَّذِينَ هُم عَنِ اللَّغْوِ مُعْرِضُونَ . وَالَّذِينَ هُمْ لِلزَّكَاةِ فَاعِلُونَ . وَالَّذِينَ هُم لِفُرُوجِهِم
حَافِظُونَ . إِلَّا عَلَىٰ أَزْوَاجِهِم أَو مَا مَلَكَتْ أَيْمَانُهُم فَإِنَّهُم غَيرُ مَلُومِينَ . فَمَنِ ٱبْتَغَىٰ
وَرَاءَ ذَٰلِكَ فَأُولَئِكَ هُمُ العَادُونَ . وَالَّذِينَ هُمْ لِأَمَانَاتِهِم وَعَهْدِهِمْ رَاعُونَ . وَالَّذِينَ
هُمْ عَلَىٰ صَلَوَاتِهِم يُحَافِظُونَ . أُولَئِكَ هُمُ الوَارِثُونَ . الَّذِينَ يَرِثُونَ الْفِرْدَوْسَ هُمْ فِيهَا
خَالِدُونَ .

VOCABULARY

humility	خُشُوعٌ	the sword	السَّيْفُ
yesterday	أَمْس	angry	غَضْبَان
conquered	مَفْتُوح , plu مَفْتُوحُونَ / مَفْتُوحِينَ		
madmen	مَجَانِين sing مَجنون		
period	فَتْرَةٌ	the prince	الأَمِير
attended	إِشْتَرَك	inaugurated	افْتَتَح
entered	دَخَل	widest gate	أَوْسَعُ الأَبْوَاب
recited	يُتْلَىٰ	discharged	يؤدى
his duties	وَاجِبَاتِه	benifit	يَنْفَعُ
prize	جَائِزَةٌ plu جَوَائِز	humanbeing	الإِنْسَانُ
conqueror	فَاتِحٌ plu فَاتِحُونَ / فَاتِحِينَ		

الَّذِينَ sing الذّى	who , that , which (a relative pronoun)
هُمْ Who sing هُوَ	pronoun. (will be dealt seperately in coming chapter).
صَلاةُ	prayer
اللَّغْوِ	Vain conversation
فُرُوْحٌ	modesty ف + رَوْحٌ
أَزْوَاجٌ sing زوج	wife or husband
مَلُوْمٌ	blameworthy
وراء ذٰلِكَ	beyond that
عَادُون sing عادٍ	transgressor
أمَانَات sing أمانة	pledge
يُحَافِظُونَ	pay heed to Protect
يَرِثُ	will inherit
خَالِدُونَ	will abide
خَاشِعٌ	state of humbleness.
مُعْرِضٌ	shun , avoid
إِلَّا	(a particle: except , some)
ابْتَغَى	saught , wished
أولَئِكَ	such people or such thing
رَاعُونْ ، رَاعِى	shapherd , protecor
عَهْدٌ .	covenant
وَارِثٌ	Heir
الفِرْدَوْس	paradise

CHAPTER 11

THE ADJECTIVES

1. A noun qualified with an adjective is called (in Arabic اَلْمُرَكَّبُ التَّوْصِيفِي (The Adjectival Compound). The noun which is to be qualified is termed as مَوْصُوفٌ 'mousuf' and the adjective is صِفَةٌ 'sifat**un**' The English simple adjectives such as 'The Long way', 'The white shirt' is translated into Arabic placing the noun first, then the adjective, thus 'The white shirt' will become 'the shirt white'; the long way will be read "the way long" and so on, thus:
The long way اَلطَّرِيقُ الطَّوِيلُ
The white shirt اَلْقَمِيصُ الأَبيضُ

2. An Arabic adjectival phrase (That is not English 'Adjective pharse') is formed by an agreement of noun with the adjective, in the quality, the number and the gender. That is, if the noun is a proper or common one the adjective will receive the same quality, e.g رَجُلٌ كَبِيرٌ a big man اَلرَّجُلُ الْكَبِيرُ the big man likewise if the noun is dual or plural, the adjective will take the Same e.g. رَجُلاَنِ كبيرانِ two big men اَلرَّجُلانِ الكَبِيرانِ the two big men. رِجالٌ كِبَارٌ big men (plural, without an article). اَلرِّجَالُ الكِبَارُ the big men (with an article).

A feminine noun will have an adjective feminised with " ة "
تا المَرْبُوطَة 'ta-almarbuta', thus:

بنتٌ صغيرةٌ	a young girl	البنتُ الصَّغيرَةُ	The Young girl.
بِنْتَانِ صَغيرَتَانِ	two Young girls	البِنْتَانِ الصَّغيرَتَانِ	The two young girls.
بَنَاتٌ صغيراتٌ	young girls	البَنَاتُ الصَّغيرَاتُ	Thy young girls.

The nouns too will be in full agreement with the adjectives as in other cases, e.g.

رَجُلٌ كبيرٌ	in nominative case	(مَرْفوعاً)
رَجُلاً كبيراً	in accusative case	(منصوباً)
رَجُلٍ كبيرٍ	in genetive case	(مَجْرُورًا)

3. If a phrase takes place of a noun it will be regarded as a proper noun. Therefore, the adjective will be particularised with the definite article أَلْ e.g.

بَيْتُ اللهِ الحرامُ	The Holy House of Allah.
مَسْجِدُ المدينةِ الكبيرُ	The big mosque of the city.

Note: An alternative of the vowelling can change the type of the phrase and give quite different meaning, e.g.

بِيْتُ اللهِ العظيمُ	baitullahil azim**u**	The great House of Allah.
بَيْتُ اللهِ العَظيمِ	baitullahil azimi	The House of great Allah.

in the first phrase ' العظيم ' "the great" is qualifying بيت 'bait', "House" and in the latter is qualifying Allah.

Adjective patterns

1. There are certain patterns for denoting an adjective, the first in the active participle which has already been dealt in previous lesson. The rest are forms which give the meaning of the active participle with some intensification in meaning. They are derived from what might be termed as 'stative verbs' that is, verbs which denote a state or condition rather than an act.

(a) فَاعِلٌ **fa ع ilun,** e.g.

صادِقٌ	sadiqun,	upright.
عادل	ع adilun,	judge
جاهِلٌ	jaahilun ,	ignorant

(b) فَعِيلٌ **fa ع eelun,** as

قَدِيرٌ	qadirun,	powerful.
كبِيرٌ	kabirun,	big.
عَظِيمٌ	azimun,	great.

(c) فَعُولٌ **fa ع oolun,** e.g.

ظَلُومٌ	zalumnn,	very opressor,
جَهُولٌ	jahoolun,	very ignorant.

(d) فَعْلان **fa ع laan,** e.g.

رحْمَان	rahmaan,	very kind, merciful
غَضْبَان	ghadbaan,	angry.

عطشان	ع atshaan	thirsty,
زَعْلاَن	za ع laan	annayed

2. Another intensive form of the active participle is فَعَّال fa ع ع aal, e.g. (from The Holy Qur'an).

فَعَّالٌ لِمَا يُرِيد	**85-16** doer (with all might) what He intends.

جبَّار	Jabbar,	compeller.

This pattern is also used to denote occupations, e.g.

خبَّازٌ	khabbazun,	baker
خيَّاطٌ	khayyatun,	tailor,
جَزَّارٌ	jazzarun,	butcher.
طَبَّاخٌ	tabbakhun,	cook.
بَقَّالٌ	baqqalun,	green grocer.

3. Another common form of adjective is that used for colours and defects. Their form for the masculine singular is أَفْعَلُ af ع alu and the feminine singular is فَعْلَاءُ fa ع laau. The plural is فُعْلٌ fu ع lun. That is used for both genders. The following table will illustrate all forms of this pattern.

Sing. Masc.	Dual. Masc.	PL. Masc.
أسْوَدُ aswadu	أسْوَدَانِ aswadane	سُودٌ soodun
أبْيَضُ abyadu	أبْيَضَان abyadane	بِيضٌ beedun
أحْمَرُ ahmaru	أحْمَرانِ ahmaraane	حُمُرٌ humurun

أَبْكَمُ abkamu	أَبْكَمَانِ abkamaane	بُكْمٌ bukmun
أَعْرَجُ aعraju	أَعْرَجَانِ aعrajaane	عُرْجٌ عurjun
أَعْمَى aعmaa	أَعْمَيَانِ aعmayaane	عُمْيٌ عumyun
أَصَمُّ asammu	أَصَمَّانِ assamaane	صُمٌّ summun

Sing. Fem.	Dual. Fem.	PL. Fem.
سَوْدَاءُ soudaaءu	سَوْدَاوَانِ soudaawaane	سُودٌ soodun
بَيْضَاءُ baidaaءu	بَيْضَاوَانِ baidaawaane	بِيضٌ beedun
حَمْرَاءُ hamraaءu	حَمْرَاوَانِ hamraawaane	حُمْرٌ humurun

Sing. Fem.	
خَرْسَاءُ	Kharsaءu
بَكْمَاءُ	bakmaaءu
عَرْجَاءُ	ع arjaaءu
عَمْيَاءُ	ع amyaaءu
صَمَّاءُ	sammaaءu

Plur. Fem.	
خُرْسٌ	Khursun
بُكْمٌ	bukmun
عُرْجٌ	عurjun
عُمْيٌ	عumyun
صُمٌّ	Summun

Note: Except plurals of the pattern, other forms (sing, dual) neither can be nonized with (تنوين) nor they can receive kasra (ـِ).

4. Pattern for the comparative and superlative of adjective is called إِسْمُ التَّفْضِيل Ismut-tafdeel that is:

sing.masc.	أَفْعَلُ	af ع alu	(The same form as that for colours and defects.)
Plu.masc.	أَفَاعِلُ	afaa ع ilu	
Sing.fem.	فُعْلَى	fu ع laa	
Plu.fem .	فعْلَيَاتٌ	fu ع layaatun.	

Though the grammarians have mentioned dual forms for masculine and feminine but these are in little use.

The singular masculine form has more frequent use than other forms because it denotes both comparative and superlative or Elative meanings e.g. الله أكْبَر Allah is great.

5. If the root has a doubled consonant as جديدٌ "jadidun" new the superlative form is أجدُّ ajaddu, (not أَجْدَدْ ajdad أَفْعَل) From قَلِيلٌ "qaleelun little", few, comes أَقلُّ aqallu, less fewer (not أَقْلَلْ aqlal)

6. The Arabic preposition for "than" such as English phrase "smaller than.." is مِنْ (min) e.g. أصْغَرُ مِن

عَلِى أصْغَرُ مِنْ أخيه	Ali is smaller than his brother.
البِنْتُ أصْغَرُ مِنْ أخيهَا	The girl is younger than her brother.
الطَّلَبَةُ فِى المَدَارِسِ الدِّينيَّةِ أقلُّ عَدَداً مِنَ الجَامِعَاتِ	Students in the religious schools are less in numbers than in the universities.

7. Sometimes, the elative is used as a noun, followed by a genetive, e.g. هُوَ أَكْبَرُ رَجُلٍ فِى المدينةِ He is the greatest man in the city. (Also see chapter 29)

Examples from the Holy Qur'an:

I.	المذكر مَرفُوعاً	Masc. Nominative

خُلُق عَظِيمٌ	**68-4** A subline moral.
كِتَابٌ مَرْقُومٌ	**83-20** A written book.
عَجُوزٌ عَقِيمٌ	**51-29** A barren old woman.
شَيطانٌ رجيمٌ	**81-25** An accursed devil.
كِتَابٌ كَرِيمٌ	**27-29** An honourable letter.
رَبٌّ غفورٌ	**34-15** A forgiving Lord.

II.	المذكر منصُوباً	Masc. Accusative

مَالاً مَمْدُودًا	**74-12** Vest riches.
سِرَاجًا وَهَّاجًا	**78-13** A shining lamp.
سَبْعًا شِدَادًا	**78-12** Seven strongs.
قَولاً مَيْسُوراً	**17-28** A gentle word.
مَاءً غَدَقاً	**72-16** The abundant water.
لَحْماً طَرِيًّا	**16-14** The fresh flesh.

مَاءً ثَجَّاجاً	**78-14** The clouds water.
كَأْسًا دِهَاقًا	**78-34** A pure cup.

III.	المذكر مجروراً	**Masc. Genetive.**

ظِلٍ ممدودٍ	**56-30** An extensive shed.
كَفَّارٍ عنيدٍ	**50-24** A rebellious ungreatful.
سِدْرٍ مَخْضودٍ	**56-28** Thornless Lote-tree.
كتابٍ مَكْنُونٍ	**56-78** A protected book.
يومٍ معلُومٍ	**56-50** An appointed day.
مَاءٍ مَهِينٍ	**77-20** Ordinary water.
ماءٍ مسكوبٍ	**56-31** Water gushing.
لوحٍ محفوظ	**85-22** A guarded tablet.

IV.	المذكر مع الألف واللام	**Masc. With a definite Article**

الفَوزُ الكبيرُ	**85-11** The great achievement.
اليَوْمُ المَوعُودُ	**85-2** The promised day.
العِهْنُ المَنْفُوش	**101-5** The carded wool.
الشَّجرُ الأَخْضَرُ	**36-80** The green tree.
النَّجمُ الثاقِبُ	**86-3** The star of piercing brightness.

V. المؤنث مع الألف واللام	Fem. With a definite Article

الآيَةُ الْكُبْرىٰ	**79-20** The mighty sign.
الطامَّةُ الكبرىٰ	**79-34** The great calamity.
النَّفْسُ المُطْمَئِنَّةُ	**89-27** The soul which is in rest
الدَّارُ الآخِرَةَ	**29-64** The home of the hereafter.

VI. الألوان والعاهات	Colours and defects
حتى يَتَبَيَّنَ لَكُمُ الخيطُ **الأبيضُ** من الخيطِ **الأسودِ**	**2-187** ... until the **white** thread becoms distinct to you from the **black** thread.
وَاضْمُمْ يَدَكَ إِلىٰ جَنَاحِكَ تَخْرُجْ **بَيْضَاءَ** مِنْ غَيرِ سُوءٍ آيَةً أُخْرَىٰ	**20-22** And thrust thy hand within thy armpit, it will come forth **white** without hurt (as) another token.
إِنَّهَا بَقَرَةٌ **صَفْرَاءُ**	**2-69** She is a yellow cow.
وَمِنَ الجِبَالِ جُدَدٌ **بِيضٌ** وَ**حُمْرٌ** مختلفٌ أَلْوانها وغَرَابِيبُ **سُودٌ**	**35-27** And among the hills are streaks **white** and **red** of diver hues, and (others) raven-black

Some Examples of Adjective Forms: Simple & Comparatives.

إِنَّهُ لَكَبِيرُكُمُ الَّذِى عَلَّمَكُمُ السِّحْرَ	**20-71** Lo! He is your chief who taught you magic.

مَالِ هَذَا الكِتَابِ لا يُغَادِرُ صَغِيرَةً وَلَا كَبِيرَةً إلا أحْصَاها	**18-49** What kind of a book is this that leaves not a small thing nor a great thing.
أطَعْنا سَادَتَنا وَكُبَرَاءَنَا	**33-67** We obeyed our masters and great men.
وَالَّذِينَ يَجْتَنِبُونَ كَبَائِرَ الإثْمِ وَالْفَوَاحِش	**42-37** And those who shun the worst of sins and indecencies.
والفِتْنَةُ أَكْبَرُ مِنَ القَتْلِ	**2-217** And persecution is worse than killing.
وَإِثْمُهُمَا أكْبَرُ مِنْ نَفْعِهِما	**2-219** And the sin of them (wine and game) is greater than their usefulness.

EXERCISE

1. **Translate into Arabic:**

A muslim wishes to follow the straight path. I love a red flower white tea and the green light. Both of them are tall men, but Nadiya and Samira are tiny ones. Girls are hard workers. Boys are good players. The big men and the big women of the world admire good cultivation. The Prophet's mosque in Madina is a beautiful mosque but the mosque of Holy Ka'ba is greater than others. There in Mecca is a good Centrre of education for blind boys, called the Institution of the Light.

Ali is more clever than his elder brother Hasan. English people have blue eyes, golden hair and white skin. Muslims do not hate any colour. They believe in brotherhood among entire human-being. The Red sea is the boundry of Arabia in the West and the South The teacher is angry with them. We are happier than lazy men.

2. Translate into English :

١ – إِنَّ الْمُسْلِمِينَ وَالْمُسْلِمَاتِ أعدَّ اللهُ لَهُمْ مَغْفِرَةً وَأجْراً عَظِيماً

٢ – هُمُ التَّائِبُونَ العابِدُونَ الْحَامِدُون السَّائِحُونَ

٣ – يَلْبَسُونَ ثِيَاباً خُضْرا

٤ – مَنْ تَابَ وَآمَنَ وَعَمِلَ عَمَلاً صَالِحاً

٥ – فَأنجيْنَاهُ وَمَنْ مَعَهُ فى الفُلْكِ المَشْحُونِ

٦ – إِنَّ رِبَّكَ لَهُوَ الْعَزِيزُ الرَّحِيمُ

٧ – صُمٌّ بُكْمٌ عُمْىٌ فَهُمْ لاَ يَرْجِعُونَ

٨ – هٰذَا لِسَانٌ عَرَبِىٌّ مبينٌ

٩ – الزَّوْجَةُ الصَّالِحَةُ نِعْمَةٌ مِنَ اللهِ

١٠ – الصَّديقُ الوَفِىُّ أَحَبُّ إلى النَّفْسِ مِنَ الْقَرِيبِ الظَّالِم

١١ – كتابُ اللهِ العَظِيمُ

١٢ – كتابُ اللهِ العظيمِ

١٣ – أَكْبَرُ شَاعِرِ البَلَدِ قادِمٌ

VOCABULARY

To follow	ان يَسْلُكَ or أنْ يَتَّبِعَ
The Path	الصِّرَاطُ
Tiny (Masc.)	قَصِيرٌ (Fem.) قَصِيرَة (plu. masc.) قُصَار
Admires	يُحِبُّ (use plural)
Clever	عَاقِلٌ
The Centre.	الْمَرْكَزُ
No cleverer than	لَيْسَ أعْقَلَ مِنْ
People	النَّاسُ
English people	الشَّعْبُ الإنْجلِيزى
Love	الحُبُّ
Golden	الذَّهبى (not on the forms of colours)
Blue	الأَزْرَقُ (use fem. & plural)
Red Sea	البَحْرُ الأَحْمَرُ
Happier than	أَكْثَرَ فَرَحًا مِنْ or أفْرَحَ مِنْ
Straight	المُسْتَقِيم
Tall (Masc.)	طَوِيلٌ (Fem.) طَوِيلَةٌ (plural) طِوَالٌ
The cultivation	التَّمَدُّنُ
The Institute of the Light.	مَعْهَدُ النُّور
Elder	أكبر من أَكْبَرُ عُمْراً

Angry	غَضْبَانَ
Lazy	كَسْلَانَ

القَانِتُ	one who obeys , from ق ن ت
الخَاشِعُ	one who bow in humbleness
أَعَدَّ	(3rd Pers. Masc.) Prepared
المَغْفِرَةُ	The forgiveness
الأَجْرُ	The reward
التَّائِبُ	one who turns repentant
العَابِدُ	one who serves Allah
الصَّائِمُ	one who fasts
الرَّاكِعُ	one who bows down
السَّاجِدُ	fall Prastrate (in worship)
الآمِرُ	enjoins
النَّاهِى	forbids
لَبِسَ	to wear
الثِّيَابُ	clothings , sing
الفُلْكُ	ark
المَشْحُونُ	laden

الرَّحِيمُ	The Merciful
العَزِيزُ	The Almighty
الغَفُورُ	The Forgiver
الحَامِدُ	one who praises Allah
اللِسانُ	The tongue , language
رَجَعَ	(3rd Pers.(Masc.) to return

CHAPTER 12

THE PRONOUNS

The Pronouns in Arabic are divided into two forms-detached and attached.

1. The detached pronouns الضَّمَائِرُ المُنْفَصِلَةُ are:

Singular		Dual		Plural	
أنَا	'ana, I			نَحْنُ	'nahnu, We
أَنْتَ	'anta, thou (you) (masc.)	أَنْتُمَا	'antuma, You (two) (masc & fem.)	أَنْتُمْ	'antum, You (masc.)
أَنْتِ	'anti, thou (you) (fem.)		-do-	أَنْتُنَّ	'antunna, You (fem.)
هُوَ	'howa, He, It	هُمَا	'huma, They (two) (masc & fem)	هُمْ	'hum, They (masc.)
هِيَ	'hiya, She		-do-	هُنَّ	hunna, They (fem.)

أَنَـا	وأنا رَبُّكُم فَاعْبُدُونِ	21-92 ... and I am your Lord, so worship Me.
	ولاَ أنا عابِدٌ ما عَبَدتُّمْ	109-4 ... and I shall not worship that which ye worship.

أَنْتَ	فَلَمَّا تَوَفَّيْتَنِى كُنْتَ أَنتَ الرقيبَ عَلَيهِم	5-117 (Jesus said) and when **thou** tookest me thou wast (كُنْتَ) the watcher over them.
	أأنتَ قلتَ للنَّاسِ	5-116 Didst **thou** say into mankind.

هُوَ	قل : هُوَ اللهُ أحَدٌ	112-1 Say: **He** is Allah The one.
	هُوَ اللهِ الّذى لاَ إِلَهَ إلا هُوَ	59-23 **He** is Allah than whom there is no other God.

Note: sometimes at the ending of a sentence it becomes **"hoo"**

هُوَ خيرٌ ثواباً	18-44 **He** is best to reward.
بَلْ هُوَ خيرٌ لَكُمْ	24-11 Nay, **it** is good for you.

هِىَ	إن هِىَ إلا حياتُنَا الدُّنيا	**23-37 It** is not but our wordly life.
	وهِىَ تَجْرِى بِهِم	**11-42** And **it** moves on with them

نَحْنُ	نَحْنُ نَرْزُقُكَ	**20-132 We** provide for thee.
	نَحْنُ أَوْلِيَاؤُكُمْ فِى الْحَيَاةِ الدُّنْيَا وَفِى الآخِرَةِ	**41-31** We are your friends in this world's life and in the hereafter.

أَنْتُمْ	قَالَ : أَنْتُمْ شَرٌّ مَكَاناً	**12-77** He said: **You** are in an evil condition.
	ثُمَّ أَنْتُمْ تُشْرِكُون	**6-64** Then **you** set up others (with Him)

هُمْ	هم لِلْكُفْرِ يَوْمَئِذٍ أَقْرَبُ مِنْهم للإيمَانِ	**3-167 They** were on that day nearer to disbelief than to belief.
	وما هُمْ بِخَارِجِينَ مِنْهَا	**5-37** And **they** are not coming forth from it.

هُنَّ	هُنَّ لِبَاسٌ لَكُمْ وَأَنْتُم لِبَاس لَهُنَّ	**2-187 They** (wives) are an apparel for you & **you** (men) are apparel for **them** (wives).

The Pronouns هُمَا huma (3rd Person Masc. & Fem.) and أَنتُمَا antuma (2nd Person Masc. & Fem.) have rare use in the Holy Quran in their absolute forms. But they are in common use in the language.

ثَانِىَ اثنين إذ هُمَا فى الغار	**9-40** he being the second of the two when they (two men) both were in the Cave.

ذاهبتان إلى البيت	هُمَا	They (two fem.) are going home.
تَستَحِقَّانِ الجَائِزَةَ	أَنتُمَا	You (two masc. & fem.) deserve the prize.
طالبانِ فى المدرسَة	أنتما	You (two masc.) are students in the school.
ذَاهِبَتَانِ إِلَى البَيْتِ	أنتما	You (two fem.) are going home

2. The attached Pronouns الضمائر المُتَّصِلَةُ are as the following:

Singular	Dual	Plural
Third Person		
ه hu. (his. him) (Masc.)	هُمَا huma. their. them	هُمْ hum. their. them (Masc.)
ها ha, her	(two. masc. or fem.)	هُنَّ hunna. their, them. (fem.)

Attached to a noun:

كِتَابُهُ Kitaabuhu, his book.	كِتَابُهُمَا Kitaabuhuma. their (two masc. & fem.) book	كِتَابُهُمْ Kitaabuhum. their (masc.) book.
كتابها Kitaabuhaa, her book	كتابهما Kitaabuhuma. their (two masc. & fem.) book.	كِتَابُهُنَّ Kitaabuhunna. their (fem) book.

Attached to a Verb:

نَصَرَهُ nasarahu, he helped him.	نَصَرَهُمَا nasarahuma, he helped (two) (Masc. & Fem.)	نَصَرَهُمْ nasarahum, he helped them (Masc.)
نَصَرَهَا nasaraha, he helped her	-do-	نصرهُنَّ nasarahunna. he helped them (fem.)

2nd Person

كَ ka, thee. they (Masc)	كُمَا kuma, your. you (Masc. & Fem.)	كُمْ kum. yours. you. (Masc.)
		كُنَّ kunna, yours. you (Fem.)

Attached to a Noun:

كِتَابُكَ	Kitaabuka. thy (Masc) book.	كِتَابُكُمَا	Kitaabukumaa. Yours (two Masc. & Fem.) book.	كِتَابُكُمْ	Kitaabukum. your (Masc.) book.
كِتَابُكِ	Kitaabuki, thy (Fem.) book.		-do-	كِتَابُكُنَّ	Kitaabukunna. Yours (Fem.) book.

Attached to a Verb:

نَصَرَكَ	nasaraka, he helped thee (Masc.)	نَصَرَكُمَا	nasarakuma, he helped you (two Masc. & Fem.)	نَصَرَكُمْ	Nasarakum, he helped you (Masc.)
نَصَرَكِ	nasaraki, he helped thee (Fem)		-do-	نَصَرَكُنَّ	nasarakunna, he helped you (Fem.)

First Person (Masc. & Fem.)

Attached to a Noun only:

ى	i, my as book.	كِتَابِى my	as plural	نا كِتَابُنَا	naa, our, as kitaabunaa, our book.
نى	ni, me, as helped me.	نَصَرَنِى he	-do-	نَصَرَنَا	nasaranaa, he helped us.

Note : The Pronouns of 3rd person ہ hu is read ہ hi. هُمَا huma becomes هِمَا hima and هُمْ hum and. هُنَّ hunna turns to هِمْ and هِنَّ hinna sounds when they are followed by a preposition thus:

كِتَابُهُ	kitaabuhu, his book.
فى كِتَابِهِ	fi kitaabehi, in his book.
نَصَرَهُمْ	nasarahum, he helped them.
هُوَ عَلَى نَصْرِهِمْ قَدِير	howa alaa nasrehim qadeer. He is most powerful **on their help.**
نَصَرَهُنَّ	nasarahunna, he helped them (fem.)
هُوَ عَلَى نَصْرِهِنَّ قَدِير	howa alaa nasrehinna qadeer, He is most powerful **on their help.**

these differences should be noted in the examples from the Holy Qur'an.

Examples from the Holy Qura'n.

Third Person (Masc.) Sing: هُوَ hu.

وَقَلْبُهُ مُطْمَئِنٌّ بِالإِيمَانِ	**16-106** And **his** heart is content with faith.
هُنَالِكَ دَعَا زَكَرِيَّا رَبَّهُ	**3-38** There did Zachariah pray to **his** Lord.

مَنْ جَاءَ بِالْحَسَنَةِ فَلَهُ خَيْرٌ مِنْهَا	**28-84** Whoever brings a good-deed **for him** is better than its worth.
فَإِذَا خِفْتِ عَلَيْهِ فَأَلْقِيهِ فِى الْيَمِّ	**28-7** An when thou fearest for **him** then cast **him** in the river.
فَلَمَّا جَاءَهُ وَقَصَّ عَلَيْهِ الْقَصَصَ	**28-25** and when he came to **him** and told **him** the (whole) story.

Third Person (Fem.) Sing: ها haa.

كُلَّمَا دَخَلَ عَلَيْهَا زَكَرِيَّا الْمِحْرَابَ وَجَدَ عِنْدَهَا رِزْقاً	**3-37** Whenever Zachariah went in the sanctuary where she was, he found that she had food.

Third Person (Masc. & Fem) Dual: هُمَا huma.

فَأَكَلاَ مِنْهَا فَبَدَتْ لَهُمَا سَوْآتُهُمَا وَطَفِقَا يَخْصِفَانِ عَلَيْهِمَا مِنْ وَرَقِ الْجَنَّةِ	**20-121** Then they twain ate therefore. so **their** shame became apparent upon them and they began to hide **them** by the leaves of the Garden.
يَنْزِعُ عَنْهُمَا لِبَاسَهُمَا	**7-27** Pulling off from them **their** clothing.

Third Person (Masc.) Plural: هُمْ hum

أَفَأَمِنُوا أَنْ تَأْتِيَهُمْ غَاشِيَةٌ مِنْ عَذَابِ اللهِ أَوْ تَأْتِيَهُمُ السَّاعَةُ بَغْتَةً وَهُمْ لاَ يَشْعُرُونَ	**12-107** Deem they themselves secure from coming on them of a pull of Allah's punishment or coming of the hour suddenly while they are unaware.
صِراطَ الَّذِينَ أَنْعَمْتَ عَلَيْهِم غَيرِ المَغْضُوبِ عَلَيهِم	**1-7** The path of those **whom** Thou hast favoured; Not (the path) of those against **whom** Thou art wrathful

Third Person (Fem.) Plural: هن hunna

وَبُعُولَتُهُنَّ أَحَقُّ بِرَدِّهِنَّ	**2-228** And **their** husbands would do better to take them back.
وَعَلَى الْمَوْلودِ له رِزْقُهُنَّ وَكِسوَتُهُنَّ بِالْمَعْرُوفِ	**2-233** and it is for the fathers to provide **them** and clothe **them** honourably.

Second Person (Masc.) Sing: كَ ka

وقُلْنَا يَا آدم اسْكُنْ أَنتَ وزوجُك الجَنَّة	**2-35** And we said: O Adam, dwell **thou** and thy wife in the Garden.

قالوا ادْعُ لَنَا رَبَّك	**2-69** They said pray for us **thy** Lord.
ولَن تَرضى عَنكَ اليَهُودُ	**2-120** And the Jews will not be pleased with **thee.**
إذ قَال الله يا عيسٰى إنى مُتَوَفِّيكَ وَرَافِعُكَ إلىَّ وَمُطَهِّرُكَ مِن الّذين كَفرُوا	**3-55** And (Remember) when Allah said: O' Jesus! Lo! I am gathering **thee** and causing **thee** to ascend into Me and cleansing **thee** of those who disbelieve.

2nd Person (Fem.) Sing: كِ	ki

قال يَا مَرْيَمُ أنّىٰ لكِ هٰذا	**3-37** he said: O' Mary: whence cometh into **thee** this?
قالَ إنَّمَا أنا رَسُولُ رَبِّكِ لأهَبَ لَكِ غلاماً زَكِيًّا	**19-19** he said: I am only a messnger of **thy** Lord that I may bestow on **thee** a faultless son.
يَا أختَ هَارُونَ مَا كانَ أبوكِ امرَأَ سَوءٍ وَمَا كانَتْ أمُّكِ بَغِيًّا	**19-28** O' Sister of Aaron! **Thy** father was not a wicked man nor was **thy** mother a harlot.

2nd Person (Masc. & Fem) Dual: كُمَا kuma

وقَالَ مَا نَهَاكُمَا رَبُّكُمَا عَنْ هَذِهِ الشَّجَرَةِ إِلَّا أَن تكونا مَلَكَيْنِ أو تكونا مِنَ الخَالِدِين . وقَاسَمَهُمَا إِنِّي لَكُمَا لَمِنَ النَّاصِحِينَ	**7-20,21** And said: **Your** Lord has forbidden **you** this tree lest you become angels or become of the immortals and he swore to them both: Surely I am a sincere adviser to you.
إِن تَتُوبَا إِلَى اللهِ فَقَدْ صَغَتْ قُلُوبُكُمَا	**66-4** If you turn to Allah, then indeed **your** hearts are inclined (to Him).

2nd Person (Masc.) Plural: كُمْ kum

يَا بَنِي إِسْرَائِيلَ ! اذْكُرُوا نِعْمَتِيَ الَّتِي أَنْعَمْتُ عَلَيْكُم وَأَنِّي فَضَّلْتُكُم عَلَى الْعَالَمِينَ	**2-47** O' children of Israel, call to mind My favour which I bestowed on **you** and that I made **you** excel the nations.
وَإِذْ نَجَّيْنَاكُم مِنْ آلِ فِرْعَوْنَ يَسُومُونَكُم سُوءَ العَذَابِ يُذَبِّحُونَ أَبْنَاءَكُم وَيَسْتَحْيُونَ نِسَاءَكُم وَفِي ذَٰلِكُم بَلَاءٌ مِن رَبِّكُم عَظِيمٌ	**2-49** And when we delivered **you** from Pharoh's people, killing **your** sons, and sparing **your** women and in this there was a great trial from **your** Lord.

2nd Person (Fem.) Plural: كُنَّ kunna

يَا أَيُّهَا النَّبِى قُلْ لأَزْوَاجِكَ : إنْ كُنْتُنَّ تُرِدْنَ الْحَيَاةَ الدُّنْيَا وَزِينَتَهَا فَتَعَالَيْنَ أُمَتِّعْكُنَّ وأُسَرِّحْكُنَّ سَرَاحًا جَمِيلاً	**33-28** O' Prophet, say to thy wives: if you desire this world's life and its adornment, come I will give you a provision and allow you to depart a goodly departing.
عَسَى رَبُّه إن طَلَّقَكُنَّ أن يُبْدِلَه أزواجاً خيراً مِنكُنَّ	**66-5** Maybe, his Lord, if he divorces **you** will give him in **your** place wives better than **you**.

First Person (Masc & Fem) Sing: ى – i

اذهبْ بكتابى هَذَا	**27-28** Take this **my** letter Or go with this letter of **mine**.
قَال ربِّ اشْرَحْ لِى صَدْرِى وَيَسِّر لى أمْرِى واحْلُلْ عُقْدَةً مِن لسَانِى يَفْقَهُوا قَولِى وَاجْعَل لِى وَزِيراً مِنْ أهْلى هَارُونَ أخى اشْدُدْ بِهِ أزْرِى وأشْرِكْهُ فى أمْرِى	**20-25/32** He said: My Lord! expand my breast for **me**, and loose the knot from **my** tongue, that they may understand **my** word and give to **me** an aider from **my** family: Aaron **my** brother. Add to **my** strength by him and make him share **my** task.

Attached to a Verb: نِى – ni

مَا قُلْتُ لَهُمْ إِلاَّ مَا أَمَرْتَنِى بِهِ	5-117 I said to them naught save as thou didst command **me**.
أَيُّكُم يَأْتِينِى بِعَرْشِهَا	27-38 which of you can bring **me** her throne?
لَئِنْ بَسَطْتَ إِلَىَّ يَدَكَ لِتَقْتُلَنِى مَا أَنَا بِبَاسِطٍ يَدِى إِلَيْكَ لأَقْتُلَكَ	5-28 If thou stretch out **thy** hand against **me** to kill **me** I shall not stretch **my** hand against **thee** to kill **thee**.

First Person (Masc. & Fem)

dual and Plural - نا - naa

قَالاَ رَبَّنَا ظَلَمْنَا أَنْفُسَنَا وَإِنْ لَمْ تَغْفِرْ لَنَا وَتَرْحَمْنَا لَنَكُونَنَّ مِنَ الخَاسِرِين	7-23 They (two) said: Our Lord, we have wronged **ourselves**; and if thou forgive **us** not, and have no mercy on **us**, we shall certainly be of the loosers.
وَاللّٰهُ أَمَرَنَا بِها	7-28 And Allah has enjoined it to **us**.
هٰذا كِتَابُنَا يَنْطِقُ عَلَيْكُمْ بِالحَقِّ	45-29 This is **our** record that speaks against you with truth.

EXERCISE

1. **Translate into Arabic:**

   For the first three Years, or rather less, of his mission, The Prophet preached only to his family and to his intimate friends, while the people of Makka as a whole regarded him as one who had become (معتوه) a little mad. The first of all his converts was his wife Khadija, the second his cousin Ali whom he had adopted. The third his servant Zaid. His old friend Abu Bakr was among those early converts with some of his slaves and dependents.

2. **Translate into English:**

أو كَالَّذِى مَرَّ عَلَىٰ قَرِيَةٍ وَهِىَ خَاوِيَةٌ عَلَىٰ عُرُوشِهَا قَالَ أَنَّىٰ يُحْيِ هَـٰذِهِ
اللهُ بَعْدَ مَوتِها فأَمَاتَهُ اللهُ مِائَةَ عَامٍ ثُمَّ بَعَثَهُ قَالَ كَمْ لَبِثْتَ قَالَ لَبِثْتُ
يَوْماً أو بَعضَ يومٍ قَالَ بَل لَبِثْتَ مائَةَ عامٍ فَانْظُر إِلَى طَعَامِكَ
وَشَرَابِكَ لَمْ يَتَسَنَّهْ وَانظُر إِلَى حِمَارِكَ وَلنجعَلَكَ آيَةً لِلنَّاسِ وانظُر إِلى
العِظَامِ كَيْفَ نُنْشِزُهَا ثُمَّ نَكْسُوهَا لَحْماً . فَلَما تَبَيَّن لَه قَال أَعْلَمُ أَنَّ
اللهَ عَلَىٰ كُلِّ شَىءٍ قَدِيرٌ

VOCABULARY

First three years	السَّنَوَاتُ الثَّلَاثُ الأُولٰى (an adjective phrase)
rater	غَالِباً
less	أَقَلُّ (منها)
mission	المُهِمَّةُ ، الرِّسَالَةُ
to preach	بَلَّغَ
family	الأسرة
intimate	الأقربون
regarded	اعتبروا
mad	معتوه
convert	الذى أسلم Plu الَّذِينَ أَسْلَمُوا
the slave	العَبْدُ Plu. الْعِبَادُ
dependent	تابع Plu. أتباع

أو	or
كَالَّذِى	ك like & الذى which, who, that = like of him who....
قَرْيَةٌ	township
خَاوِيَةٌ	fallen
عُرُوشٌ	Sing. عَرش roofs
أَنَّى	how !

أَمَاتَ		made (someone die)
أماته		made him die.
مائة		hundred
ثُمَّ		then
بَعَثَ		to bring back to the life
كَم		how long.
لَبِثَ		he tarried (3rd person Masc.)
بَلْ		but
أنظرُ	(Imperative)	see, look!
لم يَتَسَنَّهْ		did not get spoiled.
حِمَارٌ		Ass
العِظَامُ	Sing. العَظْمُ	bones.
نُنْشِزُ	(Ist person Imp. Plural)	We adjust
نكسو	-do-	We cover
فَلما		thus then
تَبَيَّنَ		(the matter) has been cleared.
قَدِيرٌ		The Powerful

CHAPTER 13

THE PLURAL

The patterns of Arabic roots have been dealt in chapter 3 and 7. The Noun patterns are also trileteral with exception of few that are supposed to b biliterac. The Plurals are divided into two catagories: (a) Solid and (b) Broken.

(A) 1. The Solid Plurals are those formed by adding و – ن in nominative sentences and by ..ين in case of accusative or genitive sentences. e.g. مُسْلِمُون Muslimoona or مُسْلِمين Muslimeen from مُسْلِمٌ Muslimun, فَاعِلُون faaعloona or فَاعِلين faaعleen from فاعِلٌ faaعlun. We have a a few examples in the following (verreses) of the Holy Qur'an.

قد أفلَحَ المُؤمنونَ	**23-1.** Successful indeed are the believers
الَّذينَ هُمْ فِي صَلاَتِهِم خَاشِعُون	**-2.** who are humble in their prayers
وَالَّذِينَ هُمْ عَنِ اللَّغْوِ مُعْرِضُونَ	**-3.** and who are shun what is vain

وَالَّذِينَ هُم لِلزَّكَاةِ فَاعِلُون	**-4.** and who act for the sake of parity
وَالَّذِينَ هُم لِفُرُوجِهِمْ حَافِظُونَ إِلاَّ عَلَى أَزْوَاجِهِم أَوْ مَا مَلَكَتْ أَيْمَانُهُمْ فَإِنَّهُمْ غَيْرُ مَلُومِين	**-5.** and who restrain their sexual passions (6. except in the presence of their mates or those whom their right hands possess, for such surely are not blameable.
فَمَنِ ابْتَغَىٰ وَرَاءَ ذٰلِكَ فَأُولَئِكَ هُمُ العَادُونَ	**-7.** but whoever seeks to go beyond that, such are transgressioners)
وَالَّذين هُم لأَمَانَاتِهِم وَعَهْدِهِم رَاعون	**-8.** And those who are keepers of their trusts and their convants,
وَالذين هُم عَلَى صَلَوَاتِهِمْ يُحَافِظُون	**-9.** and those who keep a guard on their progress
أُولَئِكَ هُمُ الوَارِثُونَ	**-10.** those are the heirs,
الَّذين يَرِثُونَ الفِردوس هُم فِيهَا خَالِدُون	**-11.** who inherit Paradise. Therein they will abide.

2. The solid plurals of the feminine is made by adding آت aat after the noun, such as مُسْلِمَاتٌ Muslimaatun from مُسْلِمَةٌ muslimatun e.g. (from The Holy Qur'an):

إنَّ المُسْلِمينَ والمسلِمَاتِ والمؤمنينَ والمؤمنـاتِ والـقَـانِتـينَ والقَانِتَاتِ والصَّادِقينَ والصَّادِقَاتِ والصَّابِرينَ والصَّابِرَاتِ والخَاشِعينَ والخَاشِعَاتِ وَالْمُتَصدِّقِينَ والْمُتَصدِّقَاتِ وَالصَّائِمينَ والصَّائِمَاتِ وَالحَافِظِينَ فُروجَهُم وَالحافِظَات والذَّاكِرِينَ اللهَ كثيراً والذَّاكِراتِ أعَدَّ الله لَهُم مَغْفِرَةً وَأجراً عظيماً .	Surely the men who submit and the women who submit, and the believing men and the believing women, and the obeying men and the obeying women, and the truthful men, and the truthful women, and the patient men and the patient women, and the humble men and the humble women, and the charitable men and the charitable women, and the fasting men, and the fasting women, and the men who guard their chestity, and the women who guard their chestity, and the men who remember ALLAH much and the women who remember ALLAH much; Allah has prepared for them forgiveness and a might Reward.

(B) 1. The solid plural is formed by a noun (derived from a triletral root) plus a suffix و – ن or ن ى in case of masculine and آت aat in case of feminine, as seen in above examples. The broken plural is that in which a noun has a prefix or an infix or both of them. To illustrate the difference between solid and broken plurals the following example will be self - explanatory:

طالبٌ taalibun (a student, a demander, a wisher) is a noun, its plural is طَالِبُون taalibun or طَالِبِين taalibeen or taalibaat, this is called a solid plural as you can see the original word طَالِبٌ is existing in its solid shape. There are some other forms of plural such as طُلَّابٌ in which an أَلِفٌ alif is fixed between second and third redicals and the second rdical ل is duplicated with Shaddamark,Thus it becomes a broken plural, because the word طالب taalib is broken by duplicating the second redical ل and adding an الف alif after ل as well as ألف 'alif' (or long vowel) after first redical is omitted.

2. **The broken plural has** many forms Grammarians divide them into two catogiries جَمْعُ القِلَّةِ Jam ع al qillah and جمع الكَثْرَةِ jam ع al kathrah. جَمْعُ القِلَّةِ (Jam ع al qillah) has four patterns and is grammatically used for a number of more than two and less than ten. These patterns are as below:

I.	أَفْعُلُ	afعulu, e.g.

أَنْهُرُ anhuru, plural of نَهْرٌ nahrun - river.

Examples from the Holy Qur'an:

أَرْجُلُ arjulu. plural of رِجْلٌ rijlun - foot.

وَتَشْهَدُ أَرْجُلُهُم	**36-65** and their feet will bear witness.

أَعْيُنُ aعyunu, plural of عَيْنٌ عainun eye

وَلَهُمْ أَعْيُنٌ لاَ يُبْصِرُونَ بِهَا	**7-179** and they have eyes wherewith they see not.

أَنْفُسُ 'anfusu, plural of نَفْسٌ nafsun - soule.

مِنَ الأَمْوالِ وَالأَنْفُسِ والثَّمَرَاتِ	**2-155** (and they may loss) of property, lives and fruits.

أَشْهُرُ ash-huru, plural of شَهْرٌ shahrun - month

فإذا انسَلَخَ الأَشْهُرُ الحُرُمُ	**9-5** so when the sacred months have passed.

II.	أفعلةٌ	'afعilatun e.g.

أَنْدِيَةٌ andiyatun, plural of نادى naadee - club.

Examples from the Holy Qur'an:

أَسْلِحَةٌ 'aslihatun plural of سِلاَحٌ silaahun-arm.

وَلْيَأْخُذُوا أَسْلِحَتَهُم	**4-102** and let them take their arms.

أجنحةٌ ‘ajnihatun, plural of جَنَاحٌ jannahun - wing

جَاعِلِ المَلَائِكَةِ رُسُلاً أُولى أَجْنِحَةٍ	**35-1** The Maker of the angels messengers flying on wings.

أفئِدة ‘af ء idatun, plural of فؤادٌ fu ء aadun - heart.

فَاجْعَلْ أَفْئِدَةً مِنَ النَّاسِ تَهوى إِلَيْهِم	**14-37** so make the hearts of some people yearn towards them.

III.	فِعْلَةٌ	Fi ع latun, e.g.

صِبيَةٌ sibyatun, plural of صَبِيٌّ sabbeyyun - a child.

عِلْيَةٌ عilyatun, plural of عالى عaali - high.

Example from the Holy Qur'an

فِتيَةٌ fityatun, plural of فتى fata - youth, young man.

إنَّهم فِتيَةٌ آمَنوا بِرَبِّهم	**18-13** Surely they were youths who believed in their Lord.

IV.	أفعالٌ	‘af عaalun e.g.

أهْدَافٌ ahdaafun, plural of هَدَفٌ hadafun, target. This

form of plural is very often used to denote meaning of a plural in a common sense not for limited numbers, though it is one of the four patterns known as أوزانُ جَمْعِ القلّةِ (forms of those plurals that point to a number ranging between three to ten).

Some Examples from the Holy Qur'an:

أنصارٌ 'ansaarun. plural of ناصِرٌ nasirun- helper

كُونُوا أنصَارَ اللهِ	**61-14** be helper (in the cause) of Allah.

أخبارٌ 'akhbaarun. plural of خبرٌ khbarun news

يومئذٍ تُحَدِّثُ أخبارَها	**99-4** on the day she will tell her news.

أقْفَالٌ 'aqfaalun, plural of قفل qufflun - lock.

أم عَلَى قُلوبٍ أقْفَالُها	**47-24** or, are there locks on the hearts.

أصحابٌ 'ashaabun, plural of صاحبٌ sahibun owner.

أولئكَ أصْحَابُ الجَنَّةِ	**2-82** these are the owners of the Garden.

3. The following are among the more common patterns of the borken plurals:

I. فُعُولٌ fu ع ulun e.g.

حُرُوفٌ hurufun, plural of حَرْفٌ harfun - letter

عُلُومٌ عulumun, plural of عِلْمٌ عlmun - knowledge.

دُرُوسٌ durusun, plural of دَرْسٌ darsun - lesson, study.

Examples from the Holy Qur'an:

مُلُوكٌ mulukun, plural of مَلِكٌ malikun - king.

قَالَتْ إنَّ المُلُوكَ إذا دَخَلُوا قَرْيَةً أفْسَدُوهَا	**27-34** she said: surely the kings, when they enter a town, ruin it.

قُلُوبٌ qulub plural of qalb heart. قَلْبٌ

ألا بِذِكْرِ اللهِ تَطْمَئِنُّ القُلُوبُ	**13-28** Surely! in Allah's rememberance do hearts find rest.

II. فِعَالٌ fiعaalun, e.g.

كِبَارٌ kibaarun, plural of كبيرٌ kabirun - big.

صِعَابٌ siعaabun, plural of صَعْبٌ saعbun - difficult.

كِلَابٌ kilaabun, plural of كَلْبٌ kalbun - dog.

Examples from the Holy Qur'an:

رِجَالٌ Rijaalun. plural of رَجُلٌ rajulun-man.

رِجَالٌ لا تُلْهِيهِم تِجَارَةٌ ولا بيعٌ عَن ذِكْرِ اللهِ	**24-37** men whom neither merchandise nor selling diverts from the rememberance of Allah.

بِحَارٌ bihaarun, plural of بَحْرٌ bahrun - sea.

وإِذَا البِحَارُ سُجِّرَتْ	**81-6** and when the seas rise.

غِلاظٌ ghilaazun, plural of غَلِيظٌ ghalizun - stern.

شِدادٌ shidaadun, plural of شَدِيدٌ shadidun-strong .

عليها ملائكةٌ غِلاظٌ شِدادٌ بِغَالٌ لا يَعصُونَ اللهَ	**66-6** over it (i.e. fire) are angels, stern and strong who do not disobey Allah

bighaalun, plural of بَغْلٌ baghlun - mule

والخَيْلَ والبِغَالَ وَالحَمِيرَ لِتَركَبُوهَا وَزِينَةً	**16-8** .. and (He made) horses and mules and asses that you might ride upon them and as an ornaments.

III. فُعُلٌ fuعulun, e.g.	

كُتُبٌ kutubun, plural of كتابٌ kitaabun - book.

سُفُنٌ sufunun, plural of سَفِينَةٌ safinatun - ship.

مُدُنٌ mudunun, plural of مدينةٌ madinatun - city.

Examples from The Holy Qur'an:

كُتُبٌ - kutubun plural of كِتَابٌ kitaabun-book

فيها كُتُبٌ قَيِّمَةٌ	**98-3** Wherein are right books.

سُبُلٌ subulun, plural of سَبِيلٌ sabilun - way.

وجَعَلَ لكم فِيها سُبُلاً	**43-10** and made in it ways for you.

حُرُمٌ hurumun. plural of حَرَمٌ haramun-sacred.

مِنْهَا أَرْبَعَةٌ حُرُمٌ	**9-36** of these (12 months) four are sacred.

فُرُشٌ furushun, plural of فِراشٌ firaashun - couch.

وفُرُشٍ مَرْفُوعة	**56-34** and exalted couches.

IV. فُعَلَاءُ fu ع alaa ء u, e.g.

وُزَرَاءُ wuzaraa ء u, plural of وزيرٌ wazirun - minister.

أُمَرَاء 'omaraa ء u, plural of أَمِيرٌ amirun - prince.

Example from the Holy Qur'an :

كُبَراء kubaraa ء u, plural of كبيرٌ kabirun - big.

وقالوا رَبَّنا إنا أطَعْنَا سَادَتَنَا وكُبَرائَنَا فأضلُّونا السَّبِيْلَ	**33-67** and they said: Our Lord, we only obeyed our leaders and our great men, so they led us astry from the path.

شُعَرَاءُ **shu** ع araa ء un, plural of شَاعِرٌ shaaعirun-poet

والشُّعَرَاءُ يَتَّبِعُهُمُ الغَاوُونَ	**26-224** and the poets - the devaitors follow them.

سفهاء sufahaa.u, plural of سفيهٌ safihun - fool.

سَيَقُولُ السُّفَهَاءُ مِنَ النَّاسِ	**2-142** the fools among the people will say ...

شُفَعَاءُ **shu**fa ع aa .u, plural of شَفِيعٌ **sh**afi ع un - intercessor

فَهل لَنا مِنْ شُفَعَاءَ فَيَشْفَعُوا لَنا	**7-53** are there any intercessors on our behalf so that they intercede for us?

V. أَفْعِلَاءُ af عilaa .u, e.g.

أَصْدِقَاءُ asdiqaa .u, plural of صديق sadiq - friend.

أَذْكِيَاءُ **adh**kiyaa .u, plural of ذَكِيٌّ **dh**akiyun - intelligent.

أَصْفِيَاءُ asfiyaa .u, plural of صَفِيٌّ safi .un - pure.

Examples from the Holy Qur'an:

أَنْبِيَاءُ ambiyaa ء u, plural of نَبِيٌّ nabiyun - prophet

إِذْ جَعَلَ فِيكُمْ أَنْبِيَاءَ	**5-20** Remember when He raised prophets among you.

أَغْنِيَاءُ aghniyaa ء u, plural of غَنِيٌّ ghaniyun - rich.

لَقَدْ سَمِعَ اللهُ قَوْلَ الَّذِينَ قَالُو إِنَّ اللهَ فَقِيرٌ وَنَحنُ أَغْنِيَاءُ	**3-181** Allah has certainly heard the saying of those who said: Allah is poor and we are rich.

أَدْعِيَاءُ ad ع iyaa ء u, plural of دَعِيٌّ da ع iyyun - 'adopted or asserted one as son'

وَمَا جَعَلَ أَدْعِيَاءَكُم أَبْنَاءَكُمْ	**33-4** and He did not made whom you assert (to be) your sons.

VI. فِعْلَان fi ع laan, e.g.

وِلْدَان wildaan, plural of وَلَدٌ waladun - child.

صبيان sibyaan, plural of صَبِيٌّ sabiyyun - infants.

Examples from the Holy Qur'an:

يَجْعَلُ الوِلْدَانَ شيباً	**73-17** (the day) which will make children grey-headed.

VII. فُعْلَان fu ع laan e.g.

بُلدان buldaan, plural of بلدٌ baladun - city.

قُضْبَانٌ qudbaanun, plural of قَضِيبٌ quadibun - a rod.

(C) Forms of the brokenplural derived from a quadriliteral (four consonants) nouns are as below :

I. فَعَالِلُ fa ع allil e.g.

مَجَالِسُ majaalisun, plural of مجلسٌ majlisun - seat, a council.

تَجَارِب tajaarib, plural of تَجْرِبَةٌ tajribatun - an experiment, trial.

Examples from The Holy Qur'an:

مساجد masaajidu, plural of مَسْجِد masjid - mosque,

ومَسَاجِدُ يُذْكَرُ فيها اسمُ اللهِ كثيراً	**22-40** and mosques in which Allah's name is much remembered.

مَسَاكِنُ masaakinu, plural of مَسْكَنٌ maskanun -dwelling.

وَمَسَاكِنُ تَرْضَوْنَهَا	**9-24** ... and dwellings you love...

مَنَازِلُ manazilu, plural of مَنْزِلٌ manzilun - dwelling, stage.

والقَمَرَ قَدَّرنَاه مَنَازِل	**36-39** and the moon we have ordaived for it stages.

مجالسُ majaalisu, plural of مَجْلِسٌ majlisun - a seat, seating place, assembly, council.

إذا قِيلَ لكُم تَفَسَّحُوا فى المَجَالِسِ فَافْسَحُوا	**58-11** When is said to you, m ake room in assemblies, make room.

II. فَعَالِيل fa ع aaleel e.g.

سلاطِينَ salaateen, plural of سلطان sultaan as a sultan, king.

مَكاتيب makaateeb, plural of مَكْتُوبٌ maktoobun - a letter.

Examples from The Holy Qur'an:

مَحَارِيب mahareeb. plural of مِحْرَابٌ mihraabun - synagogue.

تَمَاثِيلُ tamaatheelu, plural of تِمثَالٌ timthaalun image.

يَعْمَلُون لَه مَايَشَاءُ مِنْ مَحارِيبَ وتَمَاثِيلَ وجِفَانٍ كَالجَوَابِ وَقُدُورٍ رَاسِيَاتٍ	**34-13** They made for him what he pleased, of synagogues, and images, and bowls (large)-as watering-troughs, and fixed cooking-pots.

Note: The above holy verse consists of four other plurals besides the first two plural nouns which are shown in examples of the undermentioned examples. The other forms already discussed. The last one represents the form of a solid plural for active paticiple feminine رَاسِيَةٌ raasiyatun (a fixed one)

Caution:

Most of the forms for the broken plural are similar to the verbal nouns such as فُعُلٌ fu ʿulun e.g. كُتُبٌ kutubun, plural of كِتَابٌ kitaabun - a book and meantime it is a verbal pattern as نُـزُلٌ (what a guest is offered) or as فِعْلَةٌ fi ʿlatun, e.g. فِتْيَـةٌ fityatun - youth also it stands as a verbal noun as فِتْنَـةٌ fitnatun. This form is also confused with forms indicating to singularity of a noun, as مِرْيَةٌ miryatun - doubt. Students are advised to be careful while studying the Holy Qur'an. The only rule that may help them to distinguish the plural from verbal noun or other forms, is to see either the word has its singular from the same root or not; if there is a singular it means that the word is a plural, otherwise it is either a verbal noun or exceptional form for a singular.

EXERCISE

1. Transcript the following words and write down their forms in measuring letters (ف ع ل)

قُضَاةٌ – قُدُورٌ – جِفَانٍ – قَنَادِيلَ – مَكَاتِيبَ .

2. Pick up forms of the broken plural among the following words:

أَنْصَارٌ – نَاصِرِينَ – نَاشِفُ – مَخَابِزَ – تَلامِيذَ – قُرْبَانُ – نُزُلٌ .

3. Translate into English the following verses and sentences:

(١) جاءَ إِخْوَةُ يُوسُفَ فَدَخَلُوا عَلَيه فَعَرَفَهُم وَهُم لَهُ مُنْكِرُونَ

(٢) قَالُوا قُلوبُنَا غُلْفٌ بَلْ لَعَنَهُم اللهُ بِكُفْرِهِم

(٣) تِلْكَ الأَمْثَالُ نَضْرِبُهَا لِلنَّاسِ

(٤) إِنَّا عَرَضْنَا الأَمَانَةَ عَلَى السَّمٰوَاتِ وَالأَرْضِ والجِبَالِ فَأَبَيْنَ أن يَحْمِلْنَهَا وَأَشْفَقْنَ مِنْهَا وَحَمَلَهَا الإِنْسَانُ

(٥) يُخْرِجُهُم مِنَ الظُّلُمَاتِ إِلى النُّور

(٦) إنما يَعْمُرُ مَسَاجِدَ اللهِ مَن آمَنَ باللهِ

(٧) رِجَالٌ لا تُلهِيهِم تِجارَةٌ وَلاَ بَيْعٌ عَنْ ذِكْرِ اللهِ

(٨) وَبُعُولَتُهُنَّ أَحَقُّ بِرَدِّهِنَّ

(٩) وَاخْتِلاَفُ أَلْسِنَتِكُمْ وَأَلْوَانِكُمْ

(١٠) ذَهَبَ الأغنياء إلى المَصَايفِ فى بُلدانِ الْغَرْبِ

(١١) ظَهَرتْ نَتَائِجُ الامتحانِ السَّنَوى فَفَرِحَ الطَّلَبَةُ النَّاجِحُونَ . وَوَضَعُوا كُتُبَهُم القَدِيمَةِ فى الصَّنادِيقِ وَحَمَلُوا الْكُتُبَ الجَدِيدَةَ فى الشُّنَطِ الْيَدَوِيَّةِ . رَجَعَ الأساتِذَةُ إلى المَدْرَسَةِ بِعدَ قَضَاءِ الأجَازَةِ فى أوطَانِهِم .

4. Translate into Arabic :

News about the gathering of pilgrims reached the Council of ministers. New arrangements for Haj affairs are under the consideration of the council. During the early centuries of the Islamic history the mosques were the centres of the Islamic activities. To-day mosques are used for the prayers. Prayers in Islam have their own significance, they are not like worships in other religions.

Paradise is meant for further advancement. Mohammad was sent to the entire world, not for Arabs only. The Holy Qur'an has described him as a prophet for all human beings whatsoever be their colour, race, place and time.

VOCABULARY

إِخْوَةٌ	plural of أَخٌ	brother
مُنْكِرُون	plural of مُنْكِرٌ	one who does not recognize someone (Act. participle, male, singular)
قُلُوبٌ	plural of قَلْبٌ	heart
غُلُفٌ	verbal noun	closed, covered.
الأَمْثَالُ	plural of مَثَلٌ	example
عَرَضَ	(Perf. 3rd Person. Masc) offered	
السَّمٰوٰتِ	(Plural of Heaven) السماء	
الأَمَانَةَ	Trust	
الأَرْضُ	earth	
أَبَيْنَ	(Perf. 3rd Person. Fem.)	derived from أبى abaa - refused.
يَحْمِلْنَ	(Imper. 3rd Person, Plural)	derived from حَمَلَ to bear.
أَشْفَقْنَ	(Imper. 3rd Person, Plural)	derived from أشفق to be frightened.
الظُّلُمَاتُ	plural of ظلمةٌ zul matun	darkness.

يَعْمُرُ (Imp. 3rd Person, singular) inhabit, to build.				
تَلَهَّى (Imp. 3rd Person. sing.) distract.				
بُعُولٌ	plural of	بعل	ba ع l	husband.
أَلْسِنَةٌ	plural of	لِسَانٌ	lisan	tongue.
أَلْوَانٌ	plural of	لَوْنٌ	lonun	colour.
المَصَايِفُ	pluralof	مصيف	maseef	summer place.
بُلدانٌ	plural of	بلاد	bilaadun	country.
نَتَائِجُ	plural of	نَتِيجَةٌ	Natigatun	result.
صَنَادِيقُ	plural of	صَنْدُوقٌ	sanduqun	box
شُنَطٌ	plural of	شَنْطَةٌ	shuntatun	hand bag
الأَسَاتِذَةُ	plural of	أُسْتَاذٌ	ustazun	teacher
أَوطَانٌ	plural of	وَطَنٌ	watanun	homeland.
gathering	جُمُوعٌ			
pilgrims	حُجَّاجٌ			
arrangements	تَدابير	plural of arrangement.		
consideration	إِعْتِبَارٌ/فِكْرَةٌ			
advancement	تَقَدَّمَ			

CHAPTER 14

THE PRE-POSITIONS

1. The Arabic حرفُ الْجَرِّ harful jarr is similar to the English particles of the preposition. A word followed by an Arabic preposition is taken in the genetive. Consequently its last letter will be vowelled with a kasra e.g. فى fee (in), فى كتابٍ fi kitaabin - in a book, فِى الكِتَابِ filkitaabi - in the book, فى دينٍ fideenin - in a religion فى الدِّينِ fiddini - in the Religion and so on.

2. Prepositions are a) Inseparable, consisting of one letter always attached to the following word; b) separate, which stand alone and are either particles or nouns in the accusative.

(A) Inseparable Preposition

I. ب "in, by, with" etc.

verbs denoting 'to begin, adhere, seize, attach' are constructed with ب e.g. اتَّصَلَ بِه he got in contact with him. بَدَأَ به he began with him. أبدأُ باسْمِ اللهِ I start with the name of Allah; often the verb is omitted: بسمِ الله with the name of Allah.

To believe in is آمَنَ بِ e.g. آمَنَ بالله He believed

in Allah. To swear by is اقسم ب e.g. أقْسم بِيومِ الدّينِ
I swear by the Day of judgement

After ألا 'alaa, see, behold! ب is used e.g.
ألا بِذِكْرِ الله تَطْمَئِنُّ الْقُلُوبُ Behold! with the remembe-
rance of Allah the hearts find rest. (Holy Qur'an 13-28).
In negative sentences if the predicate is a noun, ب is often prefixed, e.g. ما هُوَ بِشَاعِرٍ He is not a poet. Also without ب is used as هُوَ لَيسَ شاعراً or ما هُوَ شاعرٌ but when a negative particle such as ما or لَيسَ is followed by an interogative " أ " a, the noun must be prefixed with ب e.g. أَلَيسَ الله بِأَحْكَمِ الحَاكِمِينَ 95-8 Is not Allah the Best of the Judges?

أَلَستُ بِرَبِّكُم Am I not your Lord?

II. ت 'by' in an oath only by the name of the Almighty Allah. e.g. (from The Holy Qur'an)

وَتَاللهِ لأَكِيدَنَّ أَصْنَامَكُمْ	**21-57** And, by Allah! I will certainly plan against your idols.
تَاللهِ لقد آثَرَكَ الله عَلَينا	**12-91** They said: By Allah! Allah has indeed chosen thee over us.

III. و by in an oath. e.g. وربِّ البَيْتِ By the Lord of the (Sacred) House.

والسَّماءِ ذَاتِ البُرُوجِ	By the heaven full of the stars!
وَالسَّماءِ وَالطَّارِقِ	By the heaven and the commenly night.

IV. لِ "for, to, because of"

It is used to express the Dative and denotes possession (= "have") e.g. هذا القَلَمُ لِي . This pen is mine.

لكَ هَذِهِ الدَّارُ To you belongs this house.

It denotes the English "of" when it follows an indeterminate noun, e.g. كِتَابٌ لِزَيْدٍ a book of (belonging to) Ziad. صَاحِبٌ لي a friend of me, i.e. one of my friends.

Examples from The Holy Qur'an:

لله مَا فِي السَّمٰوٰتِ وِالأَرْضِ	**2-284** To Allah belongs whatever is in heavens and whatever is in earth.
لِمَنِ المُلْكُ الْيَومَ لله الواحِدِ القَهَّارِ	**40-16** Whome to belongs the kingdom this day? To Allah, The One, The Subduer (of all).

It is used also for the writer of a book, e.g.

قِصَص النَّبيين لِأَبِى الحَسَن النَّدوِى	The stories of the prophets of (i.e. written by) Abul Hasan Al Nadwi.

It also denotes "for the benefit of" e.g. (from The Holy Qur'an)

مَن جاءَ بِالحَسَنَةِ فَلَهُ عَشْرُ أَمْثَالِهَا	**6-160** whoever brings a good deed will have tenfold like it.

Often it is used to denote 'the benefit of' (opposite of على)
e.g. (from The Holy Qur'an):

قَالُوا أَنَّى يَكُونُ لَه الْمُلْكُ عَلَيْنَا	**2-247** They said: how can he have a greater right to kingdom over us?

It is also used to denote the purpose and the cause, e.g.

قام لِنُصْرَتِه He rose for his help.

وَمَا أَرْسَلْنَا مِن رَسُولٍ إِلَّا بِلِسَانِ قَوْمِهِ لِيُبَيِّنَ لَهُمْ	**14-4** And we sent no messenger but with language of his people, so that he might explain to them.
قَد أَنْزَلَ اللهُ إِلَيْكُمْ ذِكْراً . رَسُولاً يَتْلُوا عَلَيْكُمْ آيَاتِ اللهِ مُبَيِّنَاتٍ لِيُخرِجَ الَّذِينَ آمَنُوا ...	**65-10,11** Allah has sent down to you a Reminder A messenger who recites to you the clear messages of Allah, **so that he may bring forth** those who believe....

لِيَعْلَمُوا أَنَّ اللهَ عَلَى كُلِّ شَيْءٍ قَدِيرٌ	**65-12** that you may know that Allah is Possessor of power over all things.

لِهَذَا / لِذَلِكَ / لِأَجْلِ هَذَا / لِأَجْلِ ذَلِكَ for this reason.

Note: 1. قَالَ لِـ "to say to" often means (especially in passive), to call, name, e.g. (from The Holy Qur'an)

قَالُوا سَمِعْنَا فَتًى يَذْكُرُهُمْ يُقَالُ لَهُ إِبْرَاهِيمُ	**21-60** They said: we heard a youth who **is called** Abraham, speak of them.

2. لِ (li) is changed to لَ (la) before pronominal suffixes (except with the first person), e.g. لَكُم /لَهَا/ له

V. كَ as 'like' e.g. (from The Holy Qur'an)

وَلَيْسَ الذَّكَرُ كَالْأُنْثَى	**3-36** And the male is not like the female.
أَوْ كَالَّذِي مَرَّ عَلَى قَرْيَةٍ	**2-259** Or like him who passed by a town...

(B) **Separate Prepositions**

I. إِلَى "elaa" 'untill', e.g. (from The Holy Qur'an):

ثُمَّ أَتِمُّوا الصِّيَامَ إِلَى اللَّيْلِ	**2-187** Then complete the fast untill the nightfall.

إِلَىٰ 'to', e.g. (from The Holy Qur'an):

سُبْحَانَ الَّذِى أَسْرَى بِعَبْدِهِ لَيْلاً مِنَ الْمَسْجِدِ الحَرَامِ إِلَى الْمَسْجِدِ الأَقْصَى	**17-1** Glory to Him Who carried His servant by night from the Sacred Mosque unto the Remote Mosque.

With suffixes إليه to him, إِلَيَّ to me e.g. (from The Holy Qur'an)

إِلَيْهِ يَصْعَدُ الْكَلِمُ الطَّيِّبُ	**35-10** To Him do ascend the goodly word.
ثم إِلَيَّ مَرْجِعُكُم	**3-55** Then To Me is your return.

II. حتى hatta "until, as far as" e.g. (from The Holy Qur'an):

حَتَّى إِذَا اسْتَيْأَسَ الرُّسُلُ	**12-110** until, when the messengers despair
حَتَّى إِذَا جَاءُوهَا فُتِحَتْ أَبْوَابُهَا	**39-71** until when they come to it, its door are opened.

It is not used with suffixes. Sometimes it is used to mean 'even' e.g.

سَأَلْتُ كُلَّ شَخْصٍ حَتَّى الطِّفْلَ I asked everybody even the child.

But in this case it has no influence of genetives

III على ع alaa, 'over, upon, against, through' e.g. (from The Holy Qur'an)

إِنَّ اللهَ عَلَى كُلِّ شَيْءٍ قَدِيرٌ	**2-109** surely Allah is possessor over all things.
صِرَاطَ الَّذِينَ أَنْعَمْتَ عَلَيْهِمْ	**1-7** The path of those upon whom Thou hast bestowed favours.
إِنَّ اللهَ وَمَلائِكَتَهُ يُصَلُّونَ عَلَى النَّبِى يَا أَيُّهَا الَّذِينَ آمَنُوا صَلُّوا عَلَيْهِ وَسَلِّموا تَسْلِيمًا	**33-56** Surely Allah and His angels bless the Prophet, O' you who believe call for blessings on him and salute him (as salute is performed.)
سلامٌ عليكم	**13-24** Peace be on you.
وعَلَى الَّذِين يُطِيقُونَهُ فِدْيَةٌ طَعَامُ مِسْكِينٍ	**2-184** And on those who can afford, is redemption by feeding a poor man.

عَلَى is used with suffixes as عليه , عَلَيَّ etc.

used of places: عَلَى الطَّرِيق on the way.

جَلَسَ عَلَى المَائِدَةِ he sat at the table.

sometimes is used in hostile sense, e.g.

خرج عليه he went out, against him.

Example from The Holy Qur'an:

فَأَرسَلنا عَلَيهِم رِيحاً وَجُنُوداً لم تَرَوْها	**33-9** so we sent against them a stron wind and hosts that you saw not.

IV عَنْ ع an "from about, concerning, with"

Examples from The Holy Qur'an:

وَيَسْئَلُونَكَ عَنِ الرُّوحِ	**17-85** And they ask **thee** about the soul.
الذِينَ يَصُدُّونَ عَن سَبِيلِ اللهِ	**11-19** who hinder (men) **from** the path of Allah.
وَإذا سَأَلَكَ عِبَادِى **عَنِّى** فَإِنِّى قَرِيبٌ	**2-186** And when My servants ask thee **concerning** Me, surely I am nigh
رَضِىَ اللهُ **عَنْهُمْ** وَرَضُوا **عَنْهُ**	**5-119** Allah is well pleased with them and they are well pleased with Him.

It is used of place " away from " and so is used with verbs denoting, "avoid, restrain oneself, forbid, defend" etc.

Examples from The Holy Qur'an:

(To forbid)

يَأْمُرُونَ بِالْمَعْرُوفِ وَيَنْهَوْنَ عَنِ الْمُنكَرِ	**9-71** They enjoin good and forbid evil.

(To defend)

إِنَّ اللهَ يُدَافِعُ عَنِ الَّذِينَ آمَنُوا	**22-38** surely Allah defends those who believe.

(To discover)

وكَشَفَتْ عَنْ سَاقَيْهَا	**27-44** and she bared her legs

V. فى (fi) "in"

with suffixes: فيه in him or in it, فِيَّ in me, فيكم in you or among you.

Examples from the Holy Qur'an:

لَقَدْ كَانَ لَكُمْ فِى رَسُولِ اللهِ أُسْوَةٌ حَسَنَةٌ	**33-21** Surely you have **in** the Messenger of Allah an excellent examplar.
فِيهِ رِجَالٌ يُحِبُّونَ أَن يَتَطَهَّرُوا	**9-108 In it** (the mosque) are men who love to purify themselves.
لَقَدْ مَنَّ اللهُ عَلَى الْمُؤْمِنِينَ إِذْ بَعَثَ فِيهِمْ رَسُولاً	**3-164** certainly Allah conferred a favour on the believers when he raised among them a messenger.

VI. مِن (min) 'from'

It is often interchangeable with عن and used with suffixes such as مِنْهُ from him or from it, مِنِّى from me مِنَّا from us, etc.

Examples from The Holy Qur'an:

يُخْرِجُهُم من الظُّلُمَاتِ إِلَى النُّورِ	**2-257** He brings them out of darkness into light.

It sometimes used to complete the sense of قَبْلُ 'before' and بَعْدُ 'after'. According to the grammarians this kind of (مِنْ) is called 'an additional' (مِنْ) e.g.

لِلَّهِ الْأَمْرُ مِنْ قَبْلُ وَمِنْ بَعْدُ	**30-4** Allah's is the Command before and after.

It is also used partitively (للتبعيض) followed by a definite noun in the plural to indicate an indefinite number or quantity, e.g. (from The Holy Qur'an):

ولكِنَّ اللهَ يَجْتَبِى مِن رُسُلِهِ مَن يَشَاءُ	**3-179** But Allah choses of His Messenger whom He pleases.
لِنُرِيَكَ مِن آيَاتِنا الْكُبْرى	**20-23** that We may show thee of our greater signs.

and to indicate materials e.g. كرسى من خَشَبٍ a chair of wood.

Example from The Holy Qur'an:

وَيُطَافُ عَلَيْهِمْ بِآنِيَةٍ مِنْ فِضَّةٍ	**76-15** goblets of silver are brought round for them.

It is very often used after ما (maa) to explain (للتبيين) what is intended by the particle e.g.

أنفقْتُ مَا كَان عِنْدِي من المالِ I spent of what was with me in the way of wealth.

Examples from the Holy Qur'an:

وما تُنفِقُوا مِن خيرٍ فَإنَّ اللهَ بِهِ عَلِيمٌ	**2-273** And whatever good thing you send surely Allah is knower of it.

وَمَا أَصَابَكُمْ مِن مُصِيبَةٍ فَبِمَا كَسَبَتْ أَيْدِيكُمْ وَيَعْفُوا عَن كَثِيرٍ	42-30 And whatever misfortune befell you it is on account of what your hands have earned and He pardons much.

VII. مُذْ mudh, مُنذُ mundhu 'since'

It is not used with suffixes, it is sometimes followed by the nominal, e.g.

مَا رَأَيْتُكَ مُنْذُ يَوْمِ الجمعَةِ
منذ (مذ) يومِ الجمعةِ
} I have not seen you since Friday.

3. There are a number of nouns used as prepositions, though not endorsed among them by Arab grammorians, some Western authors listed them as real prepositions, however these particles are useful for learners as they have accord in The Holy Qur'an:

(a) لَدَىٰ لَدُنْ لَدَىَّ (lada), (Ladun), (laday), 'with' (Latin 'apad') with suffixes لَدَيْهِم with him, لدىَّ with me, لَدَيْه with him, لَدُنِّى with me, to me,

Examples from the Holy Qur'an:

لا يَخافُ لَدىَّ المُرْسَلون	27-10 surely, The Messengers fear not in my presence.
وَإِنَّهُ فِى أُمِّ الكِتابِ لَدَيْنَا لَعَلِىٌّ حكيم	43-4 And it is in the Original of the Book with Us, truly elevated, full of wisdom.

آلر !كتابٌ أُحْكِمَتْ آياتهُ ثُمَّ فُصِّلَتْ من لَدُنْ حَكِيمٍ خَبِيرٍ	**11-1** A book whose verses are characterized by wisdom, then they are made plain **from One** Wise, Aware.
وَمَا كُنْتَ لَدَيْهِمْ إذْ يُلْقُونَ أَقْلاَمَهُمْ	**3-44** And thou wast not **with them** when they cast their pens.

(b) مَعَ (maع a) with, e.g. (from The Holy Qur'an):

إن الله مع الصَّابِرِينَ	**2-153** Allah is with the patients.

(c) عِنْدَ (inda) 'with, at':

used of place: جَلَسْتُ عِنْدَهُ I sat with (beside) him.

Example from The Holy Qur'an:

وَلَا تُقَاتِلُوهُم عِنْدَ المَسْجِدِ الحَرَامِ	**2-191** and fight not with them **at** the Sacred Mosque.

use of time: جاء عِنْدَ طُلوعِ الشَّمْسِ he came at sunrise. It is often used to denote the meaning "for to, near, presence"

Examples from The Holy Qur'an:

وَتَحْسَبُونَهُ هَيِّناً وَهُوَ عِنْدَ اللهِ عَظِيمٌ	**24-15** You counted it a trifle, in the sight of Allah is very great.

اُذْكُرْنِى عِنْدَ رَبِّكَ	**12-42** Remember me in presence of thy Lord.

It is also used with the meaning 'to have'.

Example from The Holy Qur'an:

مَا عِنْدَكُمْ يَنْفَدُ وَمَا عِنْدَ اللهِ بَاقٍ	**16-96** whatever you possess will pass away and what Allah has, will remain.

EXERCISE

1. Translate into Arabic :

.... in short, a life which fully represents all aspects of human existence and combines all that is best and noblest in terms of sentiments and behaviour is the life of Prophet Mohammad (Peace be upon him). The highest standard of perfection for everybody, in every respect and for all places and times. Supposing you are a rich man you have an ideal to follow in the person of the merchant of Makka and the treasurer of Bahrain. If you are poor, you must emulate the example of the internee of Shaعb Abi Talib and (latter) the guest of the people of Madina.

2. Translate into English:

١ – لَمْ يَكُنْ بَطَلُ الأبْطَالِ وَخاتَمُ النَّبِيينَ صَلَّى اللهُ عَلَيه وَسَلَّم إلاَّ بشَراً يُوحى إليه وَمَا أوتِىَ عَن طريقِ الْوَحْىِ قَد فُصِّلَتْ آياتُهُ فى الكِتابِ وَفِيما عَدا ذٰلِكَ من الأقْوَالِ والأَعْمَالِ فإنَّما هِىَ ثَمرةُ عَقْلٍ راجحٍ وَلسَانٍ فَصِيحٍ فى ذَاتٍ فَذَّةٍ

٢ ـ إنَّ أوَّل شَرط لِنَجاحِ البَائِعِ أن يُحِبَّ عَمَلَه وَأن يُوَجِّهَ إلَيه كلَّ اهْتِمامِه حَتى يُؤَدِّيه فى سُهُولَةٍ وَيُسْرٍ وعَن رضا وَارْتِيَاح عَلى أن يَكونَ البَائِعُ بِجَانِبِ ذٰلِكَ مُتَفَائِلاً . وَالابْتِسَامَةُ عَلى وَجهِ البَائِع ضَرورةٌ مِن ضَرُوراتِ هَذِهِ المِهنَةِ وَبِدُونِها لَا يَستَقِيمُ لَه عَمَلٌ .

٣ – أهَمُّ شَىء عند عَالِم كتابُه ، وعِندَ أصْحَابِ المِهَنِ اليَدَوِيَّةِ عُدَّتُهم ، وَعِندَ الجُنْدِىِّ سِلاحُهُ .

VOCABULARY

Hero of Heroes	بَطَل الأبْطَال
The Last Prophet	خاتَمَ النَّبِيِّنَ
Human being	البشر/الإنسَانُ
Revealed	أوحى
Way	طريق/ سبيل
Stated clearly	المصرَّح به
Sings	الآية

Among the saying	مِنَ الأقوال
Deeds	الأعْمَال
Front	الأمام
Wisdom	العقْل
Matured	الرَّاجح/ الناضج
Apart from that	فضلاً عن ..
Frank speaking	القولُ الصَّريح
Condition	الشَّرطُ
Success	النجاح
Merchant	التَّاجِرُ
To love Perf. أَحب Imperf. يُحِبُّ	
To Direct توجيه Perf. وَجَّه Imperf. يُوَجِّه	
attention	الاهتمامُ
In order to	لِ/ لأجْلِ
To do, Perform, discharge (duty) Imperf يؤدى ـ أدى Perf	
Easyness	السُّهُولَةُ / اليُسْرُ
Delightfully,	ابتهاجاً
Besides this	ماعَدا ذلك
Optimistic	متفائل/ التفاؤل
Smiling	التَّبَسُّم / الابتسامُ
Necessity	الضَرورَة

Profession	المِهْنَةُ
Does not stand	لا يَستَقيمُ
The Most Important thing.	أهَمّ شَىء
Tool	العُدَّة
Soldier	الجندى
Arms	السَّلاحُ
Personal	الذَّات
Unique	الفَذَّةُ
Represents	يُمَثِّلُ
Aspects الظواهرَ	Plural of ظاهِرَةٌ
Existence	الوجُود - البقَاء
Sentiments	العَواطف
Behaviour	السلُوكُ
Perfection	التَوافُق
Respect	الإحْلال
Supposing	على فرضٍ
Rich	الغَنى
Ideal	الصَنَمُ
Treasurer	الخازن
Internnee	الداخلُ

CHAPTER 15

THE IMPERATIVE

1. The Imperative فِعْلُ الأَمْرِ is a modification of the Imperfect. It is formed by :
   1. Taking away the vowel of the final radical as in case of the jussive.
   2. Dropping the pronominal prefix.
   3. Replacing it by an أَلِف alif, e.g.

      كَتَبَ to write. Imperfect - يَكْتُبُ he writes.

      Imperative - أُكْتُبْ write !
2. This أ alif may be vowelled with **damma** or **kasra**. If the second radical of the imperfect has **damma**, the prefixing alif will take **damma** otherwise it will be vowelled with **kasra.** Thus from يَنْصُرُ the imperative will be أُنْصُرْ and from يَفْتَحُ and يَضْرِبُ the imperatives will be إِفْتَحْ and إِضْرِبْ respectively.
3. In case of a weak letter in the middle radical of the imperfect such as يقول and يبيعُ no alif is prefixed, and the first radical will receive the vowel that will agree with the vowel of the middle radical, thus: قال to say. Imperfect يقول he says. Imperative: قُلْ say ! بَاعَ to sell. Imperfect يَبِيعُ he sells. Imperative : بِعْ sell !

4. The prefixing "alif of the imprative is applied at the begining of a statement, otherwise this" alif will be considered silent Consequently, the second radical will determine the pattern of the imperative :

كُلُوا وَاشْرَبُوا eat and drink ! إجْلِسْ وَاكْتُبْ sit and write !

Example from the Holy Qur'an :

اعْمَلُوا آلَ دَاوودَ شُكْرًا	O' children of David, work hard, in thanks.

5. The following conjugation of the imperative represents its common pattern :

from يكتُبُ = يَفعَلُ	from يفتح=يَفعَلُ	from=يَضْرِبُ يَفْعَلُ
Sing. 2nd pers. masc. أُكْتُبْ	إفْتَحْ	إضْرِبْ
2n pers. fem. أُكْتُبِي	إفْتَحِي	إضْرِبِي
Dual. 2nd pers. masc. & fem. أُكْتُبَا	إفْتَحَا	إضْرِبَا
Plu. Pers. masc. أُكْتُبُوا	إفْتَحُوا	إضْرِبُوا
Pers. fem. أُكْتُبْنَ	افتحن	إضْرِبْنَ

from يَقُولُ		from يَبِيعُ
Sing. 2nd Pers. Masc.	قُلْ	بِعْ

Sing, 2nd Pers. Fem.	قولى	بِيعى
Dual. Masc. & Fem.	قُولاَ	بِيعَا
Plu. 2nd pers. Masc.	قُولُوا	بِيعُوا
Plu. 2nd pers. Fem .	قُلْنَ	بِعْنَ

the negative imperative فعل النهى is formed by the 2nd person, Imperfect (Jussive) preceded by لا thus:

لا تَكْتُبْ	لا تَقُلْ	لا تَبِعْ
لا تَكْتُبِى	لا تَقُولِى	لا تَبِيعِى
لا تَكْتُبَا	لا تَقُولاَ	لا تبيعا
لا تَكْتُبُوا	لا تَقُولوا	لا تَبِيعوا
لا تَكْتُبْنَ	لا تَقُلْنَ	لا تَبِعْنَ

Examples from the Holy Qur'an :

Pattern I أُكْتُبْ from كَتَبَ to write, Imperfect يَكْتُبُ he writes

اركُضْ بِرِجْلِكَ هٰذا مُغْتَسَلٌ بارِدٌ وشرابٌ	**38-42 Urge** with they foot; here is a cool washing-place and drink.

أُكْتُبى Sing. Fem.

يا مَرْيَمُ اقْنُتى لِرَبِّكِ وَاسْجُدِى	**3-43** O' Mary, **be obedient** to thy Lord and **do** ' Sajdah

اكْتُبوا Plural, Masc.

واسْجُدوا وَاعْبُدوا رَبَّكُمْ	**22-77** And **do** sajdah and serve your Lord.

اكْتُبنَ Plural, Fem.

وَاذْكُرْنَ ما يتلى فى بيوتِكُنَّ	**33-34** And **remember** that which is recited in your houses.

Pattern II إفْتَح open, from فَتَحَ to open Imperfect : يَفْتَحُ he opens.

يا أَبَتِ افعَلْ ما تُؤمَرُ	**37-102** O' my father, **do** as thou art commanded.

إفْتَحى Sing. Fem.

وَارْكَعِى مَعَ الرَّاكعِين	**3-43** and **bow** thyself with whom who bow themselves.
وقِيلَ يَا أرْضُ ابْلعِى مَاءَكِ	**11-44** and it was said : O' earth swallow thy water.

إفتحوا Plural, masc.

وَافْعَلوا الخيرَ لَعَلَّكُم تُفْلِحُون	**22-77** and do good that you may Succeed.

Pattern III إضْرِبْ strike , Sing. Masc, From ضَرَبَ to Strike. Imperfect يَضْرِبُ

فَقُلْنا اضْرِبْ بِعَصَاكَ الحَجَرَ	**2-60** We said: strike on the rock with thy staff.

إضْرِبُوا Plural, Masc.

فَقُلْنَا اضْرِبُوهُ بِبَعْضِهَا	**2-73** So We said : strike him with it partially.

From Weak Verbs:

قُلْ Sing. Masc.

وقُلْ لَهُمَا قَولاً كَرِيماً	**17-23** and speak to them a generous word.

قُولُوا Plural. Masc.

قُل مُوتُوا بِغَيْظِكُمْ	**3-119** Say : Die in your rage.

قُلْنَ Plural, Fem.

وَقُلْنَ قَولاً مَعْرُوفاً ۝ وقَرْنَ فى بُيُوتِكُنَّ	**33-32,33** and speak a word of goodness and stay in your houses.

6. Imperative from Hamzated verbs

verbs of which the first radical is hamza such as أَكَلَ to eat'

Imperfect : يَأكُل he eats, have their imperative without an 'alif, e.g.

Sing. 2nd Pers (M) كُلْ eat, as خُذْ take e.g.

خُذْ مِنْ أَمْوَالِهِم صَدَقَةً	**9-103** take alms out of their property.

Sing. 2nd Pers. (F) كُلِى eat e.g.

فَكُلِى وَاشْرَبِى وَقَـرِّى عَيْناً	**19-26** eat and, drink and cool the eye.

Dual. 2nd Pers. (M&F) كُلاَ eat

وَكُلا منها رَغَداً	**2-35** and eat from it a plenteous (food).

Plu. 2nd Pers. (fem) as قَرْنَ ، قُلْنَ of weak verb's imperative.

Verbs hamzated in their middle radical such as سَأَلَ to ask ;

Imperfect يَسْأَلُ

The Imperative will be سَلْ ask.(Example from the Holy Qur'an):

سَلْ بَنِى إسْرَائيل ..	**2-211** Ask children of Israel.

also إسأَلْ with alif vowelled with kasra e.g. (From the Holy Qur'an)

وَاسأَلِ القَرْيَةَ التى كُنّا فِيهَا	**12-82** and ask the town where we were.

If hamza occurs in the third radical such as قَرَأَ the imperative will be : (From The Holy Qur'an) إِقْرَأْ read !

اقرأ بِاسْمِ رَبِّكَ الَّذِى خَلَقَ	**96-1** Read in the name of thy Lord.

Some Examples of the negative imperative from the Holy Qur'an

يا أَبَتِ لا تَعْبُدِ الشيطَانَ	**19-44** O' my father, **serve not** Satan.
لا تَقُمْ فِيهِ أَبَداً	**9-108 Never stand** in it.
فَلاَ تَقُل لهما أُفٍّ وَلاَ تَنْهَرْهُمَا	**17-23 Say not** "Fie" to them nor chide them.

فَلا تَدْعُ مَعَ اللهِ إِلَـٰهًا آخَرَ	**26-213** so call not upon another God with Allah.
وَلَا تَقْبَلُوا لَهُم شَهَادَةً أَبَدًا	**24-4** Never accept their evidence.
وَلَا تَقُولُوا لِمَنْ يُقْتَلُ فِي سَبِيلِ اللهِ أَمْوَاتٌ	**2-154** and call them not dead those who are killed in the way of Allah.

7. The "Emphatic Nun"

To emphasize the meaning of a verb, the imperfect has sometimes, emphatic **nun** which is suffixed without any other alternation. This type of 'nun' is called نون التوكيد nunut-tokeed. It has two kinds : a duplicated one with **shadda;** and another with sukun i.e. vowelless.

The former is termed نون الثقيلة "nun thaqila" and the latter as نون الخفيفة "nun khafifa" e.g. (from The Holy Qur'an) :

(nun thaqila)	
لأكيدَنَّ أصنامَكم	**21-57** And by Allah I will certainly plan against your idols.

(nun **khafifa**)	
لَنَسْفَعاً بالنَّاصِيَةِ	**96-15** We will seize him by the forlock.

It is also used with imperative to denote 'strict command'. Compare :

إِذْهَبْ	go !
إِذْهَبَنْ	you should go.
إِذْهَبَنَّ	you must go.

لا تَذْهَبْ	Do not go !
لا تَذْهَبَنْ	Never go !
لا تَذْهَبَنَّ	You must'nt go.

The 'emphatic nun' can be suffixed with all parts of imperfect while the imperative is made by the parts of 2nd person only. The following conjugation will show the modification of imperfect and imperative with 'emphatic nuns' :

3rd Person, Sing. Masc.	لِيَذْهَبَنَّ	he should go.
3rd Person, Sing. Fem.	لِتَذْهَبَنَّ	she should go.
2nd Person, Sing. Masc.	لِتَذْهَبَنَّ	you should go.
2nd person, Sing. Fe.	لِتَذْهَبَنَّ	you should go.
First Person, Sing.	لأذهَبَنَّ	I should go.
3rd Person, dual, Masc.	لِيَذْهَبَانِّ	They (two) should go.
3rd Person, dual, Fem.	لِتَذْهَبَانِّ	They (two) should go.

2nd Person, dual, Masc.	لِتَذْهَبَانِّ	You (two) should go.
2nd Person, dual, Fem.	لِتَذْهَبَانِّ	You (two) should go.
3rd Person, Plural, Masc.	لِتَذْهَبُنَّ	You (all) should go.
3rd Person, Plural, Fem.	لِتَذْهَبْنَ	You (all) should go.
First Person, Plural.	لِنَذْهَبَنَّ	We should go.

It is often used in the negative cases and rarely in other forms.

Examples from The Holy Qur'an :

ولا يَحْسَبَنَّ الَّذِينَ كَفَرُوا أَنَّمَا نُمْلِى لَهُمْ خَيْرٌ لِأَنْفُسِهِمْ	**3-178** And let not those who disbelieve think that our granting them respite is good for themselves.
ولا تَحْسَبَنَّ اللهَ غَافِلاً عَمَّا يَعْمَلُ الظَّالِمُون	**14-42** And think not Allah to be heedless of what the unjust do.
وَلا تَقُولَنَّ لِشَىْءٍ إِنِّى فَاعِلٌ ذَلِكَ غَداً إِلَّا أَنْ يَشَاءَ اللهُ	**18-23,24** And say not of anything : I will do that tomorrow .. unless Allah Please.
فَلَا تَمُوتُنَّ إِلَّا وَأَنْتُمْ مُسْلِمُونَ	**2-132** So die not unless your are Muslims (submitting ones)

EXERCISE

1. Distinguish difference patterns of the imperatives given below:

إبْلعى ، أقْصرى ، قُولوا ، إسألوا ، سَلْ ، قُم ، خُذْنَ ، قُولا ، إجْمَعى ،
إضْرِبُوا ، لا تَحْسَبْ ، لا تَحْسَبَنَّ

2. Is there any difference between:

إفْعَلوا ، وَافْعَلُوا ، قال : اذهَبوا ، وَقالَ اذْهَبُوا ، اذْهَبْ وَافْتَحِ البابَ ،
إذهَبْ يا وَلَدُ ، إفْتح البابَ

3. Make imperatives from the following verbs:

نَصَرَ يَنْصُرُ ، كَرُم يَكْرُمُ ، حَسِبَ يَحسَبُ ، قتل يَقْتُلُ ، بلغ يَبْلُغُ ،
جَعَلَ يَجْعَلُ .

Translate into Arabic :

1. Look! O' friends, what you have done.
2. O' boys, enter and sit by my side
3. O' believer, open your heart for good advices.
4. O' Men, do not hink Allah is heedless of your doing.
5. Never go to the evil places.
6. Do whatever you are commanded to.
7. Recite the Holy Qur'an every morning.
8. Say not what is unjust. Do pray for your parents and relatives

Translate into English :

وقُلْ جَاءَ الْحَقُّ وَزَهَقَ الْبَاطِلُ إنَّ الْبَاطِلَ كَانَ زَهُوقاً ، خُذْ منْ أمْوالِهِم صَدقَةً تُطَهِّرُهُمْ ، يا بُنَىَّ لا تُشْرِك بالله ، لا تَجْعَلُوا مع الله إلَـهًا آخَرَ ، إعْمَلوا آل دَاوودَ شُكراً ، جَاهِدِ الكُفَّارَ وَاغْلُظْ عَلَيهم ، طهِّر بَيْتِىَ لِلطَّائفينَ والعَاكِفينَ وَالرُّكَّعِ السُّجُودِ .

VOCABULARY

Look	انْظُر	from نَظَرَ يَنْظُرُ
enter	ادْخُل	from دَخَلَ يَدْخُلُ
open	إفْتح	from فتَحَ يفتح
think	فكِّر	from فكَّرَ يُفكِّرُ (derived form)
heedless	غافِلٌ	Active participle from غَفَلَ يَغْفَلُ
command	أَمْرٌ	
recite	اتْلُ	from تَلا يتْلوا (weak verb)
unjust	ظُلَّمٌ	
parents	الوالدين	duel of وَالِدٌ
Relatives	الأقْرِبَاء	Pl. of قَرِيبٌ

الحَقُّ	truth
بَاطِل	falsehood
زَهَقَ	vanished (3rd person)
زَهُوقٌ	bound to vanish (verbal noun)
صَدَقَةٌ	alms
تُطَهِّر	make clear, pure (from derived form)
لا تَرْكَنُوا	do not incline (imperative plural, masc. 3rd person)
القَبْر	tomb
جَاهِد	struggle.
اغْلُظْ	to be firm against someone.
المنافِقين	hypocrites plural of المنافق hypocrite
الطَّائِفِين	Plural of طَائِف who gets round the Holy Ka'ba.

CHAPTER 16

THE DERIVED FORMS OF THE VERBS - I,II,III

Forms derived from the triliteral roots are made by the addition of prefixes, suffixes and infixes. Throught these modifications the variations in the shade of meaning are obtained.

Arabic roots, are formed into words by addition of vowels; these added vowels and consonants make certain STOCK PATTERNS or FORMS. Each particular form produces its own particular modification of the basic meaning of the root. For instance meaning of the verb قَتَلَ "qtl" is 'to kill' thus a long vowel after the first radical ق makes it قَاتَلَ "quaatala" that means they fight each other. If the second radical of this verb قتل is duplicated to become قَتَّلَ "qattala" which means he (3rd person sing, masc) cut (someone or something) into pieces.

The total number of these derived forms is 15 and they are referred to by their serial number such as form I, II, III and so on. The important ones which are used in Qur'an are given below:

I. fa ʿala e.g. ضَرَبَ daraba - to give parable.

كَيْفَ ضَرَبَ اللّٰهُ مَثَلاً	**14-24** How Allah sets forth a parable.

fعع ala e.g. صَدَّقَ saddaqua - to verify

بل جَاءَ بالحق وَصَدَّقَ المُرْسَلِينَ	**37-37** Nay, he has brought the Truth and **verifies** the messenger.

faaع ala e.g. قَاتَلَ qaatala - they fight each other.

قَاتَلَ مَعَهُ رِبِّيُّونَ كَثِيرٌ	**3-146** Many godly men have faught with him

af ع ala e.g. أَحْسَنَ ahsana - to do good.

قَدْ أَحسَنَ الله له رِزْقاً	**65-11** Allah has indeed given him a good by sustenance.

tafaعع ala e.g. تَقَبَّلَ taqabbala - to accept.

فَتَقَبَّلَها رَبُّها بِقَبُولٍ حَسَنٍ	**3-37** so her Lord accepted her with a goodly acceptance.

tafaع ala e.g. تقاتل taqaatala - to fight.

وَمَا لَكُم لاَ تُقَاتِلُونَ فِى سَبِيلِ الله	**4-75** and what reason have you not to fight in the way of Allah.

infaع ala e.g. انطلق intalaqa - to set out.

وَانْطَلَقَ الْمَلأُ مِنهُم ...	**38-6** and chief of them started saying.

iftaع ala, e.g. اِقْتَرَبَ iqtaraba - to get high, to draw near

اقْتَرَبَ لِلنَّاسِ حِسَابُهُمْ	**21-1** Their reckoning has drawn near to the people.

if ع alla, e.g. إِسْوَدَّ iswadda - to get black

فَأَمَّا الَّذِينَ اسْوَدَّتْ وُجُوهُهُمْ	**3-106** then so to those whose faces became black.

istafعala e.g. إِسْتَغْفَرَ istaghfara - to seek forgiveness.

وَاسْتَغْفَرَ لَهُمُ الرَّسُولُ	**4-64** And the Messenger asked forgiveness of Allah.

II. The Verbal Stems II (Faعala)

1. The first stem is the absolute form of triliteral verb which stands as root-form for all described stems and it was dealt in Chapter 4.

2. The second stem is formed from the triliteral root by duplicating the second radical that is ع in فَعَلَ e.g. كَسَّرَ from كَسَرَ

This form or stem denotes:

A causative meaning e.g. عَلِمَ to know, عَلَّمَ to teach (to cause some one to know).

Example from the Holy Qur'an :

عَلَّمَ الإِنْسَانَ مَا لَمْ يَعْلَمْ	**96-5** He (i.e. Allah) taught man what he did not know.

حَمَلَ to carry حَمَّلَ to load i.e. to make some one to carry.

Example from the Holy Qur'an :

رَبَّنَا ! وَلَا تُحَمِّلْنَا مَا لَا طَاقَةَ لَنَا بِهِ	**2-286** Our Lord, impose not on us that which we have not the strength to bear.

Note: "Impose not on us" is the rendering of لَا تَحْمِلْنَا its literary translation is "do not load upon us".

3. If the verb is Intransitive in the first form, it becomes transitive in this form e.g. فَرِحَ to be glad. and فَرَّحَ to gladden; ضَعُفَ to be weak and ضَعَّفَ to weaken.

Intransitive حَكَمَ to judge.

Example from the Holy Qur'an :

إِنَّا أَنْزَلْنَا إِلَيْكَ الْكِتَابَ بِالْحَقِّ لِتَحْكُمَ بَيْنَ النَّاسِ	**4-105** We revealed to you the Book that you may judge between mankind.

Transitive : حَكَّمَ to make some one a judge,

Example from the Holy Qur'an :

فَلاَ وَرَبِّكَ لا يؤمِنُونَ حَتَّى يُحَكِّمُوكَ فِيمَا شَجَرَ بَيْنَهُمْ	**4-65** But no, by Thy LOrd, they will not believe until they make you the judge in all disputes among them.

4. Intensive meaning i.e. an act is done with great violence or continued for a long time e.g. كَسَرَ to break كَسَّرَ to break in pieces, قَطَعَ to cut قَطَّعَ to cut to pieces, قَتَلَ to kill قَتَّلَ to massacre.

Examples from the Holy Qur'an:

وقتَلَ دَاوودُ جَالوتَ	**2-251** and David Killed Goliath.

وَقُتِّلُوا تَقْتِيلاً	**33-61** They were massacred.

5. Declarative or Stimative: e.g. صَدَقَ to tell the truth. صَدَّقَ to declear that one speaks the truth

Examples from the Holy Qur'an:

قل صَدَقَ اللهُ	**3-95** Say: Allah told the truth
وصدَّقَ المُرْسَلِينَ	**37-37** And He affirmed the truth of Messengers.
فلا صَدَّقَ ولا صلَّى ولكِنْ كذَّبَ وتَوَلَّى	**75-31,32** So he accepted not The Truth nor prayed- But denied and turned back.
وَرَتِّلِ القُرْآنَ تَرْتِيلا	**73-4** and recite the Qur'an in leisurely manner.
وكَبِّرهُ تَكْبيرا	**17-111** and proclaim His greatness magnifying (Him).
وَالَّذى جَاءَ بِالصِّدقِ وَصدَّقَ بِهِ أُولَٰئِكَ هُمُ المُتَّقُونَ	**39-33** and he who brings the truth and accepts the truth - such are the duty-full
كَذٰلِكَ زَيَّنَّا لِكُلِّ أُمَّةٍ عَمَلَهُم	**6-108** thus to every peopel have we made their deeds fair-seeming.
وَلَكِنَّ اللهَ حَبَّبَ إِليكُمُ الإيمَانَ	**49-7** But Allah has endeared the faith to you and maed it seemly in your

ولا نُكذِّبَ بآيات رَبِّنَا	**6-27** and We would not reject the message of our Lord.

III. The Verbal Stem Faa ع la = Qaatala

This stem is formed by inserting an 'alif between first and second radicals of the root-form فَعَلَ fa ع ala, and it means to do something with another person. Thus form root forms:

fa ع ala فَعَلَ - he did, will be فاعَلَ faa ع la - They did something with another.

kataba كَتَبَ he wrote, will be kaataba كاتَبَ he correspondent with.

Qatala قَتَلَ he killed, will be qaatala قَاتَلَ he faught with.

sabaqa سَبَقَ he preceded, will be saabaqa سابَقَ he ran a race with.

This stem is somethimes denominative e.g. ضاعَفَ daa ع fa, to make something double, from ضِعْف de ع f. سَافَرَ saafara, to go on a journey, from سَفَر journey. قابَلَ qaabala, to be in front of, to compare one thing with another to interview.

The Passive Perfect is quotila قُوتِلَ and passive imperfect: يُقاتِلُ yoqatilo.

The conjugation of this stem كَاتَبَ "to write to, to correspond with" is as below:

Perfect	Passive	Imperfect
كَاتَبَ	كُوتِبَ	يُكَاتِبُ
قَاتَلَ	قُوتِلَ	يُقَاتِلُ
سَابَقَ	سُوبِقَ	يُسَابِقُ
جَاهُدَ	جُوهِدَ	يُجَاهِدُ

Imperative	Part Active	Part Passive
كَاتِبْ	مُكَاتِبٌ	مُكاتَبٌ
قَاتِلْ	مقاتِلٌ	مقاتَلٌ
سَابِقْ	مُسَابِقٌ	مسَابَقٌ
جَاهِدْ	مُجَاهِدٌ	مجاهَدٌ

The verbal noun has two alternative forms:

1. مكاتَبَةٌ Mukatabat (un) signifying the act of writing to, or corresponding with, anyone.
2. كتابٌ kitaab this is used as a simple noun to mean a book or a letter.

Examples from the Holy Qur'an:

يُقَاتِلُونَ فِي سَبِيلِ اللهِ **فَيَقْتُلُونَ وَيُقْتَلُونَ**	**9-111** They fight in Allah's way so they slay and are slain.
وَمَا **أُرِيدُ** أَنْ **أُخَالِفَكُمْ** إِلَىٰ مَا أَنْهَاكُمْ عَنْهُ	**11-88** and I desire not to act in opposition to you in which I forbid you.

وَمَنْ جَاهَدَ فَإِنَّمَا يُجَاهِدُ لِنَفْسِهِ	**29-6** And whoever strives hard, strives for himself.
وَالَّذِينَ اتَّخَذُوا مَسْجِداً ضِراراً وَكُفْراً وَتَفْرِيقاً بَيْنَ الْمُؤْمِنِينَ وإِرْصَاداً لِمَنْ حَارَبَ اللهَ وَرَسُولَه	**9-107** And there who built a mosque to cause harm (to Islam) and to help (disbelief) and to cause division among the believers and refuge for him who made war against Allah and His messenger before.
إِنَّمَا جَزَاءُ الَّذِينَ يُحَارِبُونَ اللهَ وَرَسُولَهُ	**5-33** The only punishment of those who wage war against Allah and His Messenger.
فَحَاسَبْنَاهَا حِسَاباً شَدِيداً	**65-8** so We called it to severe account.

EXERCISE

1. Translate into Arabic :

(*a*) Say.This is my way :I call on Allah with sure knowledge. I and whosoever follow me - glory be to Allah ! - and I am not of the idolaters.

We did not send before thee (any messenger) save men whom we inspired from among the folk of the townships - have they not travelled in the land and seen the nature of the consequence for those who were before them? And verily the abode of the Hereafter, for those who ward off (evil), is best. Have ye then no sense?

(*b*) As you know,when the war broke out last year between our Arab brothers and their Zionist enemies, our brothers advanced to the battle-field hailing the Name of God Almighty saiying Allahu Akbar Allah Akbar (God is greatest ... God is greatest), there is no deity but God. The result was that they routed their enemies in the canal zone, in the Golan Heights, which proves to the Muslims that holding firmly to their religion, ideology, faith in God and dedication to Him will bring them victory in various fields. God Willing.

(*c*) **1.** Servant, bring us fresh (new) coffee at once from the kitchen.

2. The minister commanded them to bring forward the robber.

3. I ordered them to tell their friends about this affair, but they did not believe me.

4. Man proposes, but God Disposes.

5. Send that man to me, so that I may supervise his work. He has disobeyed my orders many times.

6. Bring in the doctor so that we can consult him about the prince's condition.

7. Attack (the attack) is the best way of defence.

8. Do not mix with the people next door.

9. The government inspectors travelled to the village, greeted the shaikh, and witnessed the horse races. Then inspected the new houses.

10. We saw the bedouins round the well, from a distance, during the journey.

2. Translate into English:

يا أخِي المُسْلِمُ إنَّ اللهَ كَتَبَ عَليكَ الصِّيامَ كَما كَتَبَ عَلى الَّذينَ سَبَقُوكَ ، وَهُوَ اللهُ الَّذِى خَلَقَكَ وأرْسَلَ إلَيْكَ رَسُولاً وَأنْزَلَ عَلَيكَ كِتاباً يُصدِّقُ كُتُبَ الأوَّلينَ ، والأنْبِياءَ المُرْسَلِينَ ، فجاهِدْ فى سَبِيلِه ، ولا تُخالِفْ أمْرَهُ وساعِدْ أخيكَ المُسْلِم ، وَلاَ تَكُن مُسْرِفاً فى النَّفقَاتِ ، وَالَّذى يَعْصَى اللهَ وَرَسولَه كأنَّه يُحَارِبُ اللهَ .الَّذى جاءَ بالصِّدقِ وَصدَّقَ بِهِ فَهُوَ مُؤمِنٌ ، أحْسِنْ إلى النَّاسِ كَمَا أحسَنَ اللهُ إلَيْكَ .

VOCABULARY

To call	call on دعا إلى –يدعو imperf. –دَعَا
Sure knowledge	بَصِيرةٌ
Folk	أهْلٌ
Twon ship	قَرْيَةٌ
To travel	سار/ سافر يسير / يسافر
consequence	عَاقِبَةٌ Pl. عواقب (verb. III يعاقِب عاقَب)

abode	حياةٌ
ward off أَعْرَضَ / IV	يُعْرِضُ
to have sense شَعَرَ	يَشْعُرُ
broke out / VII	إنفَجَرَ
enemies أَعْداء Pl. of.	عَدُوٌّ
to advance / V تَقَدَّمَ	يَتَقَدَّمُ
Battle field	مَيْدانُ الحربِ
to hail II	يُكَبِّرُ - كَبَّرَ verbal noun تَكْبِيرٌ
Diety	إلٰه
to rout out	يَسْتَأْصِلُ - اسْتَأْصَلَ
canal نَهْرٌ - قناه	Pl. أَنْهَارٌ - قنوات
zone	مِنْطَقَةٌ
Ideology عَقِيدَةٌ	Pl. عَقَائِدُ
Faith	الإيمانُ
Dedication / VIII	(يلتجىءُ - التجأ) الالتجاء
Victory	الفتح
Various	مُتَنَوِّعٌ - مُخْتَلِفٌ
God Willing	إنشاء الله
fresh	طَازِجٌ
kitchen	مَطْبَخٌ

propose	يَقْصِدُ يُصَمِّمُ يَقْتَرِحُ	
dispose / IV	يُبْطِلُ	
so that use preposition	لِـ	
disobey	يَعْصِي	
condition	الحَالُ	
attack (imperative)	هاجِمْ	verbal noun. الْهجُومُ
mix	اختَلَطَ يَختَلِطُ	
government	الحكومة	
inspector	مُرَاقِبٌ	
village	قَرْيَةٌ	
to greet	حَيَّى يُحَيِّي	
race	مسابقةٌ	
bedouins	البَدْوُ	
well	بئْرٌ	
distance	بُعْدٌ	

كَتَبَ	to write (here use prescribed)
سَبَقَ	pass before
جاهد	strive
خَالَفَ	to oppose

الْمُسْرِفُ	who exceed the limits (especially in expendi tures.)
كَأَنَّهُ	as he
الصِّدْقُ	the truth
صَدَّقَ	to believe
أَحْسِنْ	(Imperative) ; do the good - behave nicely

CHAPTER 17

DERIVED STEMS IV, V, VI

The Verbal Stem IV : أَفْعَلَ afعla

أَخْرَجَ akhraja

This stem is formed by prefixing an alif vocalized with **fatha** to the root-form. Thus فَعَلَ faعala becomes afعala, خَرَجَ kharaja, becomes أَخْرَجَ akhraja.

1. The meaning of the fourth stem is "causative" e.g. if "kharaja" - "to go out," is diverted to أَخْرَجَ akhraja, will mean : to take out, to drive out.

Examples from The Holy Qur'an:

كما **أَخْرَجَكَ** رَبُّكَ من بَيْتِكَ بِالْحَقِّ	**8-5** Just as Thy Lord took thee out of thy house, in truth.

From the root-form ذهب **dh**ahaba, to go أَذْهَبَ a**dh**aba, to take out, e.g.

وقالوا : الحَمدُ لله الذى **أذهَبَ** عنا الحَزَنَ	**35-34** And they will say : Praise be to Allah Who removed from us (all sorrow).

From نَزَلَ nazala, to descend أَنْزَلَ anzala, to take or bring down :

وبِالْحَقِّ أَنْزَلْنَاهُ وَبالحَقِّ نَزَلَ	**17-105** We sent down the (Qur'an) in truth and in truth has it descended.

2. With a slight difference, often this stem has the meaning of Root-form e.g.

خَبَّرَ khabara means to inform as does أَخْبَرَ akhbara of Stem IV. Likewise صَلَّحَ sallaha-to repair أَصْلَحَ to rectify, reform. عَلِمَ to know أَعْلَمَ to inform.

3. There are a few intransitive of this Stem e.g. أَسْلَمَ to surrender to the will of Allah, (or to become a Muslim). In Qur'anic words:

قَالَ أَسْلَمتُ لِرَبِّ العَالَمِينَ	**2-131** He Said ! I surrendered to the Lord of the Worlds.

أَرْسَلَ to send e.g.

هُوَ الَّذِى أَرْسَلَ رَسُولَه بِالهُدىٰ	**9-33** It is He who sent His Messenger with the guidance.

أَقْبَلَ to approach, to come forward, e.g.

قَالُوا وَأَقْبَلُوا عَلَيْهِم : مَاذَا تَفْقِدُونَ	**12-71** They said, and came forward, what are you seeking for?

The conjugation of this stem will be as below. The verb of example is أَخْرَجَ akhraja, that is derived from خَرَجَ kharaja.

	Perfect	Passive Perfect	Imperfect	Passive Imp.	Imperative
3rd Pers. Masc.	أَخْرَجَ	أُخْرِجَ	تُخْرِجُ	يُخْرَجُ	
3rd Pers. Fem.	أخرجَتْ	أُخْرِجَتْ	تُخْرِجُ	تُخْرَجُ	
2nd Pers. masc.	أخرجتَ	أُخْرِجْتَ	تُخْرِجُ	تُخْرَجُ	أَخْرِجْ
2nd Pers. Fem.	أخرَجتِ	أُخْرِجتِ	تُخْرِجِينَ	تُخْرَجِينَ	أَخْرِجِى
1st Pers.	أَخْرَجْتُ	أُخْرِجْتُ	أُخْرِجُ	أُخْرَجُ	

Part Act: مُخْرِجٌ mukhrijun

Part passive: مُخْرَجٌ mukhrajun

Verbal noun is: الإِخْرَاجُ

The Verbal Stem V تَفَعَّلَ Tafaعّala

تَقَبَّلَ Taqabbala

This stem is formed from the second stem: فَعَّلَ = صَدَّقَ by prefixing the syllable, تَ thus صَدَّقَ will become تَصَدَّقَ

The meaning of this stem is most frequently the reflexing of II stem e.g. فَرَّقَ to separate تَفَرَّقَ (to separate oneself), to scatter, عَلَّمَ to teach, تَعَلَّمَ (to teach oneself) to learn. ذَكَّرَ to remind تَذَكَّرَ (to be reminded), to remember.

Examples from the Holy Qur'an:

Verbs of Stem II فَعَّلَ

مَا يُفرِّقُونَ بِهِ بَيْنَ الْمَرْءِ وَزَوْجِهِ	**2-102** They cause division between man and his wife
عَلَّمَ الإِنْسَانَ مَا لَمْ يَعْلَمْ	**96-5** He taught man what they did not know
وَذَكِّرْ (Imperative) فَإِنَّ الذكرىٰ تَنْفَعُ المؤمنين	**51-55** Remind! For re-memberance benefits the believers.

Verbs of Stem V تَفَعَّلَ

وما تَفَرَّقَ الَّذِينَ أُوتُوا الكتابَ إلا مِنْ بَعْدِ ما جاءَتْهُمُ الْبَيِّنَةُ	**98-4** The people of the Scripture did not divid until the clear proof came unto them.
وَيَتَعلَّمون ما يَضُرُّهُم وَلا يَنْفَعُهُمْ	**2-102** And they learn what harms them and profits them not.
وَمَا يَتَذَكَّرُ إِلَّا مَنْ يُنِيبُ	**40-13** Only those remember who turn (to Allah).

4. This stem is also used to form Verbs from Nouns, especially Nouns of Quality or Status e.g.

From نَصْرانى a Christian تَنَصَّرَ to become a Christian,
يهودى a jew to become a Jew. تَهَوَّدَ

5. It also means thinking or representing oneself to have certain quality or status which he does not actually possess, e.g.

كبير great تَكَبَّرَ to think oneself great , to be proud.
نَبِىٌّ prophet تَنَبَّأَ to represent oneself to be a Prophet.

Conjugation of تَعَلَّمَ to learn , is as below:

	Perfect	Imperfect	Imperative	Part/ Act	Part / Passive
3rd Pers (M)	تَعَلَّمَ	يَتَعَلَّمُ		مُتَعَلِّمٌ	مُتَعَلَّمٌ
3rd Pers (F)	تَعَلَّمَتْ	تَتَعَلَّمُ			
2nd Pers (M)	تَعَلَّمْتَ	تَتَعَلَّمُ	تَعَلَّمْ		
2nd Pers (F)	تَعَلَّمْتِ	تَتَعَلَّمِين	تَعَلَّمِى		
1st Person	تَعَلَّمْتُ	أَتَعَلَّمُ			
Verbal Noun التَّعَلُّمْ					

Examples from the Holy Qur'an:

رَبَّنا ! تَقَبَّل مِنّا	**2-127**·(Imperative) Our Lord! accept from us.

ولكن ما تعمّدت قلوبُكم	**33-5** and but what your heart purpose.
وتقطّعتْ بِهِمُ الأسبابُ	**2-166** and their ties are cut as under.
قد نرى تقلُّبَ وجْهِكَ فى السَّماء	**2-144** Indeed We see the turning of thy face to heaven.
تتجافى جُنُوبُهم عَنِ الْمَضَاجع	**32-16** They forsake their beds.
إذْ تسوَّروا المِحْرَاب	**38-21** When they climbed the wall to the chamber.
تُكَلِّمُ النَّاسَ فِي المَهْدِ	**5-110** Thou spokest to people in the cardle.

The Verbal Stem VI تَفَاعَلَ tafaa ع ala

تَجَاوَبَ tajaawaba to respond to one another.

This stem is formed from the Stem V by adding an 'alif after the first radical. Thus تَفَعَّلَ tafa ع ع ala becomes tafaa ع ala; تَقَبَّلَ taqabbala تقابل taqaabala and تَقَرَّبَ taqarraba تقارَبَ taqaaraba. Pertaining to the meaning, this stem tends to be reflexive of steem III e.g.

قَاتَلَ	to fight	تَقَاتَلَ	to fight each other
حارَبَ	to fight	تَحارَبَ	to fight each other
عاوَنَ	to cooperate with	تَعاوَنَ	to cooperate together
وافَقَ	to agree with	تَوَافَقَ	to agree together.

Examples from The Holy Qur'an:

وتَعَاوَنُوا على البِرِّ والتَّقْوَى ولا تَعَاونوا عَلَى الإثمِ والعُدْوَانِ	**5-2** Help ye one another in righteousne and piety and help ye not one another in sin and rancour
وَلَوْ تَوَاعدتُّمْ لَاخْتَلَفتم فى المِيعَاد	**8-42** Even if ye had promised each other (to meet) ye would certainly have failed in the appointment.
وَلَو أَرَاكَهُمْ كثيراً لَفَشِلْتُم ولتنازَعْتُم فى الأمْرِ	**8-43** If he had shown them to thee as many, ye wou,d, surdly, have been discouraged and ye woudl have disputed each other in decision.
فَلَمَّا ترآءتِ الفئتانِ نَكَصَ على عَقِبَيْهِ	**8-48** But·when the two forces came in sight of each other.
فليقَاتِل فى سَبِيلِ اللهِ الَّذِينَ يَشْرُونَ الْحَيَاةَ الدُّنْيَا بِالآخِرَةِ وَمَن يُقَاتِلْ فى سَبِيلِ اللهِ فَيُقْتَلْ أو يَغْلِبْ فَسَوْفَ نُؤتِيهِ أجراً عَظِيماً	**4-74** Let those fight in the cause of who sell the life of this world for the hereafter. To him who fight in the cause of God whether he is slain or gets victory. We shall give him very soon a reward of great value.

مَا لَكُمْ لا تَنَاصَرُونَ	**37-25** What is the matter with you that ye help not each other.
إلاَّ الَّذِين آمَنوا وعَمِلوا الصَّالِحَاتِ وتَوَاصوا بالحَقِّ وَتَوَاصوا بِالصَّبْرِ	**103-3** Except such as have faith and do righteous deeds and join together in the mutual teaching of truth, and of patience and constancy.

Some Verbs of Stem V:

تَعَاوَنَ	to cooperate together
تفارَق	to disperse.
تواعَدَ	to promise each other.
تَظَاهَرَ	to show , to demonstrate ,
توافَقَ	to agree togother.
تحادَثَ	to converse together
تقابَلَ	to meet each other.

EXERCISE

1. Translate into Arabic :

(a) .We conversed about this matter this evening, but did not agree. The Muslims and Christians fought each other a long time ago, but they agree to-day on many things. The learned ones were talking together about Islam. They expect our advance from this side.

(b) 1. These countries had only one system of education and that was the purely religious Islamic system.

2. But the religious schools retained their old method and curriculum and did not catch up with the demands of the time.

3. When English domination was fully established in the nineteenth centry, the ruleers introduced modern schools and started English and modern branches of learning as required subjects in schools.

4. People got more interested in modern schools, because those who graduated from them and received academic certificates, were appointed as officials and government jobs.

5. The certificates which are given to the graduates are not accepted either in offices or in modern schools or government agencies.

6. They were not able to preserve the old standard because the

old subjects which were taught in traditionsal schools did not leave any time for other subjects.

7. Thus it was necessary to reduce the number of traditional subjects so that modern subject could be accommodated.

2. Translate into English:

أمَرَنَا رَبُّنَا أنْ نَتَعَاوَنَ عَلَى البِرِّ والتَّقْوَىٰ

المُسلمونَ لاَ يَتَقاتَلُونَ فِيمَا بينهم

أيها المُسْلِمُونَ ، مَا لَكُم لاَ تَنَاصرون . تعاونوا فى أَدَاءِ الوَاجب

اللُّغَةُ العَرَبيَّة سَهْلَة غَنِيَّةٌ بالْكَلِمَاتِ وَالمعَانى ، إنَّ أعْداءَ اللُّغةِ العَرَبيةِ يُظْهِرُون صُعُوبَاتٍ كَثِيرَةً فى تَعَلُّمِهَا لِغَرَضٍ فى أنفسِهم

تَرَكْنَا أَصْدِقَاءَنَا فى الحَدِيقَةِ وَهُم يَتَحادَثُونَ

* * *

قُلْ مَن يَرْزُقُكُمْ مِنَ السَّماءِ والأرضِ ، أمَّن يَملِكُ السَّمْعَ والأبْصَارَ وَمنْ يُخْرِجُ الْحَىَّ مِنَ المَيِّتِ وَيُخرِجُ الْمَيِّتَ مِنَ الحَىْ وَمنْ يُدبِّر الأَمْر فَسَيَقُولُونَ اللهَ فَقُل أفلاَ تَعْقِلون .

وَمِنْهُم مَن يؤمِنُ بِهِ وَمِنهُمْ مَن لاَ يُؤمِنُ بِهِ وربُّكَ أَعْلَمُ بِالمُفْسِدِين .

VOCABULARY

to converse / V	تحدث	يتحدث also VI /	تحادث
to agree / III	وافق		
system	منهج		
to retain / V	تمسك به	يتمسك	
curriculum	المناهج الدراسية		
to catch up	أخذ به	الإدراك	أدرك به
Domination	الاستعمار		
Branches	فروع	Pl. of	فرع
require / VII	احتاج إلى		
graduate (verb) / V	تخرج	يتخرج	
certificate	الشهادة	شهادات	
to appoint	use passive case	عُيِّنَ	
to accomodiate	يوضع	passive of	يضع

البر .	good deeds
التقوى	God fearing
تَقَاتَلَ	VI - to fight each other

تناصر	VI to help each other (against enemies)
سهلة	easy
غنى - غنية	(Fem.) Rich
صعوبات	Pl. of صعوبة difficulty
ترك	left
تحادث يتحادثون	to converse
أم - مَن	or who is .. ?
السمع	the sense of hearing
يملك	possess
البصر	the sense of seeing
يُخرج	Brings forth
يدبر	plans, proposes,decideds, etc.

CHAPTER 18

DERIVED STEMS—VII TO X

Stem VII إِنْفَعَلَ infaعala:

This stem is formed from the first stem فَعَلَ faعala by prefixing the syllable إِنْ "in" Thus كَسَرَ "kasara" becomes إِنْكَسَرَ inkasara.

It means the passive of the first stem e.g. فَعَلَ to do, كَسَرَ to break قَطَعَ to cut, when is altered to this stem as إِنْفَعَلَ infaعala, إِنْكَسَرَ inkasara and إِنْقَطَعَ inqatعa, will mean - to be done, to be broken, to be cut off respectively.

There are certainly a difference between the passive verb, which is formed from the changing of vowels e.g. كُسِرَ kusira to be broken and verb of this stem (inkasara) which is translated in same way; "to be broken" infact passive verb indicates that the act has taken place by someone discoverable while in the verb of this stem the act is done either through a human agency or automatically or through an unknown inner cause, to illustrate the difference the following example should be carefully observed:

انْقَطَعَتِ الأَسْبَابُ
قُطِعَتِ الأَسْبَابُ } The means were cut down (eliminated)

In first form the verb suggests no reason or hidden hand behind the cutting of the means, while the second form shows involvement of some reason or hand though it is not discoverable. Take another example.

إنْكَسَرَ البابُ The door was broken

كُسِرَ البابُ The door was broken

In first form, the verb suggests that the door was broken by any undiscoverable way, say it might have happened by itself, due to being very old or by wind blow, etc. While the second form indicates that there was some who broken the door but his name was not mentioned here.

Examples from the Holy Qur'an:

3rd Pers. Masc.	
وَانطَلَقَ المَلأُ مِنْهُم أن امْشُوا واصْبِروا عَلىٰ آلِهتكم ، إنَّ هٰذا لَشَىءٌ يُراد	**38-6** The chiefs among them go about exhorting: Go and be staunch to your gods. Lo! this is a thing designed.

3rd Pers. Dual, Masc.	
فَانطَلَقَا حتّى إذَا رَكِبَا فى السَّفِينة خَرَقَها	**18-71** So the twin **set out** till when were in the ship he made a hole therein.

3rd Pers. Pl. Masc

وَإِذَا **انْقَلَبُوا** إِلَى أَهْلِهِم **انْقَلَبُوا** فَكِهِينَ	**83-31** And when they **returned** to their own folk they returned jesting.

3rd Pers. Fem.

فَانْبَجَسَتْ منه اثْنَتَا عَشْرَةَ عَيْنًا	**7-160** And there **gushed forth** therefrom twelve springs.

3rd Pers. Masc.

ثُمَّ ارْجِعِ الْبَصَرَ كَرَّتَيْنِ يَنْقَلِبْ إِلَيكَ الْبَصَرُ خَاسِئاً وَهُوَ حَسِيرٌ	**67-4** Then look again and yet again thy sight will return into thee weakened and made dim.

3rd Pers. Fem. Verbal noun

إِذَا السَّمَاءُ انْفَطَرَتْ	**82-1** When the heaven is cleft asunder.
فَمَنْ يَكْفُرْ بِالطَّاغُوتِ وَيُؤْمِنْ بِاللهِ فَقَدِ اسْتَمْسَكَ بِالْعُرْوَةِ الْوُثْقَىٰ . لَا **انْفِصَامَ** لَهَا	**2-256** And he who'rejects false dieties and believes in Allah has grasped the most trust-worthy handhold - with no breakdown.

Imperative :

انْطَلِقُوا إِلَىٰ مَا كُنْتُم بِهِ تُكَذِّبُونَ	**77-29** Deposit to that which you used to reject.

Part. active : Plu. Masc.	
والمُشْرِكين مُنفكّين	**98-1** and .. the polytheists were not going to depart

(From فكّ to depart the second redical is duplicated)

Part passive. Sing. Fem.	
والمُنْخنِقَةُ وَالموقُوذَةُ	**5-3** That which has been killed by strangling or killed by a violent blow

	Perfect	**Imperfect**	**Imperative**	**Verbal Noun**
Masc.	إنْكسَرَ	يَنْكَسِرُ	إنْكَسِرْ	الإنكِسارُ
Fem.	إنكسرَتْ	تَنْكَسِرُ	إنكَسِرى	
Part. Active	مُنْكَسِرٌ			

Note: the variation of vowel in the second redical that is س in the verb.

Part. Passive

Can not be formed because this stem denates that the work is done by itself while posne indicates to some one caused to do that

Some other verbs of this stem :

إنْقِطَاعٌ	to be cut off	إنْبعَاثٌ	to march
إنْصِرَافٌ	to get away	إنْحصَارٌ	to surround
إنْقِلَابٌ	to get turned up side down		

Stem VIII إِفْتَعَلَ ifta ع ala

1. This stem is formed from the first stem fa ala by prefixing a hamza vowelled with kasra and infixing a ت 'ta' after the first redical. Thus فَعَلَ will be shaped in this stem as افتعل ifta ع ala and جَمَعَ jam ع a اجْتَمَعَ ijtama ع a, خَبَرَ khabara اخْتَبَرَ ikhtabara, نَصَرَ nasara إِنْتَصَرَ intasara.

Examples from The Holy Qur'an:

أَنَّه اسْتَمَعَ نَفَرٌ من الجِنِّ	**72-1** A company of Jinns listened.

(The verb إِسْتَمَعَ , istam ع a is derived from سَمِعَ , to hear)

فَاحْتَمَلَ السَّيْلُ زَبَدًا رَابِيًا	**13-17** The torrent bears away the foam that mounts up to the surface.

(The word إِحْتَمَلَ 3rd pers. masc., to bear is derived from حَمَلَ (hamala to carry.)

وَإِنَّ الَّذِين **اخْتَلَفُوا** فى الكِتَابِ لَفى شِقَاقٍ بَعِيدٍ	**2-176** Those who causes of dispute in the book are in schism far (from the purpose)

(The verb اختلف to dispute, to disagree or to cause a dispute
(is drawn from خَلَفُوا 3rd person, plural, masc. to succeed someone)

وَآخَرُونَ اعْتَرَفُوا بِذُنُوبِهِم	**9-102** (There are) who have acknowledged their wrong doings.

(In this verse the verb اعترفوا they acknowledged, is derived (from عَرَفوا, 3rd Pers. plural, masc, to recognize, todistinct)

وَاعْتَصِمُوا بِحَبْلِ اللهِ جَمِيعاً	**3-103** hold fast all together by the rope of Allah.

The verb اعتصموا is the imprative form, plural, masc. that means:

(Hold!, is derived from عَصَموا to protect some thing or someone)

2. If the first redical (that is ف in فَعَلَ ، ج in جَمَعَ jamعa and ن nun in نَصَرَ nasara) is one of the emphatic letters (i.e. ظ ، ط ، ض ، ص). The following additional letter will be ط instead of ت . e.g. in The Holy Qur'an :

فَاعْبُدْهُ واصْطَبِرْ لِعِبَادَتِه	**19- 65** Therefore, worship Him and be steadfast in his service.

Note: the verb اصْطَبِرْ imperative, 2nd per. sing. masc., 'be steadfast' was supposed to be اصْتَبِرْ with ت instead of ط but because of ص that is the first redical of this verb, and one of four imphatic letters the ت(t) is changed to ط (ṭ) Likewise t. ~e is in the Holy Qur'an .

وَاصْطَنَعْتُكَ لِنَفْسِى	**20-41** And I have attached thee to Myself.

(The verb اصطنعت 1st pers, sing, which is derived from "صَنَعْتُ I made" -Note the changing of ت to ط)

إِلَّا مَا اضْطُرِرْتُمْ إِلَيْهِ	**6-119** Except under compulsion of necessity.

The verb, passive, 2nd pers, plural, masc, is derived from the root form of ضَرَرَ but in this the infixed ت was changed to ط to agree with the emphetic letter of the first redical.

3. Conjugation of افتعل = اجتمع to assemble.

	Perf.	Imperf.	Imperative	Part Active	Part Passive
3rd Pers. Sing. Masc.	إِجْتَمَعَ	يَجْتَمِعُ		مُجْتَمِعٌ	مُجْتَمَعٌ
3rd Pers. Sing. Fem.	إِجْتَمَعَتْ	تَجْتَمِعُ		(Note the second redical is vowelled with Kasra)	(It is with Fatha).
2nd Pers. Sing. Masc.	إِجْتَمَعْتَ	تَجْتَمِعُ	إِجْتَمِعْ		
2nd Pers. Sing. Fem.	إِجْتَمَعْتِ	تَجْتَمِعِينَ	إِجْتَمِعِى		
1st Pers. Sing.	إِجتمعتُ	أَجْتَمِعُ			
1st Pers. Plural.	إِجتَمَعْنا	نَجْتَمِعُ			

(*a*) The meaning of this stem is like VII, i.e. reflexive of the simple verb first stem e.g. جَمَعَ jama ع a to collect, اجتمع ijtam ع a to collect themselves, assemble (hence الإِجْتِمَاع the meeting).

سَمِعَ Sami ع a to hear إِسْتَمِعَ istami ع a to listen.

شَغَلَ shaghala to occupy, keep busy; إِشْتَغَلَ to be busy, to work.

(*b*) It also has the sens of doing something for oneself e.g.

كَسَبَ kasab, to acquire اِكْتَسَبَ iktasaba, to gain

كَشَفَ kashafa, to uncover إِكْتَشَفَ iktashafa, to discover

بَدَعَ bada ع a, to initiate ابْتَدَعَ ibtada ع a, invet

(*c*) Sometimes, it seems to be reserved for odd by ways of meaning e.g.: ضَرَبَ ḍarab, to strike إِضْطَرَبَ idtaraba, to be disturbed, shaken. حَمَلَ ḥamala, to carry احتَمَلَ to bear, with sense of endure, to be proble. حَرَمَ ḥarama, to forbid, إِحْتَرَمَ ihtarama, to respect.

(*d*) It often has the same meaning as the root form e.g.

بَسَمَ basama إِبْتَسَمَ ibtasama, to smile.

Examples from The Holy Qur'an:

لَهَا مَا كَسَبَتْ ، وعليها ما اكْتَسَبَتْ	**2-286** For it (any soul) is that which it earns (for good) and against it that it works (of evil).
وَاخْتِلَافِ اللَّيْلِ وَالنَّهَارِ	**3-190** .... and (in) the alternation of the night and the earth .....
إِلَّا مَنِ اغْتَرَفَ غُرْفَةً بِيَدِهِ	**2-249** except he who takes a handful in (water) with his hand.

اقْتَرَبَتِ السَّاعَةُ وَانْشَقَّ الْقَمَرُ	**54-1** The hour (of Judgment) is nigh, and the moon is cleft usunder.
إِنَّ اللهَ اصْطَفَاكِ	**3-42** (O Mary!) God hath chosen thee.

Stem IX إفعَلَّ **if**ع**alla** إحْمَرَّ **ihmarra**

This stem is formed from the first (root) or by prefixing a "Hamza" vowelled with Kasra and doubling the third redical e.g.

إحْمَرَّ ihmarra to be, or to become red.

This stem is used only to express colours and effects e.g.

إخْضَرَّ to be, or to become green.

إسْوَدَّ to be, or become black.

إبْيَضَّ to be, or become white (see chapter 11).

The conjugation of this stem is as following:

(Note: There is no passive form in this stem)

Pers. of the subject	Number of Person	Perfect	Imperfect	Imperative	Part Active	Part passive
3rd Pers. Masc.	Singular	إحْمَرَّ	يَحْمَرُّ		مُحْمَرّ	مُحْمَرّ
3rd Pers. Fem.		إحْمَرَّتْ	تَحْمَرُّ		مُحْمَرَةٌ	مُحْمَرَّةٌ
2nd Pers. Masc.		إحمررتَ	تَحْمَرُّ	إحْمَرِرْ		
2nd Pers. Fem.		إحمررتِ	تَحْمَرِّينَ	إحْمَرِّى		
1st Pers. M & F.		إحمررتُ	أحْمَرُّ			

Pers. of the subject	Number of Person	Perfect	Imperfect	Imperative	Part Active	Part Passive
3rd Pers. Masc.	Dual	إحْمَرَّا	يَحْمَرَّانِ		مُحْمِرَّان	مُحْمَرَّان
3rd Pers. Fem.		إحْمَرَّتا	تَحْمَرَّانِ		مُحْمِرَّتَان	مُحْمَرَّتَانِ
2nd Pers. Masc.		إحْمَرَرْتُمَا				
2nd Pers. Fem.		إحْمَرَرْتُمَا				
3rd Pers. Masc.	Plural	إحْمَرُّوا	يَحْمَرُّونَ		مُحْمِرُّونَ	مُحْمَرُّونَ
3rd Pers. Fem.		إحْمَرَرْنَ	يَحْمَرِرْنَ		مُحْمِرَّاتٌ	مُحْمَرَّاتٌ
2nd Pers. Masc.		إحْمَرَرْتُم	تَحْمَرُّونَ			
2nd Pers. Fem.		إحْمَرَرْنَ	تَحْمَرَرْنَ			
1st Pers. Masc. & Fem.		نَحْمَرُّ				

Examples from The Holy Qur'an:

يوم تَبيَضُّ وجوهٌ وَتَسْوَدُّ وُجُوه فَأَمَّا الذينَ اسْوَدَّتْ وُجُوهُهُم : أكَفَرتُم بعدَ إيمانِكم فذوقوا العذاب بما كنتم تكفرون وَأَمَّا الذين ابْيَضَّتْ وُجُوهُهُم فَفِي رَحْمَةِ الله هُمْ فيها خالِدُونَ .	3-106,107 On the day when some faces will be (lit up with) white, and some faces will be (in the gloom of) black. To those whose faces will be black: did you reject faith after accepting it? Taste themthe penalty for rejection faith. But those whose faces will be(lit with) white they will be in the light of Allah's mercy, therein to dwell (for ever).

وَابْيَضَّتْ عَيناه من الْحُزْنِ فَهُوَ كَظِيمٌ	**12-84** And his eyes become white with sorrow.
فَتُصْبِحُ الأرض مُخْضَرَّةً	**22-63** The earth becomes clothed with green.
ظَلَّ وَجْهُهُ مُسْوَدًا	**16-58** His face becomes darkens.

Stem X إِسْتَفْعَلَ **istaf ع ala** إِسْتَقْبَلَ **istaqbala**

This stem is formed from the root form فَعَلَ by prefixing the syllable of three letters إِسْتَ e.g. from قَبِلَ إستقبل from نَصَرَ إِسْتَنْصَرَ etc. The meaning of the verb of this stem is :

1. The reflexive of the IV stem أَفْعَلَ Thus

   أَخْبَرَ to inform, إِسْتَخْبَرَ to be made known,

   أَسْلَمَ to give up, or to deliver إِسْتَسْلَمَ to give oneself up, to surrender.

2. This stem also indicates that a person thinks that a certain thing possesses the quality expressed by the root form e.g.

   عَظُمَ to be great إِسْتَعْظَمَ to regard something as great,

   حَسُنَ to be handsome إِسْتَحْسَنَ to regard something as good

   ثَقُلَ to be heavy إِسْتَثْقَلَ to find something heavy.

3. The stem often expresses the seeking, asking or demanding what is expressed by the root form e.g.

رَجَعَ to return إِسْتَرْجَعَ to reclaim, to recall.

غَفَرَ to pardon إِسْتَغْفَرَ to ask for pardon,

أَذِنَ to permit إِسْتَأْذَنَ to ask permission.

4. Sometimes this stem gives a causative meaning e.g.

خَرَجَ to get out إِسْتَخْرَجَ to draw out, to extract.

5. This stem is also demonative in which case it invites factitive and reflexive e.g.

خَلَفَ to succeed إِسْتَخْلَفَ to appoint one as successor or caliph (خَلِيفَةٌ)

حجر a stone اسْتَحْجَرَ to become like stone.

The following are the conjugation of this stem:

person of the Subject	Perfect	Imperfect	Imperative	Past active	Past Passive
3 masculine	استَقْبَلَ	يَسْتَقْبِلُ		مُسْتَقْبِلٌ	مُسْتَقْبَلٌ
3 feminine	استَقْبَلَتْ	تَسْتَقْبِلُ		مُسْتَقْبِلَةٌ	مُسْتَقْبَلَةٌ
2 masculine	استَقْبَلْتِ		استَقْبِلْ		
2 feminine	استَقْبَلْتُ	تَسْتَقْبِلِينَ	استَقْبِلِي		
1 mas. fem.	استَقْبَلْتَ	استَقْبِلَ			
3 masculine	استَقْبَلا	يَسْتَقْبِلاَن		مُسْتَقْبِلان	مُسْتَقْبَلاَن
3 feminine	استَقْبَلَتَا	تَسْتَقْبِلاَن	استَقْبِلا	مُسْتَقْبِلَتان	مُسْتَقْبَلَتَانِ
2 masculine	استَقْبَلْتُمَا				
2 feminine					
1 mas. fem.	استَقْبَلْنَا	نَسْتَقْبِلُ			
3 masculine	استَقْبَلُوا	يَسْتَقْبِلُونَ	استَقْبِلوا	مُسْتَقْبِلون	مُسْتَقْبَلُونَ
3 feminine	استَقْبَلْنَ	يَسْتَقْبِلْنَ	استَقْبُلْنَ	مُسْتَقْبِلاتٌ	مُسْتَقْبَلاَتٌ
2 masculine	استَقْبَلْتُمَا	تَسْتَقْبِلاَن			
2 feminine					
1 mas. fem.	نَسْتَقْبِلُ	نَسْتَقْبِل			

Examples from The Holy Qur'an:

قَالَ : أَتَسْتَبْدِلُونَ الَّذى هُوَ أدْنىٰ بالَّذى هُوَ خَيْرٌ	**2-61** He said would you exchange that is higher for which is **lower?**
إذ تَسْتَغِيثُونَ رَبَّكُمْ فاسْتَجابَ لكُمْ	**8-9** When you sought help of your Lord and he answered you.
وَيَسْتَخرِجَا كَنْزَهُا رَحْمَةً مِن رَبِّكَ	**18-82** And (they) should bring forth their treasure as a mercy from their Lord.
يَسْتَبْشِرون بِنِعْمَةٍ من اللهْ وفَضْلٍ وأن الله **لا يُضِيعُ** أجْرَ المؤمنين. الذين **استجابوا** لله والرَّسولِ مِن بَعْدِ ما أصابَهُم **القَرْحُ** للذين **أَحْسَنُوا** منهم وَاتَّقوا أجْرٌ عَظِيمٌ	**3- 171, 172** They rejoice because of favour from Allah and kindness, and that Allah wastes not the wages of the believers. As for those who heard the call of Allah and the Messenger after the befell them (in the fight); for such of them as do right and ward off (evil) there is great reward.
وَاستَشْهِدوا شهيدَينِ من رِجالكم	**2-282** And call two witnesses from among your men.

وَإِنْ أَرَدتُّمْ أَن تَسْتَرْضِعُوا أَولادَكم فلا جُنَاحَ عليكم	**2-233** And if you wish to give your children out to nurse, it is no sin for you.
فاستبشِروا ببيعِكم الذى بَايَعتُمْ به	**9-111** (Imperative) Rejoice them in your bargain that you have made.
وكانوا مُسْتَبْصِرِينَ	**29- 38** And they were keen observers. (Part active)
وُجُوهٌ يَومئِذٍ مُسْفِرَةٌ ضاحِكَةٌ مُسْتَبْشِرَةٌ	**80-38 , 39** On that day faces will be bright as dawn, laughing, rejoicing at good news. (Part activ)

EXERCISE

Translate into Arabic:

I. It was during that last pilgrimage, that the surah "Succour" was revealed, which he received as an announcement of approaching death. Soon after his return to Al-Madinah he fell ill. The tidings of his illness caused dismay throughout Arabia and anguish to the folk of AL-Madinah, Mecca and Taif, the hometowns. At early dawn on the last day of his earthly life he came out from his room beside the mosque at AL-Madinah and joined the public prayer, which Abu Bakr had been leading since his illness. And there was great relief among the people who supposed him well again. When, later in the day, the rumour grew that he was dead, Omar threatened those who spread the rumour with dire punishment, declaring it a crime to think that the messenger of God could die. He was storming at the people in this strain when Abu Bakr came into the mosque and over heard him.

II. How many hours have you been waiting for your friend?
Write a letter to your father with all respect.
How do you work in the month of Ramadhan.
The Government has recognized women right in election.
Arabs were victorious in their war against Israel.
Go away, girl, and occupy yourself in the kitchen.

There is apolitical disturbance in some of the European countries.

The elders think that the youth of today are lazy.

The Western pattern of life is hardly acceptable in an Islamic society

III. Two white cars stopped at traffic light when it was red. A boy in a white paint went to the market alongwith his sister in a red shirt.

Translate into English :

١ - إنْقَلَبت سَيَّارةٌ فى الطَّريقِ وَلَم ينكَشفْ السَّبَبَ الرَّئيسى لِهَذَا الحادِثِ .

٢ - إنْتَحَر شَابٌ فِى لَندن وَلَمْ يُعْلَم بَعدُ سَبَبَ إنتحارِه .

٣ - إسْتَفْسَرَت المَحْكَمَةُ العُليا مِن الشُّرطَةِ عَنِ الحَادِثِ .

٤ - تَمَّ إنتِخَابُ عَالِمٍ كبيرٍ رئيسًا لمجْمع إسْلامى مَعْروفٍ .

٥ - جَاءَ فِى القرآنِ الكريم : لَو كنتَ فَظًّا غليظَ القَلْب لَانفضُّوا مِنْ حَولِك .

٦ - وقَّع الموظَفُونَ قَبْلَ إنْصِرافِهم عَلى سِجلِّ الحُضُورِ .

٧ - إنْقَطَع التَّيارُ الكَهْرُبائِى مَساءَ أمْسِ .

٨ - زَارَ المملكة مَلِكٌ مِن ملوكِ العَالَم واسْتُقْبِلَ إستقبالاً حافلاً .

٩ - خرج الطَّلَبَةُ مُسْتَبْشِرين بِنَتَائج إختبارهم السَّنَوى .

١٠ - إسْتَوضَحَ الطَّالِبُ مِنَ المُدَرِّسِ المَواضِعَ الصَّعْبَةِ مِنْ دُرُوسِهِ .

VOCABULARY

انتحر	VII to suicide
انْقَلَبَ	VII to be over turned
انْكَشَفَ	to be disclose
السَّبَبُ	VII reason
الرَّئيسى	main
انْتِخَاب	VII (v. n.) to elect , election
رَئِيسٌ	Chief , President
فَظٌّ	rude
غَلِيظٌ	anguish , of thick blood
إنْفَضَّ	VII to desperse
وَقَّعَ	II to sign (signature)
إنْصِرَاف	(v.n.) leaving back
سِجِلٌّ	Register
انْقَطَعَ	VII to cut off , to be off
أمْسِ	yesterday
اسْتُقْبِلَ	was received (pass of اسْتَقْبَلَ X to receive)
المُسْتَبْشِرُ	one who gets good news , (Act Part X)
اسْتَفْسَرَ	X to enquire
إسْتَوضَحَ	X to ask for details , to ask clearfecation.

duration	أثناء
pilgrimage	الحَجُّ
Announcement	الإعْلَانُ
Approaching	قُرْب الوُصول - القُرْبُ
News - tiding	أخْبار
grieveness	الْحُزْنُ - الأسى
earthly life	الحَيَاةُ الدنْيَوِيَّةُ
Relief.	الطمَأْنِينَةُ

CHAPTER 19

THE UNSOUND VERBS

Arabic verbs are divided into:

(a) Sound verbs

(b) Unsound verbs

The stems of former have been discussed in previous chapters. Now we start learning the forms of unsound verbs that is comprising:

1. Verbs constructed by all consonants but some of them have one of the three radicals duplicated e.g. مَدَدَ which is pronounced with assimilation إدغام i.e. two radicals are writeen as one with 'shaddah' e.g. مَدَّ instead of writing or saying مَدَدَ some other forms are those a 'hamza' takes place of a radical e.g.

In	أَسِفَ	the first radical is a hamza
In	سَأَلَ	the second radical is a hamza
In	بَرَّأَ	the third radical is a hamza.

contrasting the consonantal verbs either hamzited or duplicated redicals, is verbs colified with irregular (مُعْتَل) that means either (و) **waw** or (ى) **ya** has occurred in place of one of the redicals that caused certain changes in all forms and stems of the verbs.

2. **Ther Verbs of duplicated redicals.**

When a word has cluster of two consonant as مَدَدَ ـ مَدَّ it will be pronounced with **shaddah**, if it has a short vowel i.e. fatha, damma or kasra, otherwise i.e. in case of ending the word on a sukun ْ bothe will be sounded without assimilation e.g. رَدَّ (to restore, to reply) رَدّوا they replied.

but when it is followed by a ت or ن the assimilation will be left, and will be pronounced as مَدَدْتُ ، رَدَدْتَ or مَدَدْنَ ، رَدَدْنَ etc .

in the imperfect, this necessitates shifting the vowel forward from the second radical e.g. يَمُدُّ he extends, but in case of Jussive يَمْدُدْ **yamdud.** As a rule the assimilation does not take place where the third radical has **sukun** e.g.

مَدَدْنَا	We extended
مَدَدْنَ	they (fem) extended
لَمْ يَمْدُدْ	they (Masc.) did not extend.
لَمْ نَمْدُدْ	We (Masc. & Fem.) did not extend.
لَمْ أَمْدُدْ	I (Masc. - Fem) did not extend.

Where the second redical is separated from the third by a long vowel no assimilation can take place, e.g.

مَرْدُودٌ	Passive Participle	one who was turned out.

إِرْدَادٌ	Verbal noun	to turn out.

Conjugation of مَدَّ

1. Perfect:

		Dual	Plural
Sing. 3rd Person ,(M).	مَدَّ	مَدَّا	مَدُّوا
Sing. 3rd Person , (F).	مَدَّتْ	مَدَّتَا	مَدَدْنَ
Sing. 2nd Person , (M).	مَدَدْتَ	مَدَدْتُمَا	مَدَدْتُم
Sing. 2nd Person , (F).	مَدَدْتِ		مَدَدْتُنَّ
1st Person , (M). & (F).	مَدَدْتُ		مَدَدْنَا

2. Imperfect:

Indic	Subj	Juss
يَمُدُّ	يَمُدَّ	يَمْدُدْ
تَمُدُّ	تَمُدَّ	تَمْدُدْ
تَمُدِّينَ	تَمُدِّى	تَمْدُدِي
أَمُدُّ	أَمُدَّ	أَمْدُدْ

	Imperative	Negative Imperative:
Masc.	أُمْدُدْ مُدَّ	لا تَمُدَّ
Fem.	أُمْدُدِى مُدِّى	لا تَمُدِّى

Part. Active	مَادٌّ	Part Passive	مَمْدُودٌ

3. Hamzated verbs

The hamza, which is written on the 'alif (as أَ ، إِ ، أُ) oron between two letters (as ء) or separately after a final letter as بَطْحَاءُ ـ حمراء etc., is counted in verbs as a consonant, and as such may be the initial, middle or final radicals e.g. The Initial : أَجَرَ to reward, to recompense; أَكَلَ to eat; أَخَذَ to take. The Middle as in سَأَلَ to ask. سَئِمَ to be disgusted at. The final redical as in قَرَأَ to read, خَطَأَ to transgress; and بَطُوءَ to be slow.

(a) Hamza as Initial Radical :

In certain verbs أخذ to take أَمَرَ to command أَكَلَ to eat, the initial Hamza is dropped in the imperative e.g.

Imperative

Root form Verb	Masc. Sing	Fem. Sing.	Dual	Plural Masc.	Plural Fem.
أَخَذَ	خُذْ	خُذِي	خُذَا	خُذُوا	خُذْنَ
أَمَرَ	مُرْ	مُرِى	مُرَا	مُرُوا	مُرْنَ
أَكَلَ	كُلْ	كُلِى	كُلَا	كُلُوا	كُلْنَ

The conjugation of أَمَرَ to command is as below :

	Perf.	Imper. Indic.	Subj	Juss
3rd Pers. (M).	أَمَرَ	يَأْمُرُ	يَأْمُرَ	يَأْمُرْ
3rd Pers. (F).	أَمَرَتْ	تَأْمُرُ	تَأْمُرَ	تَأْمُرْ
2nd Pers. (M).	أَمَرْتَ	تَأْمُرُ	تَأْمُرَ	تَأْمُرْ

2nd Pers. (F).	أَمَرْتِ	تَأْمُرِينَ	تَأْمُرِي	تَأْمُرِي
1st Pers. Common.	أَمَرْتُ	آمُرُ	آمُرَ	آمُرْ

	Part Active	Part Passive
Sing. (M).	آمِرٌ	مَأْمُورٌ
Sing. (F).	آمِرَةٌ	مأمورةٌ
PL. (M).	آمِرُونَ	مأْمُورونَ
PL. (F).	آمِرَاتٌ	مَأمورَاتٌ

Passive Perfect أُمِرَ

Imperfect يُؤْمَرُ

Verbal Noun الأَمْرُ ـ أمْرٌ

Note: When this initial hamza is followed by an 'alif the latter is replaced by a prolonged vowel called **madda** e.g. in 1st Person Imperfect an 'alif is prefixed to indicate imperfect as usual, thus the hamza of initial Radical and this alif got together, therefore, the two were assimulated in one with **madda** sound as you see in the last row of the above conjugation.

In case of imperative the conjugation from أَمَرَ has already been given above. From other roots such as أَكَلَ the same rule will apply as :

أخذ = خُذْ ، أَكَلَ = كُلْ

Examples from The Holy Qur'an:

1. Verbal Noun : الأمْر or أمْر order, matter, duty, command, plan, task etc.

مرفوعاً Nominative :

أتاها أمْرُنا ليلاً أو نهاراً	**10-24** There reaches it our command by night or by day.
حتى إذا جَاءَ أمرُنا	**11-40** But when there came our command.

مَنْصُوباً Accusative :

وَلا أعْصِى لَكَ أَمْرًا	**18-69** And I shall not disobey thee in aught.
فَأجمِعُوا أمْرَكُمْ وشرَكاءَكُمْ	**10-71** Get ye then an agreement about your plan and among your partners.

مجروراً Genetive :

وَآتَيْناهُم بيِّنات مِنَ الأمْرِ	**45-17** And we granted them clean signs in affairs.

2. Perfect.

لا يَعصُونَ اللهَ ما أمَرهُمْ	**66-6** They flinch not (from executing) what Allah hath commanded them.

أمَرَ ألَّا تَعْبُدوا إلَّا إيَّاهُ	**12-40** (3rd Pers. Masc.) He hath commanded that ye worship none but He.
ما قلت لهم إلَّا ما أمرتَنِى به	**5-117** (2nd Pers. Masc.) Never said I to them ought except what thou commanded me.
ما مَنَعَكَ ألاَّ تَسْجُدَ إذ **أمَرْتُكَ**	**7-12** (Allah said:) what prevented thee from bowing when I commanded thee?

3. Imperfect:

إنَّ الله **يأمُرُ** بالعدلِ والإحْسَان	**16-90** Allah commands Justice and the doing of goods.
وَكانَ **يَأمُرُ** أهله بالصَّلاةِ	**19-55** And He used to command his people for prayer.
فانْظُرِى ماذَا تَأمُرِينَ	**27-33** (2nd Pers. Imperf.) So consider what than command.
ويقتلون الذين يأمُرُونَ بالقِسْطِ مِنَ النَّاسِ	**3-21** And slay those who teach just dealing with mankind.
أتأمُرُونَ النَّاس بالبِرِّ وتَنْسونَ أنْفُسَكُم	**2-44** (1st Pers. Perf.) Do you command people or sight conduct and forget yourselves.

Passive Perfect :

قُل إنما أُمِرْتُ أن أَعْبُدَ اللهَ ولا أشرك بِهِ	**13-36** (2nd Pers. Imperf) Say I am commanded to worship Allah and not join partners with Him.

Imperfect :

فاصْدَع بما تُؤْمَرُ	**15-94** Therefore, expound openly what you are commanded.
يا أبَتِ افْعَل ما تُؤمَرَ	**37-102** O'my father Do as thou art commanded.
فَافْعَلوا مَا تُؤمَرُونَ	**2-68** (Now) do what you are commanded.

Imperf. Assimilated case :

وَلَئِن لَمْ يَفْعَلْ مَا آمُرُهُ	**12-32** And if he does not say what I command him ...

Imperative : With 'alif :

وأمُرْ أهْلَكَ بالصَّلاةِ وَاصْطَبِر عَليها	**20-132** And command on your people for prayer and be constant there in.

(b) Hamza as Middle Radical :

The Middle Radical may be vowelled with ḍamma, fatha or Kasra.

In this case a hamza will be written over 'alif.

Conjugation of سَأَلَ sa ء ala , to ask :

	Perf.	Imperf. Indic.	Subj.	Jussive
3rd Pers. Masc.	سَأَلَ	يَسْأَلُ	يَسْأَلَ	يَسْأَلْ
3rd Pers. Fem.	سَأَلَتْ	تَسْأَلُ	تَسْأَلَ	تَسْأَلْ
2nd Pers. Masc.	سَأَلْتَ	تَسْأَلُ	تَسْأَلَ	تَسْأَلْ
2nd Pers. Fem.	سألتِ	تَسْألين	تَسْألي	تَسْألي
1st Pers. Common.	سَأَلْتُ	أَسْئَلُ	أَسْئَلَ	أسألْ

Imperative :

2nd Pers. Sing Masc.	إِسْأَلْ or سَلْ
2nd Pers. Sing. Fem.	إِسْألي or سَلي

Part Active سَائِلٌ
Part Passive مَسْئُولٌ
Passive Perfect سُئِلَ Imperfect يُسْأَلُ

Examples from The Holy Qur'an :

Past Perfect :

3rd Pers. Sing. Masc.

سَأَلَ سَائِلٌ بِعَذَابٍ واقِع	**70-1** A questioner has asked about the chestiment to befall.

سَأَلَهُمْ خَزَنَتُهَا : أَلَمْ يَأْتِكُم نَذِيرٌ	**67-8** Its keepers ask them, did not come to you a warner?
اليوم يَئِسَ الذين كفروا	**5-3** This day have those who disbelieve dispaired of your Religion.
كما يَئِسَ الكُفَّارُ من أصْحَابِ القُبُورِ	**60-13** as the disbelievers despaire of those in the graves.

3rd Pers, Plu. Masc.

فقد سَأَلُوا موسىٰ أكبرَ من ذلك	**4-153** They demanded Moses a greater thing than that.
أُولَـٰئِكَ يَئِسوا مِن رَحْمَتِى	**29-23** They are who dispaired of My Mercy.

2nd Pers. Sing. Masc.

وَلَئِن سَأَلْتَهُم	**29-61** And if thous ask them

1st Pers. Sing.

إنْ سَأَلْتُكَ عن شيء بَعْدَهَا فلا تُصَاحِبْنِى	**18-76** He said: if I ask thee about any thing after this, keep not company with me.

Imperfect - Indic:

3rd Pers. Sing Masc.

يَسْأَلُكَ أهْلُ الكتابِ	**4-153** The people of the Book ask thee.

يَسْأَلُ أَيَّانَ يومُ القيامةِ	**75-6** He asks: when is the day of resurrection?
لا يَسْأَمُ الإنسانُ من دُعَاءِ الخَيْرِ	**41-49** Man tires not of praying for good:

(From root «س ء م» to get tired)

3rd Pers. Plur. Masc.

يَسْأَلُونَكَ عَنِ الأهِلَّةِ	**2-189** They ask thee of the new moons.
وهم لا يَسْأَمُونَ	**41-38** And they tire not.

1st Pers. Sing. Masc.

وما أسألُكُم عليه من أجْرٍ	**26-180** And I ask of you no reward for it.

Imperfect Acc.

لِيَسْأَلَ الصَّادقين عَن صِدْقِهم	**33-8** That he may question the truthful of their truth.
قَالَ رَبِّ إِنِّى أَعُوذُ بِكَ أَنْ أَسْأَلَكَ مَا لَيْسَ لِى بِهِ عِلْمٌ	**11-47** He said, O' my Lord! I seek refuge in Thee to ask you for that I have no knowledge about it
أم تريدون أَنْ تَسْأَلُوا رسولَكُمْ	**2-108** Or you wish to question to your messenger.

Genetive

أَفَلَمْ يَيْأَسِ الذين آمنوا	**13-31** Do not those who believe, convince that...

Passive Perfect:

كما سُئِلَ موسى	**2-108** as Moses was questioned.
وإذا المؤءودةُ سُئِلَتْ	**81-8** and when the one buried alive is asked.

(Root form و/ء/د (وأد) to bury alive)

Passive Imperfect:

ولا تُسْأَلُ عن أصحابِ الجَحِيم	**2-119** And thou will not be called upon to answer for the companions of the flaming fire.
ولا تُسْأَلُونَ عما كانوا يَعْمَلُون	**2-141** And you will not be asked of what they did.

Imperfect with emphatic (Nun)

تالله لَتُسْأَلُنَّ	**16-56** By Allah! you shall certainly be questioned.

Part Active:

Singular: وَأَمَّا السَّائل فلا تنهر	**93-10** And him who asks, chide not
Plural: آياتٌ للسَّائِلين	**12-7** Signs for the inquirers.

Part Passive:

Singular: أُولَٰئِكَ كَانَ عَنْهُ **مَسْئُولاً**	**17-36** All of these will be asked.
Plural: وقِفُوهمْ إِنَّهُم مسئولون	**37-24** And stop them, for they will be questioned.

Verbal Noun:

قال لَقَد ظَلَمَكَ بسُؤَالِ نَعْجَتِكَ	**38-24** He said, surely he wronged thee in demanding thy ewe.
وأَنْزَلْنَا الحَدِيدَ فِيهِ **بأسٌ** شَدِيدٌ	**57-25** And We sent down iron wherein is a great violence.

(c) Hamza as Final Radical:

Conjugation of قَرَأَ qara ء a, to read:

	Perf.	**Imperf. Indic.**	**Subj.**	**Jussive**
3rd Pers. Masc.	قَرَأَ	يَقْرَأُ	يَقْرَأَ	يَقْرَءْ
3rd Pers. Fem.	قَرَأَتْ	تَقْرَأُ	تَقْرَأَ	تَقْرَءْ
2nd Pers. Masc.	قَرَأْتَ	تَقْرَأُ	تَقْرَأَ	تَقْرَءْ
2nd Pers. Fem.	قَرَأْتِ	تَقْرَئِينَ	تَقْرَئِي	تَقْرَئِي
1st Pers. Common.	قَرَأْتُ	أَقْرَأُ	أَقْرَأَ	أَقْرَأْ

Imperative:

2nd Pers. Sing. Masc. اِقْرَأْ

2nd Pers. Sing. Fem. اِقْرَئِى

Part Active قَارِئٌ ، ..ari ، ..un or قارى qaari

Part Passive مَقْرُوءٌ

Passive Perfect قُرِىءَ

Passive Imperfect يُقْرَأُ يُقْرَأُ يُقْرَأُ

Examples from The Holy Qur'an:

Perfect:

3rd Pers. Sing. Masc.

كيف بَدَأَ الخَلْقَ	**29-20** How He makes the first creation.
فَقَرَأَه عَلَيهم	**26-199** And he had read it to them

2nd Pers. Sing. Masc.

فإذا قَرَأْتَ القُرآنَ	**16-98** So when we recite it, follow its recitation.

1st Pers. Plur. Common.

كما بَدَأْنَا أوّلَ خَلْقٍ نُعِيدُهُ	**21-104** As We began the first creation We shall reproduce it.
فإذَا قَرَأْنَاهُ فَاتَّبِعْ قُرْآنَهُ	**75-18** So when We recite it, follow its recitation.

Imperfect:

3rd Pers. Sing. Masc.

إِنَّه يَبْدَأُ الخَلْقَ	**10-4** He starts creation.

3rd Pers. Plur. Masc.

يَقْرَأُون الكتاب	**10-94** They read The Book.

2nd Pers. Masc. (Acc.)

وقرآناً فَرَقْنَاه **لِتَقْرَأَه** على الناس	**17-106** And it is a Qur'an We have made distinct so that mayest read it to the people.

Imperative:

اقْرَأْ بِاسْمِ رَبِّكَ الَّذى خَلَقَ	**96-1** Read in the name of Thy Lord, Who creates ...

Verbal Noun:

القُرآن Qur'an

فَاتَّبِعْ قُرْآنَهُ	**75-18** follow thou the reading.
وَقُرآناً فَرَقْنَاه	**17-106** and (it is) a Qur'an that We have divided.

EXERCISE

1. Translate into English:

قال رَبِّ اشْرَحْ لِى صَدْرِى وَيَسِّرْ لِى أمْرِى وَاحْلُلْ عُقْدَةً مِن لِسَانِى
يَفْقَهُوا قَولِى وَاجْعَل لِى وَزِيراً مِنْ أهلِى هَارُونَ أخِى اشْدُدْ بِهِ أزْرِى
وَأشْرِكْهُ فِى أمْرِى كَىْ نُسَبِّحَكَ كَثِيراً وَنَذْكُرَكَ كَثِيراً إنَّكَ كُنتَ بِنَا
بَصِيراً ، قَال قَد أوتِيتَ سُؤْلَكَ يَا مُوسىٰ

١ - يجب أن نقرأ القرآن ، ونتدبَّر مَعَانِيه ، وَنَعْمَل بِأوامِرِ الدِّين
الإسلامى ، حَتَّى نَفوزَ بالسَّعَادَةِ فى الدُّنْيا وَالآخِرَة .

٢ - إتَّصِفْ بِالأمَانَةِ وَالصِّدقِ فى مُعَامَلَتِكَ لِلنَّاسِ ، فَلَقد عُرِفَ
الرَّسُولُ صَلَّى اللهُ عَليه وسَلَّم بهاتَيْنِ الصِّفَتَيْنِ ، وَنُودِىَ بَيْنَ قَومِهِ
بالصَّادِقِ الأمِينِ .

2. Translate into Arabic:

The teacher has explained the lesson for the students.
The Minister has Written long reports on the matter.
Al motamar al Islami resolved (قَرَّر) to establish
a Department for Islamic jurisprudence.
The government has been requested to do some thing for the deserving officials.

Help your friend. in time of anxiety (الشِّدة)

I passed (مررتُ بـ) many fine buildings during my visit to Riyadh.

Affairs have settled down in the foreign companies.

It pleased me (أعجبنى) very much to see you here this morning.

The Holy Qur'an says : Allah has not made two hearts in one body which means one can not love two things equally. When the love of wealth occupies the heart of man, it does not leave enough space for the love of anything else. All considerations other than wealth become submerged and subservient to love of wealth. A great preacher of Islam is quoted saying : It is not a sin to keep wealth at home, it is not sin to keep wealth in the hand but it is sin to keep wealth in the heart.

VOCABULARY

إِشْرَحْ	(Imperative of) يَشْرَحُ ـ شَرَحَ
صَدْرٌ	breast , heart. Plu : صُدُورٌ
يَسِّرْ	(Imperative of) يَسَّرَ II يُيَسِّرُ to make easy
أَمْرٌ	matter , affairs Plu. أُمُورٌ
أُحْلُلْ	(Imperative of) يَحُلُّ ـ حَلَّ to Loose
عُقْدَةٌ	knot Pl. عُقَدٌ
يَفْقَهُ	understand

إجْعَلْ	(Imperative of) يَجْعَلُ — جَعَلَ to make
وَزِيرٌ	Aider , supporten
أشْدُدْ	(Imperative of) يَشُدُّ — شَدَّ
أزْرٌ	arm
أشْرِكْ	(Imperative of) يُشْرِكُ — أَشْرَكَ
كَىْ	in order to , so that
نُسَبِّحُ	II Imperative of سَبَّحَ to Glorify
أوتِيتَ	IV Passive case of أتَى يؤتى to give
سُئْولٌ	Plural of سُؤَالٌ demand request ,.
نَذْكُرَ	we remember from يَذْكُرُ — ذَكَرَ
يَجِبُ	To owe يَجِبُ أن (suljunelioe)
تُدَبِّرٌ	to think over
أوَامِرٌ	Plural of أمْرٌ order , command.
حتَى	in order to
فَوْزٌ	success
سَعَادَةٌ	Prospenity , happiness
إتَّصَفَ	to be described by , from يَصِفُ وَصَفَ
الأَمَانَةُ	trustworthy
مُعَامَلَةٌ	Affairs
عُرِفَ	Passive of عَرَّفَ to know

نُودِىَ	Passive of نَادَى to call , to announce ,
قَوْمٌ	Folk , People
صَادِقٌ	Truthful
الأمين	Trustworthy

Report	تَقْرِير	Pl	تقارير	
to establish	أسَّسَ	يُؤَسِّسُ	، أقَامَ	يُقِيمُ
Jurisprudence	الفِقْهُ			
Deserving	الْمُسْتَحَقُّ			
Companies	إلشَّرِكَاتُ	Pl of	شركة	
equally	بِالْمُسَاوَاةِ			
wealth	المَالُ			
To occupy	شَغَلَ	— يَشْغَلُ		
Place	مَكَانٌ			
Consideration	الإعْتِبَارُ	VIII	إعْتَبَرَ	
to submerge	يَحْجَبُ			
subsurrient	تَابِعٌ			
to explain	يَشْرَحُ	— شَرَحَ		

CHAPTER 20

THE NUMERALS

The Cardinal Numbers

All numerals are not governed by a single rule, but in general term they are treated as the declinable nouns; as their ending vowels are changed according to their cases, thus:

1. وَاحِدٌ **'one'** (in Nominative case مَرْفُوعاً) H.Q.

أَنَّمَا إِلَـٰهُكُمْ إِلَـٰهٌ واحدٌ	**18-110** .. that your God is One God.

(In Accosative case مَنْصُوباً) :

وما أُمِرُوا إِلَّا لِيَعْبُدوا إِلٰهاً وَاحِداً	**9-31** And they are enjoined that they should serve one God only.

(In the Genitive case مَجْرُوراً) :

وَإِذْ قُلْتُمْ يَا مُوسىٰ لَنْ نَصْبِرَ عَلَى طَعَامٍ وَاحِدٍ	**2-61** And when you said O Musa (Moses) we can not bear with one food.

The feminine form of وَاحِدٌ is وَاحِدَةٌ i.e. with a feminine ending e.g.

Nom. فَإِنَّمَا هِيَ زَجْرَةٌ وَاحِدَةٌ	**37-19** so it shall only be a single chiding

Acc. كَانَ النَّاسُ أُمَّةً **وَاحِدَةً**	**2-213** (all) People are a single nation.
Gen. مِنْ نَفْسٍ **واحِدَةٍ**	**4-1** .. From a single being

There is another form for 'One' that is read أحد e.g.

Nom. قُلْ هُوَ اللهُ أَحَدٌ	**112-1** say He God is **one.**
Acc. وَلاَ يُشْرِكُ فِى حُكْمِهِ **أَحَدًا**	**18-26** And He does not make anyone of His associate in His Judgement.
Gen. هَلْ يَرَاكُمْ مِنْ **أَحَدٍ**	**9-127** Does anyone see you?

(إِحْدَى) (with alif maqsura) is feminine of أَحَدٌ , e.g.

وَإِذْ يَعِدُكُمُ اللهُ **إِحْدَى** الطَّائِفَتَيْنِ	**8-7** And when Allah promised you **one** of two parties.

It is written with normal أَلِف as أَحَدًا when a pronoun is attehed to it e.g.

قَالَتْ **إِحدَاهُمَا** : يا أَبَتِ ..	**28-26** said one of two girls: O my father...

2. Nom إِثْنَانِ / Acc & Gen إِثْنَيْنِ } two (masc.) — **Nom** إِثْنَتَانِ / Acc & Gen إِثْنَتَيْنِ } two (fem)

Examples from the Holy Quran :

إِثْنَانِ ذَوَا عَدْلٍ مِنْكُمْ	**5-106** two just persons from among you.

مِنَ الضَّأْنِ اثْنَيْنِ وَمِنَ الْمَعْزِ اثْنَيْنِ	**6-143** two of sheep and two of goats.
فَإِنْ كُنَّ نِسَاءً فَوْقَ اثْنَتَيْنِ	**4-11** But if there are more than two females ...

3. From 3 to 10

	Masc.	Fem.	
3	ثَلَاثَةٌ	ثَلَاثٌ	(also written as ثَلٰثَةٌ and ثَلٰثٌ)
4	أَرْبَعَةٌ	أَرْبَعٌ	
5	خَمْسَةٌ	خَمْسٌ	
6	سِتَّةٌ	سِتٌّ	
7	سَبْعَةٌ	سَبْعٌ	
8	ثَمَانِيَةٌ	ثَمَانٍ	(also written as ثَمٰنِيَةٌ and ثَمٰنٍ)
9	تِسْعَةٌ	تِسْعٌ	
10	عَشَرَةٌ	عَشْرٌ	

I. it is to be noted that these numbers reserve the genders. adding the "taa" murbata for masculine fom.

II. As stated at beginning, they are all nouns, when not standing alone as a Predicate, take the noun to which they refer as genitive plurals in idaafa (الإضافة) :

ثَلَاثَ لَيَالٍ **19-10** three nights	ثَلَاثَةِ أَيَّامٍ **2-196** three days
أَرْبَعُ شَهَادَاتٍ **24-6** Four witnesses	أَرْبَعَةِ أَيَّامٍ **41-10** Four days

(Not From H.Q.) خَمْسَ مرَّاتٍ Five times

خَمْسَةٌ ، سادِسُهُم كَلْبُهُم	**18 -22** (they are) five, the sixth is their dog
سِتَّةِ أَيَّام	**7-53** (in) six days

(Not From H.Q.) سِتَّ لَيَالٍ six nights

سَبْعَ بَقَراتٍ **12-43** seven cows	سَبْعَةُ أَبْوابٍ **15-44** seven doors
ثَمَانِيَةَ أَزْوَاجٍ **6-143** Eight pairs	ثَمَانِيَةَ أَيَّامٍ **69-7** Eight days
تِسعَ آياتٍ **17 -101**Nine sings.	تِسْعَةُ رَهْطٍ **27-48** Nine persons
عَشْرُ أمثالِها **6-160** ten like it.	عَشَرَةِ مَسَاكِينَ **5-89** ten poor men

Note: The gender of the numerals depends on the singular of the noun, not on its plural. For example. بَابٌ is masculine but plural أَبْوابٌ is grammatically singular, Nevertheless, the Quran says: سبعةُ أبوابٍ Seven dors, treating the noun as masculine. In case of a broken plural the feminine noune the numeral is put in the feminine e.g.

تِسْعَ آياتٍ Nine signs, آياتٌ is a broke plural of a feminine noun as well as أَيَّامٌ that is a broken plural of a masculine noune يوم "day"

4. 11, & 12

Masc.	Fem.	
أَحَدَ عَشَرَ	إِحْدَى عَشَرَةَ	
إِثْنَا عَشَرَ	إِثْنَتَا عَشَرَةَ	in the Nominative case

In the Accusative case: إِثْنَى عَشَرَ masc, and إِثْنَتَى عَشْرَةَ for fem.

Example from the Holy Qur'an :

Non	Masc أَحَدَ عَشَرَ كَوْكَبًا	**12-4** eleven stars
	Masc إِثْنَا عَشَرَ شَهْرًا	**9-36** twelve months
	Fem إِثْنَتَا عَشْرَةَ عَيْنًا	**2-60** Twelve springs
Acc	وبَعَثْنَا مِنْهُم اثْنَىْ عَشَرَ نَقِيبًا	**5-12** and raised up among them twelve chief tains
	وَقَطَّعْنَاهُمُ اثْنَتَى عَشْرَةَ أَسْبَاطاً	**7-160** And we divided in to twelve tribes.

5. From 13 to 19

13	Masc.	ثَلاثَةَ عَشَرَ	Fem.	ثَلاثَ عَشْرَةَ
14	Masc.	أَرْبَعَةَ عَشَرَ	Fem.	أَرْبَعَ عَشْرَةَ
15	Masc.	خَمْسَةَ عَشَرَ	Fem.	خَمْسَ عَشْرَةَ
16	Masc.	سِتَّةَ عَشَرَ	Fem.	سِتَّ عَشْرَةَ
17	Masc.	سَبْعَةَ عَشَرَ	Fem.	سَبْعَ عَشْرَةَ
18	Masc.	ثَمَانِيَةَ عَشَرَ	Fem.	ثَمَانِي عَشْرَةَ
19	Masc.	تِسْعَةَ عَشَرَ	Fem.	تِسْعَ عَشْرَةَ

All the neumurals from 11 to 99 are followed by a **singular noun in the Accusative** as they are تمييز specification. e.g.

ثلاثَ عَشْرَةَ طالِبَةً	13 (male) students
أَرْبَعَ عَشْرَةَ بِنْتاً	14 boys
ثَلاثَةَ عَشَرَ طَالِباً	13 (Female) students
أَرْبَعَةَ عَشَرَ وَلَداً	14 girls.

Note: All these are indeclinable i.e. their ending vowels can not be changed due to their preceeding elements. Thus

قرأتُ ثلاثة عَشَرَ كِتَاباً	I read 13 books
وَجَدْتُ فى ثلاثَةَ عَشَرَ كِتَاباً	I found in 13 books

6. From 20 to 90

The tens from 20 to 90 are cymmon to masculine and feminine:

	Nominative	Accusative and genitine
20	عِشْرُونَ	عِشْرِينَ
30	ثَلاثُونَ	ثَلاثِينَ
40	أَرْبَعُونَ	أَرْبَعِينَ
50	خَمْسُونَ	خَمْسِينَ
60	سِتُّونَ	سِتِّينَ
70	سَبْعُونَ	سَبْعِينَ
80	ثَمَانُونَ	ثَمَانِينَ
90	تِسْعُونَ	تِسْعِينَ

All these numbers from 20 to 99, like these from 11 to 19, are followed by a noun of **Tamiz** (Noun of specification) in the Accasative singular.

Examples from The Holy Qur'an:

وَفِصَالُهُ ثَلاثُون شَهْراً	**46-15** And the weaning of him was thirty months.
وَوَاعَدْنا موسٰى ثَلاثِين لَيْلَةً	**7-142** And we appointed with Musa a time of thirty nights.
وإذْ واعَدْنَا مُوسى أربَعِينَ لَيْلَةً	**2-51** And when we appointed with Musa a time of forty nights
وبَلَغَ أربَعِين سَنَةً	**46-15** .. and reaches 40 years
إلّا خَمْسِينَ عَاماً	**29-14** excluding 50 year
فإطْعَامُ سِتِّينَ مِسكِيناً	**58-4** so feeding of 60 poors.
ذَرْعُهَا سَبعُونَ ذِرَاعاً	**69-32** The length of which is seventy cubits.
وَاخْتَارَ موسٰى قَومَه سَبْعِين رَجُلاً	**7-155** And Musa chose out of his people seventy men..

7. From 21 to 99

Masc.	Fem.
أحد وعشرون	إحْدَى وَعِشْرُونَ
إثْنَانِ وَعِشْرُون	إثْنَتَانِ وَعِشْرُون

and so on

8. From 100 upwards.

100 مِئَةٌ , Also written مَائَةٌ

From 200 upward

200 (مائتانِ) مِئَتان

300 ثَلاثُ مِئَةٍ

400 أرْبَع مِئَةٍ

500 خَمْسُ مئةٍ

600 ستُّ مئةٍ

700 سبعُ مِئَةٍ

800 ثَمَانى مِئَةٍ

900 تِسْعُ مِئَةٍ

1000 أَلْفٌ

2000 أَلْفَانِ

3000 ثَلاثَةَ آلافٍ

etc. to 10.000

100,000 مئَةُ ألف

Million مِلْيُون Pl. مَلايين

Note: These numerals from 100 are nouns and take their following noun in the Genitive Singular

In compound numerals over 100 the noun follows the rule governing its relation to the last element and the number.

Thus "103 men" the rule for 3 must be followed:

Therefore the noun must be in the Genitive plural e.g.

مائةٌ وثلاثَةُ أولادٍ   103 boys.

The ordinal Numbers

1. The ordinal numbers from 1 to 10 are formed on the Pattern of the active participle, فاعِلٌ , derived from cardinals:

Masc.	الأَوَّلُ	Fem.	الأُولى	
Masc.	الثَّانى	Fem	الثَّانيَةُ	without article ثَانٍ
Masc.	الثَّالِثُ	Fem.	الثَّالِثَةُ	the Third
Masc.	الرَّابِعُ	Fem.	الرَّابِعَةُ	the Fourth
Masc.	الخَامِسُ	Fem.	الخَامِسَةُ	the Fifth
Masc.	السَّادِسُ	Fem.	السَّادِسَةُ	the Sixth
Masc.	السَّابِعُ	Fem.	السَّابِعَةُ	the Seventh
Masc.	الثَّامِنُ	Fem.	الثَّامِنَةُ	the Eighth
Masc.	التَّاسِعُ	Fem.	التَّاسِعَةُ	the Ninth
Masc.	العَاشِرُ	Fem.	العَاشِرَةُ	the Tenth

The ending vowels of the above or changing according to their declansion, e.g.

هُوَ الأَوَّلُ وَالآخِرُ	**57-3** He is the **First** and the Last
ثَانِى اثْنَيْنِ إِذْ هُمَا فِى الْغَارِ	**9-40** the **Second** of the two when they ware in the cave

فَعَزَّزْنَا بِثَالِثٍ	**36-14** then We strengthened them with a **third**
ثَلاثَةٌ رَابِعُهُم كَلْبُهُمْ	**18-22** (they are) Three, **fourth** of them is their dog
وَالخَامِسَةُ أَنَّ لَعْنَةَ اللهِ عَلَيه إِنْ كَانَ مِنَ الْكَاذِبِين	24-7 And **Fifth** (time) that the curse of Allah be one him if he is one of the liar
سَادِسُهُمْ كَلْبُهمْ	**18-22** Their **Sixth** is their dog

After 10, the cardinal numbers are used as Ordinals, save in so far as the above numbers are included in them.

Masc. الحادى عَشَرَ Fem. الحادِيَةَ عَشْرَةَ The eleventh

Masc. الثَّانِى عَشَرَ Fem. الثَّانِيَةَ عَشْرَةَ The twelth

Masc. الثَّالِثَ عَشَرَ Fem. الثَّالِثَةَ عَشْرَةَ the Thirteenth

Masc. الرَّابِعَ عَشَرَ Fem. الرَّابِعَةَ عَشْرَةَ The fourteenth

Higher numbers run as follows:

twentieth العِشْرُونَ for both Masc. and Fem.

Masc. الحَادِى وَالْعِشْرُونَ Fem. الحَادِيَةُ وَالْعِشْرُونَ the twenty first

Masc. الثَّانِى وَالْعِشْرُونَ Fem. الثَّانِيَةُ وَالْعِشْرُون the twenty second

Masc. الثَّالِثُ وَالْعِشْرُونَ Fem. الثَّالِثَةُ وَالْعِشْرُون the twenty third

المئة Masc. & Fem. the hundredth

EXERCISE

A. **Translate into Arabic :**

The Holy Qur'an is divided into **one hundred and fourteen chapters;**
each of which is called a **surah** سُورة These chapters or suwar سُوَر (plural of سُوَرة) are not of **equal** Length. The highest number of verses in a chapter is **two hundred eighty six** and the smallest only **three verses**. The total number of verses in the Holy Quran is **six thousand, four hundred , fourty seven**. For the purpose of recitationthe Holy Quran is also divided into **thirty** parts of equal length , called a جزء every part being again sub divided into **four quarters**. But these divisions have nothing to do with the subject-matter of the Holy Quran , and so also the division into **seven "manazil"** or portions , which is meant only for the completion of the recital of the Holy Quran in **seven days**. The Quran was revealed piecemeal during a period of **twenty three** years. The **First** Chapter of the Quran is سورة الفاتحة Suratul fateha that means " opening "
It consists of **seven verses**. The second chapter is known as :
سورة البقرة Suratul baqra (Cow) the suratul " Anfal " سورة الأنفال (The Accession) is the eighth and سورة التوبة Surat "Taubah" (The Immunity) is the ninth among the chapters of the Quran.

B. Translate into English :

وُلِدَ مُحَمَّدٌ صَلَّى اللهُ عَلَيْهِ وَسَلَّم يَتِيماً ومَاتَتْ أُمُّهُ وَهُوَ ابْنٌ **لِثَلاثِ سَنَواتٍ** وكَفَلَه عَمُّه أبو طَالِب ، تَزَوَّجَ السَّيدةَ خَدِيجةَ بِنْتِ خُوَيْلِدٍ عِنْدَمَا بَلَغَ **الْخَامِسةَ وَالْعِشْرِين** مِنْ عُمْرِه .وكَانَ عُمْرُ السَّيِّدَةَ خَدِيجةَ آنذاكَ **أربَعِين عَاماً** . وَبَعَثَهُ اللهُ نَبِيًّا وَأنزَلَ عَلَيْه أوَّلَ وَحْى عِنْدَمَا بَلَغَ **أرْبَعِين عَامًا** مِنْ عُمْرِه . وبَقِى بِمَكَّةَ الْمُكَرَّمَة **ثَلاَثَ عَشْرَة** سَنَةً . ثُمَّ هَاجَرَ إلى المدِينَةِالمنورة حَيْثُ عاشَ **عَشْرَةَ سَنَواتٍ** . وقَبلَ أن يُهَاجِرَ إلَى المَدِينَةِ عَاشَ **ثَلاث سَنَوات** فِى شِعْبِ أبى طَالِب ، عِندَمَا قَاطَعَتْهُ قريشٌ .

قَد فَرَضَ اللهُ عَلَى المُسْلِمينَ الصَّومَ فِى **العَامِ الثَّانى** لِلْهِجْرَةِ ، وَوَقَعَتْ مَعْرَكَةُ «بَدْرٍ» فِى العَام نَفْسِهِ وَبَعد **سَنَةٍ واحدةٍ** وَقَعَتْ مَعْرَكَةُ أُحُد .

وَتَمَّ فَتْح مَكَّةَ الْمُكَرَّمَةَ فى **العَام العَاشِرِ** مِنَ الْهِجْرَة ، وَتُوُفِّىَ رَسُولُ الله صَلَّى اللهُ عَليه وسَلَّم فِى **الثَّالِثَة وَالسِّتِين** مِنْ عُمْرِهِ ، وَقَدْ أكملَ اللهُ لَه الدِّين وَأتَمَّ عَلَيه نِعْمَته وَرَضِىَ لَهُ الإسْلاَمَ دِيناً .

VOCABULARY

Divided	مُوَزَّعٌ Passive Participle of وَزَّعَ II also تقسم
the division	التَّقْسِيمُ - التَّوْزِيع
Equal	مُتَسَاوٍ Act. part. تسَاوى VI to be equal سَوَّى
Length	الطُّولُ
the highest number	أَكْبَرُ عَدَدٍ
the smallest number	أَصْغَرُ عددٍ
total	المجموع
Nothing to do with	لا صِلَةَ لَه بِ - عَدِيمُ الصِّلَةِ بِ
portion	حِصَصٌ Pl. حِصَّةٌ
completion	تَكْمِلَةٌ (v.n.) or إِتْمَامٌ (v.n.) of IV
piecemeal	نجوما Pl. of نجم or قطعة

orphan	يَتِيمٌ
Birthday , Time of Birth	مَوْلِدٌ
took him in his guardianship	كَفَلَهُ
married	تَزَوَّجَ
the then	آنَذَاكَ
sent as a messenger	بَعَثَ

Revealation	الْوَحْيُ
Immigrated	هَاجَرَ
Lived	عَاشَ
to boycott	قَاطَعَ
Battle	مَعْرَكَةٌ
Conquest	فَتْحٌ
Died	تُوُفِّيَ
completed	أَكْمَلَ
fulfilled	أَتَمَّ
agreed	رَضِيَ

CHAPTER 21

PRONOUNS: DEMONSTRATIVE, RELATIVE AND INTERROGATIVE

A. Demonstrative Pronouns: إِسْمُ الإِشَارَة ismul ishara have two forms, one for near distance and another for far-distance.

1. إِسْمُ الإِشَارَةِ لِلْقَرِيب Demonstrative Pronouns for near distance are as below:

	Masc.		Fem.		
Singular, all cases	هٰذَا	haadha	هٰذِهِ	haadhihi	This
Dual, Nominative	هٰذَانِ	haadhaane	هَاتَانِ	haataani	These
Dual, accusative, Dual, gentive	هٰذَيْنِ	haadhayni	هَاتَيْنِ	haatayni	These
Plural - all cases	هٰؤُلَاءِ	haa ،ulaa ،i. these, they.			

It is to be noted that haadhaa هٰذَا is not written with a full 'alif, after ه as it was supposed to, but instead of هَاذَا it is written with a short vertical stroke above the letter: ه — هٰذَا We have a plural form common to both of the gender that is هٰؤُلَاءِ but it is used only for human being, otherwise, هٰذِهِ singular form of the feminine is enough to refer to the collective or plural nouns. The following examples from The Holy Qur'an will illustrate the rules:

هٰذَا	
وَهٰذَا كِتَابٌ مُصَدِّقٌ	**46-12** And, this is a Book that verifies (previous devine books)
وهٰذَا بَعْلِي شَيْخاً	**11-72** And this is my husband, an old man.
أَنَا يُوسُفُ وَهٰذَا أَخِي	**12-90** I am Joseph and this is my brother.

هٰذَانِ	
قَالُوا إِنْ هٰذَان لَسَاحِران	**20-63** They said: These are two enchanters.

هٰذِهِ	
قُلْ هٰذِهِ سبيلى	**12-108** Say: This is my way.
إِنَّ هٰذِهِ أُمَّتُكُمْ أُمَّةً واحِدَةً	**21-92** Surely, This your community is a single community.
ما هٰذِهِ التَّمَاثِيلُ الَّتِي أَنْتُمْ لَهَا عَاكِفُونَ	**21-52** What are these images to whose worship you cleave.

Note:

سَبِيلٌ way is a feminine noun.

أُمَّةٌ is a collective noun.

تَمَاثِيلُ plural of تِمْثَالٌ image.

dual Fem for the accusative and gentive cases, e.g. (From The Holy Qur'an):

هاتَيْنِ	
إِحْدَى ابْنَتَيَّ هَاتَيْنِ	**28-27** One of these two daughters.

هؤلاء	
كُلاًّ نُمِدُّ هٰؤُلاَءِ وَهٰؤُلاَءِ مِنْ عَطَاءِ رَبِّكَ	**17-20** All do We aid-these as well as those out of the bounty of thy Lord.
يا قومِ هٰؤُلاَءِ بَنَاتِي هُنَّ أَطْهَرُ لَكُمْ	**11-78** O' my people! these are my daughters, they are purer for you.

2. اسمُ الإشَارَةِ لِلْبَعِيد Demonstrative pronouns for a far distance are as the following:

Masc. Sing. ذٰلِكَ also written as ذَالِكَ dhaalika, that, e.g. (from The Holy Qur'an):

ذٰلِكَ مَا كُنَّا نَبْغِ	**18-64** This was what we wanted.

It is also used for things of the near distance in order to emphasise the greatness or seriousness of the object pointed at, e.g. (from The Holy Qur'an):

ذٰلِكَ الْكِتَابُ لاَ رَيْبَ فِيه	**2-2** That is The Book-No doubt in it.

Further this pronoun is basically a combination of ذَا **dha** that is real pronoun and لَكَ 'for you'. Consequently if the addressee is more than one it could be changed from ذَالِكَ to ذَالِكُم **dh**aalikum i. e. This is to be demonstrated for you people, e. g. (from the Holy Qur'an):

ذٰلِكُم وَصَّاكُم بِهِ	**6-151** That is what He enjoins you.

Fem. Sing. تِلْكَ tilka, that, this, e.g. : (From the Holy Qur'an)

تِلكَ أُمَّةٌ قَدْ خَلَتْ	**2-134** Those are a people who have passed away.
تِلْكَ الرُّسُلُ فَضَّلْنَا بَعضَهُمْ عَلى بَعْضٍ	**2-253** Those are the messengers we made some of them excel others.
ومَا تِلْكَ بِيَمِينِكَ يَا مُوسٰى	**20-17** and what is this in thy right hand, O' Moses?

In the Arabic usage there are forms for duals such as ذانِكَ **dh**anika, ذَينِكَ **dh**ainaka for Masculine and تَانَكَ taanika and تِينَكَ teenaka for Feminine, but these forms neither have accord in the Holy Qur'an nor exist in the modern use.

The plural form common to the Masculine and Feminine is أولائِك ءulaaءika that is written as أولٰئِكَ e.g. (From the Holy Qur'an):

أُولَـٰئِكَ عَلى هُدًى مِن رَبِّهِم وَأُولَـٰئِكَ هُمُ الْمُفلِحُونَ	**2-5** These are on a right course from their Lord and These are successful.

B. **The Relative Pronoun** الإسْم المَوْصُول alismul-mousul, is expressed by الذى alladhi that has a delined form as follows:

	Sing.	Dual	Plural
Masc. Nominal	اَلَّذى	اَللَّذَانِ	اَلَّذِينَ
Accusative and Genetive	اَلَّذى	اَللَّـذَيـنِ	اَلَّذِينَ
Fem. Nominal	اَلَّتى	اَللَّتَان	اَللائى or اَللاتى
Accusative and Genetive	اَلَّتى	اَللَّتَينِ	اَللائى

Examples from The Holy Qur'an:

الذى هُو الذى أرْسَلَ رسُولَه بالهُدى	**48-28** He is who hath sent His messenger with the guidance.
وَالَّذِى جَاء بالصِّدقِ وَصَدَّقَ بِهِ أُولَـٰئِكَ هُـمُ المُتَّقُونَ	**39-33** And whose bringeth the truth and believeth therein, such are the dutiful.
الله الَّذِى لاَ إله إلا هُو	**59-22** He is Allah then whom there is no other God.

اللذانِ : (dual, Nominative case)

واللّذان يأتيانِهَا مِنكم فآذوهُمَا	**4-16** And as far two of you who are guilty of it give them both a slight punishment.

اللَّذَيْنِ : (dual, accusative case)

رَبَّنَا أَرِنَا **اللَّذَيْنِ** أَضَلَّانَا	**41-29** Our Lord! show us those (two) who led us astray.

الَّذِينَ : (Plural - in all cases)

وَالَّذِين آمَنُوا أَشَدُّ حُبًّا لِلهِ	**2-165** and those who believe, are stronger in their love for Allah.
وَلَو يَرَى **الَّذين** ظَلَمُوا إِذْ يَرَونَ الْعَذَابَ أَنَّ الْقُوَّةَ لِلهِ جَمِيعاً	**2-165** ... and O' that the wrongdoers had seen, when they see the chastisement, that power is wholly 'Allah'
إِذ تَبَرَّأَ **الَّذين** اتُّبِعُوا من **الَّذين** اتَّبَعُوا	**2-166** When those who were followed renounce those who followed.
وقال **الذين** اتَّبَعُوا لَو أَنَّ لَنا كَرَّةً	**2-167** And those who followed will say: If we could have our return.

الَّتِي : (Fem. for all cases):

إِدْفَعْ بالتى هِيَ أحسن	**41-34** Repel (evil) with what is best.
وَالَّتِى لَمْ تَمُتْ فى مَنامِها	**39-42** and that (soul) which dieth not (yet) in its sleep.

اللاتى and اللائى allaa-ii (Plural of التى Fem):

وَالَّتى يأتينَ الْفَاحِشَةَ من نِسَائِكُم	**4-15** and as for those of your women who are guilty of indecency.
وَالَّئى يئسن من المحيض	**65-4** and those (women) who despair of a menstruation.
وَالَّئى لَمْ يَحِضْنَ	**65-4** and those who have not (yet) menstruation

C. Interrogative Pronouns : (إسم الاستفهام 'ismul estifhaam,) are:

I. مَنْ 'man' who, e.g. (From The Holy Qur'an):

مَنْ خَلَقَ السَّموات وَالأرضَ	**29-61** Who created the heaven and the earth?
مَنْ فَعَلَ هٰذَا بِآلِهَتِنَا	**21-59** Who has done this to our gods?
قُلْ فَمَنْ يَمْلِكُ مِنَ اللهِ شَيْئًا	**5-17** Say: who then can control anything as against Allah?

Sometimes a demonstrative pronoun ذَا **dha** is attached after مَنْ to denote implied negative meaning, e.g. (From The Holy Qur'an):

مَن ذَا الَّذى يَشْفَعُ عِنْدَه إلا بإِذْنِهِ	**2-255** Who is he that can intercede with Him but by His permission.

It is also sometimes, preceded by a particle of preposition or conjunction and in this case the مِنْ min of مَنْ "man" is assimilated with a final letter of that particle thus: the combination of عَنْ and من is عَمَّنْ ع amman, from whom, or it is combined with أمْ of conjunction, 'or' as أمَّنْ "amman " or how?, e.g. (from The Hloy Qur'an):

أمَّنْ هُوَ قَانِتٌ آناءَ الليلِ	**39-9** or is he who is obedient during hours of the night?
قُلْ مَنْ يَرْزُقُكُم مِنَ السَّماءِ وَالأرْضِ أمَّنْ يَمْلِكُ السَّمْعَ وَالأبْصارَ ومَن يُخْرِجُ الحَىَّ مِنَ المَيِّتِ وَيُخْرِجُ المَيِّتَ مِنَ الحَىِّ وَمن يُدَبِّرُ الأمْرَ	**10-31** Say: **Who** gives you sustenance from the heaven and the earth , or **who** controls the hearing and the sight , and **Who** brings forth the living from the dead and brings forth the dead from the living and **Who** regulates the affairs ?

Besides denoting the meaning of an introgative pronoun مَنْ is also a particle of the relative noun, that gives the meaning of 'who' that or which e.g. (from The Holy Qur'an):

وقد خَابَ مَنْ افْتَرىٰ	**20-61** And he fails indeed **who** forges **(a lie)**
من خَشِى الرحمٰن بالغَيْبِ وَجاء بِقلْبٍ مُنيبٍ	**50-33** Who fears Rahmaan in secret and comes with a contrite heart.

فَمَن شَرِبَ مِنْهُ فَلَيسَ مِنِّى وَمَنْ لَمْ يَطْعَمْهُ فَإِنَّهُ مِنِّى إِلا مَنِ اغْتَرَفَ غُرْفَةً بِيَدِهِ	**2-249** Whoever drinks from it he is not of me and whoever tastes it not, he is surely of me except who he takes handful with his hand.

II. ما 'what' e.g. (From the Holy Qur'an):

قَالُوا وَمَا الرَّحْمَٰنُ	**25-60** ... they say: what is Rahman?
مَا هَٰذِهِ التَّمَاثِيلُ	**21-52** What are these images?

A particle of the demonstrative ذا **dha** is placed after ما 'if the interrogative sentence begins with a verb e.g. (from The Holy Qur'an):

فأرُونِى مَاذَا خَلَقَ	**31-11** then show me what he has created.
مَاذَا أَرَادَ اللهُ بِهَٰذَا مَثَلاً	**2-26** what is it that Allah means by this parable!
أرُونِى مَاذا خَلَقُوا مِنَ الأَرضِ	**35-40** Show me what they created from the earth.

After some preposition it is sometimes written مَ (i.e. with a short vowel 'fatha' instead of a long vowel: ألف) as لِمَ 'for what' why? (For لِمَا lima or لِمَاذا **limadha**) likewise after عن as عَمَّ i.e. عن + ما = عَمَّا shortened to عَمَّ 'of what', what about

But only in case of a question e.g. (From The Holy Qur'an):

لِمَ أذِنْتَ لَهم	9 - 43 **Why** didst thou permit them.
عَمَّ يَتَسَاءلُون	78 - 1 Of what they ask one another ?

other wise the ألف of (ما) remains even after pre fixing عن or لِ e.g. (From the Holy Qur'an)

وَلَا تَقُولُوا لِمَا تَصِفُ أَلْسِنَتُكُم الْكَذِب	**16-116** and Say not Concerning that where in your tongues utter a lie.
وَلاَ تَحْسَبَنَّ الله غافِلاً عَمَّا يَعْمَلُ الظَّالِمُونَ	**14-42** And deem not Allah negligent **of that** which the wrong doers work.

Students may note that there are three usages of (ما):

1. as negative **particle as**:

   ما فَعَلْتُ هذا بِأمْرِي I did not do it with my own decision.

2. as **interrogative** particle as

   ما تلك بيمينك What is This in thy right hand

3. as a relative noun as

   هَذا مَا وَعَدَ الرَّحْمَنُ This is what Allah had promised.

Apart from the contents, the meaning of ' ما ' can be known by its place with a noun or verb, if it is placed before past tens it will denote a negtive as مافعل he did not do ,if it is before a noun, then it means an interrogation as ما هو what is he? or after an imperfect verb ما يَفْعَلُ الله بعَذَابِكُمْ what shall Allah do by giving you punishment? For relative pronoun it is always placed before a verb, thus:

لها مَا كَسَبَتْ وَعَلَيها مَا اكْتَسَبَتْ	**2-286** For it is **that which it** earns (for good) and against it that it works (of evil)
أفرأيتم مَا تُمْنُونَ	**56-58** See you that which you emit?
أفرأيتم مَا تَحْرُثُون	**56-63** See you what you sow?
هٰـذا مَا وَعَـدَ الرَّحْمَـٰنُ وَصَدَقَ المُرْسَلُون	**36-52** This what Allah (Rahman) promised and messengers told the truth.

III. أىُّ ayyun, Fem: أيَّةٌ ayyatun, which, is declinable (مُعْرَب) and is treated as a noun so takes a following noun in genetive, e.g. أىُّ رَجُلٍ which man أيَّةُ بنتٍ which girl?.

Examples from The Holy Qur'an :

وسَيَعْلَمُ الَّذين ظَلَموا أىَّ مُنْقَلَبٍ يَنْقَلِبُون	**26-227** And they who do wrong, will know **to what** final place of turning they will turn back.

بِأَيِّكُمُ المَفْتُونُ	**68-6 Which** of you is mad.
أَيُّكُمْ زَادَتْهُ هٰذِهِ إِيمَاناً	**9-124** Which of you has it strengthened in faith.

IV. هَلْ 'hal', what. It forms an interrogative sentence with a verb or pronoun e.g.

هل رأيتَ أحداً	did you see anyone?
هل أنتَ طَالبُ عِلمٍ	are you a student (seeker of knowledge)

Examples From The Holy Qur'an

قُلْ هَل تَرَبَّصُون بِنَا إلَّا إحدَى الْحُسْنَيَيْنِ	**9-52** Say: Do you wait for us but one of two most excellent things?
وَهلْ أتاكَ نَبَؤُ الخَصْمِ	**38-21** and has the story of the adversaries came to thee?
هَل أتاكَ حَدِيثُ الْغَاشِيَةِ	**88-1** Has there come to thee the news of the overwhelming events?

EXERCISE

A. Translate into Arabic:

1. Did you know that famous poet? Yes I know his name; he was Iqbal of Pakistan.
2. This is a good man and that (Fem.) is his sister.
3. The tree has good shade.
4. These Arab are nice persons.
5. Those men have not arrived so far.
6. This woman returned from England yesterday.
7. Which men killed a dog yesterday?
8. How many persons attended the Juma-prayer in that village?
9. What did you demand of (مِنْ) your student in the University?
10. This is the great mosque of the City.
11. I found these books in Maktaba of Harmain at Mecca.
12. This is a great building of a merchant.
13. Whose son is Abdul Hamid?
14. Is he a minister's son?
15. These two men are friends and those two are enemies.
16. The daughter of a teacher has memorized Holy Qur'an by heart.
17. This is the man who won the 1st prize.
18. This is that girl who failed in the examination.
19. This is that boy who got first position in the Examination.
20. This is the girl who arrived yesterday from Baghdad.

slate into English:

مَن جاءَ بِالحَسَنَةِ فَلَهُ عَشرُ أمثَالِهَا . مَن قَالَ لاَ إلَهَ إلاَّ الله دخَلَ
الجَنَّةَ . مَنْ صلَّى صَلاتَنَا وأكَلَ ذَبِيحتنَا فَهُوَ مِنَّا . مَنْ لَمْ يَرْحَمْ صَغِيرَنَا
وَلَمْ يُوَقِّر كَبِيرَنا فَلَيْس مِنَّا. مَنْ جاءَ مِنَ المَدِينَةِ المنَوَّرةِ أمْسِ ؟ مَاذا تُرِيدُ
مِنَ المُعَلّم أكثَرَ مِنَ التَّعْلِيمِ ؟ مَنْ هُوَ وَرَاءَكَ ؟ هَلْ أنتَ شاعِرٌ ؟ من فَعَلَ
هَذَا ؟ مَن دَخَلَ الْبيتَ فَهُوَ آمِن ، هٰذا هُوَ الكَلْبُ الَّذى أكَلَ القِطَّ الَّذى
أكَلَ الفأرَ الَّذى قَتَلْتُه أمْسِ. هَل هِيَ أختُكَ الَّتى حَفِظَتِ القرآن الكَرِيمَ
وَفَازَتْ بالجائِزَةِ ؟

VOCABULARY

Famous	المعروفُ
Tree	الشَّجَرَةُ
Shade	الظِّلُّ
Nice	طَيِّب
Arrived	وَصَلَ
Demand	طالَبَ
Building	العِمَارَةُ
Merchant	التَّاجِرُ
Enemy	العَدُوُّ

To memorize	الحِفْظُ
By heart	بِظَهْرِ الْقَلْبِ
Prize	الجَائِزَةُ
To win	فَازَ بِـ
Examination	الإِخْتِبَارُ
Position	الدَّرَجَةُ

الحَسَنَةُ	a good deed
أَمْثَالٌ	plural of مَثَلٌ parable
يَرْحَمُ ـ رَحِمَ	to be merciful
يُوَقِّرُ	to regard
أَمِنَ	To be safe

CHAPTER 22

THE DECLENSION

The Noun is generally divided into two groups: Those are: –

1. **Declinable:** i.e. governed by their preceding elements consequently changing their ending vowels, called: مُعْرَب Muعrab, e. g.

Nominative Case:	صَدَقَ الرَّسولُ	The Messenger spoke the Truth.
Accusative Case:	صَدَّقوا الرَّسُولَ	They verified the Messenger.
Genetive Case:	صحابَةُ الرَّسُولِ	The companions of the Messenger.

2. Those which have stationery state of their ending vowels and do not accept any influence of عوامل (element), called: مَبْنِى Mabni, e.g.

Nominative Case:	صَدَقَ موسٰى	Moses spoke the truth.
Accusative Case:	صَدَّقُوا موسٰى	They verified Moses.
Genetive Case:	صَحَابَةُ موسٰى	The companions of Moses.

2. A There are certain classes of noun that are not fully declined. This class of noun is called غير منصرف ghair munsarif. According to European grammarians it may be termed as

'Diptotes' that opposes triptotes. However, the declination of this class would be as following:

قالَ فرعونُ	pheron said.
كَذَّبوا فرعونَ	They denied pheron
أصحابُ فرعونَ	The companions of pheron

It is to be noted that Diptotes differ from other declinable nouns in two respects - First: there is no Nunization (i.e. a sound of "an", un' or in') Second: there are only two different vowel endings; The Accusative and Genetive both having (فتحه) "Fatha."

As most Arabic nouns are declinable which has several types and classes they will be dealt with separately in the following chapters.

indeclinable Nouns: Words of indeclinable group are as following:

(a) All forms of Perfect as قالَ ، قُلْتُ ، سَمِعْتَ . شَرِبْتَ etc.

(b) Particles like عَلَى ، مَنْ ، قَدْ ، مَتَى etc.

(c) Words ending in 'alif but spelled with ending Yaa as موسى Moosaa, عِيسى Eisaa etc. This type of 'alif is called ألف مقصورة 'alif Maqsoora, likewise:

كُبْرَى Kubraa. Fem. Elative of أكبر Biggest one, e.g. from The Holy Qur'an:

لقد رَأىٰ مِنْ آياتِ رَبِّهِ **الْكُبْرىٰ**	**53-18** Certainly he saw of the greatest sign of his Lord.

ذِكْرى **dhi**kraa, recollection, e.g.:

فلا تَقْعُدْ بعد **الذِّكْرَىٰ** مَعَ القَومِ الظالِمينَ	**6-68** Then sit not after recollection with the unjust people.

هُدَى hudaa, guide, e.g.:

هُدًى لِلْمُتَّقِينَ	**2-2** (This book is) a guide to those who fear (Allah)

عصا ع asaa, stick, e.g.:

إضْرِبْ بِعَصَاكَ الحَجَرَ	**2-60** strike the rock with thy stick (staff).

(d) The Masculine singular, elative and colour-defect nouns of the form . أفْعَل e.g. أحْسَنَ the most beutiful, e.g. from the Holy Qur'an:

فَحَيُّوا بِأحْسَنَ مِنْها	**4-86** greet with better than it.

(e) Adjective of the form فَعْلان as غَضْبَان ghadbaan, angry, e.g. (from The Holy Qur'an):

وَلَمَّا رَجَعَ مُوسىٰ إلىٰ قَومِه غَضْبَانَ أسِفًا	**7-150** and when Moses returned to his people wrathful, grieved.

Diptotes غير منصرف

(a) Most proper names whether personal or geographical are diptotes as:

فرعون	قال المَلأُ مِنْ قَومِ فرعونَ	**7-109** the chief of Fir ع on's (Pharaon), people said ...
سليمان	إنَّه مِنْ سُلَيمانَ	**27-30** It is from Sulaimaan (Solomon).
هاروت ماروت بابل	وما أُنْزِلَ على المَلَكَيْنِ بِبَابِلَ هاروتَ وماروتَ	**2-102** And it was not revealed to the two angels in Babel, Haaroot and Maaroot.
مَدْيَنَ	وَإِلَىٰ مَدْيَنَ أخاهم شُعَيْبًا	**7-85** And to Midian (We sent) their brother **Shu** ع **aib**
ثَمُودَ	وَإِلَىٰ ثَمُودَ أخَاهُم صَٰلِحًا	**7-73** And to Thamood (We sent) their brother Saaleh.

(b) Broken Plurals of the following patterns:

fa ع laa ء u, as وُزَراء Wuzaraa ء u, ministers, e.g. From the Holy Qur'an:

شُفَعاءُ	هؤُلاءِ شُفَعَاؤُنَا	**10-18** These are our intercesors.

رُحَمَاءُ	
رُحَمَاءُ بَيْنَهُمْ	**48-29** compassionate among themselves.

عُلَمَاءُ	
عُلَمَاءُ بنى إسرائيلَ	**26-197** Learned men of the children of Israel.

فَعْلَىٰ fa ع laa as مَرْضَىٰ murdaa, plural of مريض patient, e.g. from the Holy Qur'an:

عَلِمَ أنْ سَيكونُ منكم مَرْضَىٰ	**73-20** He knew that there will be some sick among you.

فعائِلُ fa ع a ء elu as مَدَائِنُ madaa ء enu, plural of مَدِينَة madina, city, e.g. from the Holy Qur'an:

وَأَرْسِلْ فى المدائِنِ حاشِرِينَ	**7-111** and send (summoners) in the cities.

فعالىٰ fa ع aalaa, as يتامىٰ yataama, plural of يتيم yatim, orphan, e.g. from the Holy Qur'an:

وَيَسْألونَكَ عَنِ اليَتَامىٰ	**2-220** and they ask thee concerning the orphans.

فَعَالِلُ fa ع aalilu as دَرَاهِمُ daraahimu, plural of دِرْهَم dirham, silver coin, e.g. from the Holy Qur'an:

وَشَرَوْهُ بِثَمَنٍ بَخْسٍ دَرَاهِمَ معدودةٍ	**12-20** and they sold him for a small price a few pieces of silver.

فَعَالِيل fa ع aal:l, as خنازير khanazier, plural of خنزير khinzir, pig, e.g. from The Holy Qur'an:

وجَعَلَ منهم القِرَدَةَ والْخَنَازِيرَ .	**5-60** (and of whom) He made apes and pigs.

Diptotes are treated as triptote (منصرف) when they are made definite in any way, e.g.

فى المدائِنِ التى سكنوها	In the cities they dwell.
من مدائِنِ العَرَبِ	From the Cities of Arabia.

EXERCISE

A. Translate into Arabic:

1. Islam orders its followers to look after widows and orphans..
2. When our Prophet was three years old his mother had died.
3. His father died before he was born.
4. We see in big cities of the world people travel by under ground trains.
5. The helping and guidance of blind men is among the duties recommended to Muslims.
6. He had many pigs, apart from his cows and sheeps.
7. He met a white girl, so he took her into employment as a servant girl in a black man's house. But she deserted him suddenly without permission two days later.
8. They followed the enemy and found them hesitating in the sand. So they destroyed them straight away.

9. England had many colonies in the past and her sailors were famous.
10. I saw you on my right hand and Lozely on my left.
11. I knew from the perspiration flowing on his forehead that his endeavors had tired him.
12. I met a lame man and a tall Muslim in the street and I did not know when they had come.

B. Translate into English:

لَيسَ عَلَى الأعْمَى حَرَجٌ ولا عَلَى الأعْرَجِ حَرَجٌ ـ الشُّعَرَاءُ يَتَّبِعُهُمُ الْغَاوونَ ، أَلَمْ تَرَ أَنَّهُم فى كُلِّ وَادٍ يَهِيمُونَ ـ قَالَتْ كُبْرَى الْبَنَاتِ لِأُخْتِهَا الصَّغِيرَةِ لاتَتْرُكِى عَمَلَ الْيَومِ لِلْغدِ ـ سَمِعتُ العَصَافِيرَ تُغَرِّدُ عَلَى الأغْصَانِ ـ كَمْ أَخًا لَكَ وَكَمْ أُختًا ـ كَمْ مِنْ قَرْيَةٍ أَهْلَكَهَا اللهُ ـ كُلاًّ نُمِدُّ هٰؤلاءِ وَهٰؤلاءِ مِنْ عَطَاءِ رَبِّكَ ـ إرْحَمُوا اليتامى فَإِنَّهُمْ فَقَدُوا آباءهُم ـ إعملوا المَعْرُوفَ نَحْوَ الأرَامِلِ ، الأرْمَلَةُ وَالمَرِيضُ وَالفَقِيرُ أَحَقُّ بالإحْسَانِ مِنْ غَيرِهِم ـ القرآنُ يَهْدِى لِلَّتِى هِيَ أَقْوَمُ ، رَسُولُ اللهِ صَادِقٌ أمِينٌ ، بُعِثَ لِلْبَشَرِيَّةِ جَمْعَاء ـ الأبْيَضُ وَالأسْوَدُ عِندَ اللهِ سَوَاءٌ ، إنَّ اللهَ لا يَنْظُرُ إلى صُوَرِكُم وألوانكم ، إنَّ اللهَ يَنْظُرُ إلى قُلُوبِكُم وَأعْمَالِكُمْ .

VOCABULARY

To look after	رَعَى ـ يَرْعَى	ra ع a, - yar ع a.
under-ground.	النَّفَقُ	تَحتَ الأَرْضِ
Train	القِطَار	
To recommend	شَفَعَ ـ يَشْفَعُ	
Pig.	الخِنْزِيرُ	
cow	البَقَرة	
sheep	الغَنَمُ	
employment	الوظيفة الخِدْمَةُ	
servant girl	الخَادِمَةُ	
To desert	هَرَبَ ـ يَهْرِبُ	or أبق ـ يأبق
suddenly	فَجْأةً	
permission	الإِذْنُ	
To follow	أتبَعَ ـ يُتبعُ	IV
colonies	المُسْتَعمَرَاتُ plural of	مستعمرة colony X
Prespiration	التَعَرُّقْ	(V verbal noun)
forehead	الجَبينُ	
endeavour	الجُهُودُ	
To tire	أتْعَبَ ـ يتعب	

الأَعْرَجُ	Lame
الأعمى	Blind man.
حَرَجٌ	harm. objection.
الغاوون	Act. Part. Plural of غاوٍ mislead.
وَادٍ	Field, valley.
هَام . يَهِيم	to wander.
كُبْرَى البَنَاتِ	the elder daughter
العصفورة	bird
يُغَرِّدُ	singing
اليَوْمَ	to day
الغَدُ	tomorrow
مَدَّ - يَمُدُّ	1st Pers. IMP. (double radicals) to extend, to help.
أَرَامِل	Widows plural of أرملة widow
أَقْوَمُ	(Elevate) rightest
صَادِقٌ	The truthful
الأَمِينُ	Trustworthy
جَمْعَاء	All of them
صُوَرٌ	Plural of صورةٌ Face.
أَلْوَانٌ	plural of لَوْنٌ Colour

CHAPTER 23

NOUNS : DECLINABLE الأسماء المعربة

As already stated, the noun is either declinable or indeclinable. In previous chapter the indeclinable was treated. In chapter-8 we have mentioned that the Imperfect has three moods which are distinguished through the declnsion. Again the dclnsion is the result of the preceding letters or nouns which are placed for modification of the forms.

Let us recollect here once again that a noun has three cases:

Nominative	Indicated by	ضَمَّه ـُ
Accusative	Indicated by	فتحه ـَ
Genitive	Indicated by	كسره ـِ

1- A. The nominative is used:

(a) For the subject of a verbal sentence, e.g.

خَلَقَ اللهُ السَّمٰوات والأرْضَ	Allah has created the heavens and the earth.

(b) For the subject of a nominal sentence (termed مبتدأ mubtada, see chapter 2), e.g.

الرسولُ صادقٌ	The Messenger is true (man)

(c) As the predicate of a nominal sentence. صَادِقٌ is the predicate is termed as خبر **kh**abar

(d) As the predicate of إنَّ ، أنَّ ، لَعَلَّ ، لَيْتَ , e.g.

إنَّ ربَّكَ كريمٌ	Verily your Lord is kind (God)
ألَمْ أقُلْ لَّكَ أنَّ اللهَ على كل شيءٍ قَدِيرٌ	did not I say you **that** Allah is most powerful on every thing?

It is important for students to note that إنَّ and أنَّ both are used to emphasise the meaning of predicate but إنَّ is used only in the begining of a sentence while أنَّ indicates to the statement, e.g. I told you that ....

قلتُ لَك أنَّ صَدِيقَكَ قَادِمٌ	I told you **that** your friend is coming.

لَيْتَ would that, e.g.

يا لَيْتَنِى كُنْتُ تُرَابا	O' would that I were dust.

لَعَلَّ la ع alla, may, perhaps, e.g.

لا تَدْرِى لَعَلَّ اللهَ يُحْدِثُ بَعْدَ ذٰلِكَ أمْراً	**65-1** Thou knowest not that Allah may after that bring an event.

The above particles are termed as حُرُوفٌ مُشَبَّهَةٌ بِالْفِعْلِ 'letters resembling verbs' and referred to as:
(إِنَّ and sisters)

(e) After the vocative particle أَيُّهَا (always used with the Article, e.g. أيها النّاسُ O' people! also after يا , in the singular without nonation, e.g. يا رَجُلُ O' man. يا عَلِى O' ἑAli.

(f) For the adjective or a noun in opposition to another nominative, e.g.

قالَ اللّهُ العظيمُ	said Allah The Great.
صَدَقَ اللّهُ ورَسُولُه	Allah and His prophet told the turth.

1-B. Arab Grammerians divide the declension into two types - one is by vowells that is الإعْرَاب بالحَرَكَاتِ and another is declension by letters الإعْرابُ بِالحُرُوفِ

Here are letters or dipthongs that take place for the vowels:

In case of Nominative و "waw" will take place of damma.

In case of Accusative ألف "alif" will take place of Fatha.

In case of genitive ى "Yaa" will take place of kasra These declensions are traditionally represented in nouns:

Nominative :

أبو abu e. g.	
أبونا شيخٌ كبيرٌ	**28-23** our father is a very old man.

أخو akhu e. g.	
أنا أخُوكَ	**12-69** I am thy brother.

ذو dhu e. g.	
وَرَبُّكَ الغَفُورُ ذُو الرحمة	**18-58** and thy Lord is forgiving, full of mercy.

Accusative :

أبا abaa e. g.	
وَجَاءُوا أبَاهُم	**12-16** They came to their father.

أخا akhaa e. g.	
نَحْفَظُ أخَانَا	**12-65** We protect our brother.

ذا dha e. g.	
حَتّى إذا فَتَحْنَا عليهم باباً ذَا عَذَابٍ	**23-77** untill when we opened a door of chestisement.

Genitive :

أبي Abi e. g.	
قَالَ يُوسُفُ لِأَبِيهِ	**12-4** Joseph said to his father.

أخي Akhi e. g.	
أنا يُوسُفُ وَهٰذا أخي	**12-90** I am Joseph and he is my brother.

ذي dhi e. g.	
يَسْئَلُونَكَ عَنْ ذي الْقَرنَيْنِ	**18-83** They ask thee about Dhulqarnain.

EXERCISE

1. Translate into Arabic:

Among (بين) all the religious books of the world, The HolyQur'an, isthe only book which has the pure text. Every word and letter of the Holy book is revealed. There is only one Qur'an that is read in the East and in the West. There is no different texts of the Holy Book. This is memorized by heart.

Thousands of Muslims read its text every day. They try to comprehend the meaning of the Qur'an. They know that Qur'an was revealed to Syyidana Mohammad. May peace and blessing of Allah be upon him (صلى الله عليه وسلم)

Qur'an has told us the real story of Joseph; when he said to his father, " I saw eleven stars and the sun and the moon bowing to me.

2. Translate into English

أَذِنَ لَهُ الرَّحْمَنُ . لَن تغنى عَنْهُم أمْوَالهم ، لَنْ يَقْدِرَ عليه أحد ، لَنْ تُغْنِىَ عَنْكُم فِئَتُكُم ، أحَاطَ بِهِم سُرادِقُها ، كَبُرَ عَلَيْك إعْرَاضُهُم ، يَطُوفُ عَلَيهم غِلمانٌ ، طالَ عَلَيهُمُ الأَمدُ ، كَبُرَ عَلَيكُمْ مقَامى ، لاَ يَحُضُ عَلَى طَعَام الْمِسكين . صَدُّوا عَنْ سَبِيل الله ، أتمَّها على أبَوَيكَ ، تَبَّتْ يَدا أبِى لَهَبٍ ، جاء إخوَةُيُوسُفَ ، إنَّمَا الْمُؤمِنُونَ إخوَةٌ ، أخَذَ بِرَأْسِ أخِيهِ ، قَدَ سَرَقَ أَخٌ لَه مِنْ قَبْلُ .

3. Pick up subjects of the sentences in the following verses:

سَوفَ يؤتى اللهُ أجرَ المؤمنينَ ، لَقَد نَادانَا نوحٌ ، لَم يَطْمِثْهُنَّ إنسٌ ، لَنْ تَنْفَعكُم أرْحَامكُمْ . لن تَمَسَّنَا النَّارُ ، أخَذَهُ اللهُ ، كَذَّبَتْ قومُ نوحٍ المُرْسَلِين ، يمحُ اللهُ البَاطِلَ .

VOCABULARY

Religion	دين Religious book الكُتُب الدِينِيَّةُ
Text	النَّصُّ
Pure	الخَالِصُ
Revealed	أُوحِيَ Passive case for the Perfect Stem IV.
...is read	يُقْرَأُ Passive case for Imperfect (Hamzated).
To memorize	حَفِظَ — يَحفَظُ
Thousands	آلافٌ
comprehend	وَعىٰ — يَعِي
Real story	القِصَّةُ الوَاقِعِيَّةُ

أَذِنَ	To permit
لَنْ تُغْنِي	will never avail (stem V) ought against....
لَنْ يَقْدِر	will never have power upon
أَحَاطَ	surrounded IV
سُرَادِقٌ	chambers
كَبُرَ	It was hard to...

إعَرَاضٌ	to get off. IV
يَطُوفُ	to circulate
غِلْمَانٌ	boys, plural of غُلامٌ boy.
الأمَدُ	limited time.
الْمُقَامُ	end, Place.
كَذَّبَ	to deny. II
الحَقُّ	The truth.

CHAPTER 24

DECLENSION OF THE NOUN

Accusative Case = Objects

The Accusative mark نَصْبٌ is used for the objects of a verb. There are five kinds of objects:

1. Direct object مَفْعُولٌ بِهِ e.g.

خَلَقَ اللهُ الأَرْضَ	Allah has created the earth
قرأتُ كِتَاباً	I read a book

Some verbs take two objects, e.g.

أَرْسَلَ اللهُ مُحَمَّداً رَسُولاً	Allah has sent Mohammad (as a) Messenger.

Some verbs which in English take direct objects, are said in Arabic to be transitive مُتَعَدٍّ by means of a preposition, e.g.

إِنِّى ذَاهِبٌ إِلَى رَبِّى	I am going to my Lord.
ذَهَبَ بِمَالِى	He went off with my money.
أَتَانِى بِكِتَابِهِ	He brought me his book (Lit. He came to me with his book).

Examples from the Holy Qur'an:

فَقَدَرَ عَلَيهِ رِزْقَهُ	**89-16** Then straighten to **him** his subsistence.
إبتَلاهُ رَبُّه	**89-15** His Lord tried **him.**
وَسَوفَ يُؤْتِ اللهُ المؤمنين أجراً عَظِيماً	**4-146** And Allah will soon grant the believers a mighty reward.
قَد فَرَضَ اللهُ لَكُم تَحِلَّةَ أَيمانِكُمْ	**66-2** Allah has indeed sanctioned for you the expiration of your oaths.
لقد جِئْتِ شَيئاً فَرِيًّا	**19-27** (O' Mary) thou hast indeed brought a strange thing.
خلَقَكَ فَسَوَّاكَ فَعَدَلَكَ	**82-7** (Who) created thee, then made thee complete, then made thee in a right good state.
لَقَدْ أَضَلَّ مِنْكُمْ جِبِلًّا كَثِيراً	**36-62** He hath led astray of you a great multitude.
ولِمَن خَافَ مَقامَ رَبِّهِ	**55-46** And for who fears to stand before his Lord.
ونَهَى النَّفْسَ عَنِ الهَوَى	**79-40** And restrains himself from low designs.

2. As the absolute object الْمَفْعُولُ الْمُطْلَقُ

The verbal noun is placed in the accusative after its own verb as a sort of adverb, to describe the manner, times, and sometimes to denote that verb of sentence is meant by speaker in its real and complete sense, e.g.

فَصَّلْنَاهُ تَفْصِيلًا	17-12 We have explained it completely.
فَسَوْفَ يُحَاسَبُ حِسَابًا يَسِيرًا	84-8 His account will be taken by an easy reckoning.

It sometimes confuses students to see a verbal noun is repeated in accusative without any change in the meaning, thes to them:

فَرِحَ فَرِحاً	he was glad
ضَرَبَ ضرباً	he struck

have same meaning as فَرِحَ and ضَرَبَ Some European authors like Harywood / Nahmad observed that the absolute object serves "to balance the sentence from the musical point of view"

This type of confusion could be raised if the correct sense of this type of object is known. As the real sense of فرح فرحاً is he was really glad and likewise ضرب ضرباً means that someone has physically struck.

Examples from The Holy Qur'an:

وَمَهَّدتُّ لَه تَمْهِيداً	**74-14** And I made (life) smoth.
يَنْسِفُهَا رَبِّى نَسْفاً	**20-105** Say: My Lord will scatter them as scattered dust.
يُفَجِّرونَها تفجيراً	**76-6** They will make it flow in abundance.
أَنَّا صَبَبْنَا الْمَاءَ صَبًّا	**80-25** We have poured down abundant water.

It qualifies an adjective to specify the type of action, e.g.

وتُحِبُّونَ الْمَالَ حُبًّا جَمًّا	**89-20** And you love wealth with exceeding love.
ولِيُبْلِىَ الْمُؤمِنِينَ مِنْهُ بَلاءً حَسَناً	**8-17** He might test the believers by a fair test.
إِنَّا فَتَحْنَا لَكَ فَتْحاً مُبِيناً	**48-1** Surely We have granted thee a clear victory.
وَأُسَرِّحْكُنَّ سَرَاحاً جَمِيلاً	**33-28** And will release you a fair release.
أَقْرَضْتُمُ اللهَ قَرضاً حَسَناً	**5-12** lend unto Allah a kindly loan.
فَيَمِيلُونَ عَلَيْكُم مَيْلَةً وَاحِدَةً	**4-102** That they may attack you once for all.

Sometimes it comes after a verb of passive case, e.g.

زُلْزِلَتِ الأَرْضُ زِلْزَالَها	**99-1** When earth is shaken with her (final) earthquake.
كَلَّا إِذَا دُكَّتِ الأَرْضُ دَكًّا دَكًّا	**89-21** Nay! But when the earth is ground to atoms, grinding, grinding.
وَبُسَّتِ الْجِبَالُ بَسًّا	**56-5** And the hills are ground to powder.
وَذُلِّلَتْ قُطُوفُهَا تَذْلِيلاً	**76-14** And the clustered fruits thereof bow down.

3. Object for Time and Place المفعول فيه e.g.

سَيَعْلَمُونَ غَداً	**54-26** They will know tomorrow
ونُدْخِلْكُم مُدخلاً كَرِيماً	**4-31** and we cause you enter an honourable place of eternity.
انْتَبَذَتْ مِنْ أَهْلِهَا مَكَانًا شَرْقِيًّا	**19-16** She drew aside from her family to an eastern place.
قال لَبِثْتُ يَوماً أو بَعْضَ يَومٍ	**2-259** He said I have tarried a day or a part of a day.
فاللهُ يَحْكُمُ بَيْنَكُمْ يَومَ الْقِيَامَةِ	**4-141** And Allah will judge between you on the day of Resurrection.

Such Accusatives may be placed by prepositional phrases.

وتَرَكْنَا يُوسُفَ عِنْدَ مَتَاعِنَا	**12-17** And left joseph by our goods.
وأَلْفَيَا سَيِّدَهَا لَدَى الْبَابِ	**12-25** and they met her husband at the door.
لِيُحَاجُّوكُم بِهِ عِنْدَ رَبِّكُمْ	**2-76** that they may contend with you by this before your Lord.
عاهَدتُّمْ عِندَ المَسْجِدِ الحَرَامِ	**9-7** You made an agreement at the sacred mosque.

They also are placed by particles devoting meaning of "sides", e.g.

خَلْفٌ behind

ومِن **خَلْفِهِم** سَدًّا	**36-9** and a barrier behind them.

فَوقَ above

وَفَوْقَ كُلِّ ذِى عِلْمٍ عَلِيمٌ	**12-76** and above every possessed of knowledge in the All-knowing one.

تَحْتَ beneath. under

قَد جَعَلَ رَبُّكِ **تَحتَكِ** سَرِيًّا	**19-24** Surely thy Lord has provided a stream beneath thee.

أَسْفَلَ lower

والرَّكْبُ أسفل مِنْكُم	**8-42** While the carvan was in a lower place than you.

اليمين right hand

الشمال left hand

وتَرَى الشَّمْسَ إذا طَلَعَتْ تَزَاوَرُ عَن كَهْفِهِمْ ذَاتَ اليَمِينِ وإذا غَرَبَتْ تَقْرِضُهُمْ ذاتَ الشِّمَالِ	**18-17** and thou mightest see the sun, when it rose, decline from their cave to the right and when it set leave them behind on the left

وراء behind

وكان وَرَاءهم مَلِكٌ	**18-79** and there was behind them a king.

4. Object for expressing 'aim' and 'purpose' **المَفْعُول لَهُ** or This is expressed by a verbal Noun in the Accusative, e.g.

قُمتُ إكراماً لَهُ I rose to honour him.

Examples from The Holy Qur'an:

فَأَتْبَعَهُمْ فِرْعَونُ وَجُنُودُهُ بَغْيًا وَعَدْوًا .	**10-90** Then Pharaoh and his hosts followed them **for** oppression and tyranny.
بَدَّلوا نِعْمَةَ اللهِ كُفْراً	**14-28** (who) changed Allah's favour **for** disbelief.

وأَعْيُنُهم تَفِيضُ مِنَ الدَّمْعِ حَزَناً	**9-92** and their eyes overflowed with tears of grief.

Sometimes, a phrase or clause is placed with a verbal noun in the accusative. e.g. (from The Holy Qur'an):

والَّذين يُنْفِقُونَ أموالَهم رِئَاءَ النَّاسِ	**4-38** and those who spend their wealth **to be seen** of men
يَجْعَلُونَ أصابِعَهم في آذانِهم مِنَ الصَّواعِقِ حَذَرَ المَوْتِ	**2-19** they put their fingers into their ears because of the thunder-peal, for fear of death.

5. Object for denoting meaning of 'with' 'by' or 'during', e.g. From The Holy Qur'an: **المفعول معه**

فَأَجْمِعُوا أَمْرَكُم وَشُرَكَاءَكُمْ	**10-71** So decide upon your course of action, you and your partners.
قُوا أَنْفُسَكُمْ وَأَهْلِيكُمْ نَارًا	**66-6** Ward off from yourselves and your families a Fire.....

EXERCISE

1. Translate into Arabic :

Allah has revealed this Book to sayyidana (سيدنا) Mohammad, may peace and blessing of Allah be upon him. A Muslim recites the Holy Qur'an every morning. They fast during the month of Ramadan, pay poor-due (زكاة) and perform Hajj to the sacred House of Allah.

A man who killed his enemy was caught by Police and his head was cut off at the main gate of Haram. Islamic Law abolishes the criminal activities of evils. My friend came to see me last night. They went along with their families. Arabic is a richest language from the vocabulary point of view, every verb has tens of modifications. We love Arabic as it is the Language of The Holy Qur'an, traditions of the Holy Prophet and it would be the language of paradise. Your father has brought a good pen for you.

2. Distinguish kinds of objects مَفْعُولات within the following sentences:

My brother has come along with his friend.

He has done a lot for the sake of Islam.

His father was seen in the Market.

Last Friday I offered Juma prayer in Haram.

He was actually very glad to see his mother.

3. **Translate into English :**

أَرْسَلَ اللهُ نُوحاً إِلَى قَومِهِ فَدَعَا نُوحٌ قَومَه إلى عِبَادَةِ اللهِ وتَقْوَاه وَطَاعَتِهِ ، فَلَم يُؤمِن إِلَّا عَدَدٌ قَلِيْلٌ مِنْهُم وَعَصَى الْبَاقِى وازدَادُوا عِصْيَاناً ، وَلَمَّا يَئِسَ مِنْهُم دَعَا عَلَيهم وقَال :

« رَبِّ لا تَذَرْ عَلى الأَرْضِ مِنَ الكافِرِينَ دَيَّارًا ، إِنَّكَ إِن تَذَرْهُمْ يُضِلُّوا عِبَادَكَ وَلَا يَلِدُوا إِلَّا فَاجِراً كفاراً » .

VOCABULARY

Recites	يَتْلُوا - تَلا
Fasts	يَصُومُ - صَامَ
Performs	يُؤَدِّى - أَدَّى
Cut off	يَقْطَعُ - قَطَعَ (Use Passive case)
Criminal	المُجرِمَةُ ـ الإجْرامِيَةُ
Activity	النَّشاطُ
Rich	غَنى Richest أغْنَى
Point of View	مِنْ نَاحِيَةٍ
Vocabulary	الكلِمَاتُ ـ المُفْرَدَاتُ
Modification	الأنوَاعُ ـ والأشكالُ
For the sake of	لِأجلِ

أرْسَلَ	To send أَرْسَلَ ـ يُرْسِلُ IV
قَوْمٌ	Nation, People.
عِبَادَةٌ	Worship, service.
تَقْوى	God fearing
طَاعَةٌ	obedience. أَطَاعَ ـ يُطيعُ IV

عَصَى	Disobey عَصَى – يَعْصِي
ازداد	Exceeded
عِصْيَان	Disobedience.
يَئِسَ	To Dispair يَئِسَ – يَيْئَسُ
دَعَا عليه	Curse
لا تَذَر	Do no leave (May thou leave not)
دَيَّارٌ	Inhabitant
يُضِلُّ	Mislead
فاجِرٌ	Sin-doer
كَفَّارٌ	Disbeliever

CHAPTER 25

HAAL

Some other Accusative cases:

1. **حال** 'Haal' is an Arabic grammatical term that means the circumstances obtaining at the time when the action of the main verb takes place. It is expressed by an accusative or by a Finite verb, e.g.

جاءَ رَجُلٌ ساعياً or جاء رَجُلٌ **يَسْعىٰ** A man came running.

Such a Haal Accusative is usually placed after a direct object, e.g. from The Holy Qur'an:

تَرَكُوكَ قَائماً	**62-11** ... leave thee standing.
سخَّر لكم الشَّمسَ والقَمَرَ دَائِبَين	**121-33** He has made subservient to you the Sun and the Moon, pursuing their courses.
يَمْشِى **مُكِبًّا** علىٰ وَجْهِهِ	**67-22** He who goes prone upon his face, or He who walks upright on a straight path.
قُومُوا للهِ قَانِتِينَ	**2-238** Stand up truly obedient to Allah.

يَمُرُّونَ عَلَيْهَا وَهُمْ عَنْهَا مُعْرِضُونَ	**12-105** Do they pass by! yet they turn away from it.

It often refers to the subject of the sentence as:

يذكرون الله **قِياماً وقُعُوداً** but it could refer to object as:

تركوكَ **قائماً** or to some genitive as:

ونزعنا ما فى صُدُورِهِمْ مِنْ غِلٍّ **إخْوَاناً**	**15-47** And we shall root out whatever of rancour is in their breasts - as brothren.

Such a Haal may take its own direct object as:

خَرَجَ مِنها **خائفاً يَترقَّبُ**	**28-21** He went forth therefrom, fearing, awaiting,
سِيقَ الذين اتَّقَوْا رَبَّهم إلى الجَنَّةِ **زُمَرا**	**39-73** Those who keep their duty to their Lord are conveyed to the garden in companies.
وَلَّى **مُدْبِراً** وَلَمْ يُعَقِّبْ	**27-10** He turned back retreating and did not return.

The Accusative Haal is nearly always an active participle, it may also be a passive participle, e.g.

يَنْقَلِبُ إِلىٰ أَهْلِهِ **مَسْرُوراً**	**84-9** He will go back to his people rejoicing.
يَصْلَاهَا **مَذْمُوماً مَدْحُوراً**	**17-18** He will enter it (Hell) despised, driven away.

يَجِدُونه مكتوباً	**7-157** They find him mentioned.

Also a verbal noun may replace the active participle. e.g.

ولَّوا عَلىٰ أَدْبَارِهِمْ نُفُورا	**17-41** They turn their backs in avertion.
يَذْكُرونَ الله قِيامًا وقُعُودًا	**3-191** Those who remember Allah standing and sitting.
وعِبَادُ الرَّحمٰنِ الَّذينَ يَمْشُونَ على الأَرْضِ هَونًا	**25-63** And the servants of The Beneficient are they who walk on the earth in humility.

The verbal **Haal** occasionally refers not to any specific part of previous sentence (i.e. subject, object etc.) but to the whole statement, e.g.

أَوَلَمْ يَروا إلى ما خَلَقَ الله من شَيء يَتَفَيَّؤا ظِلالُه عن اليَمينِ والشَّمَائِلِ سُجَّداً للهِ وهم دَاخِرونَ	**16-48** Have they not observed all things that Allah hath created, how their shadows incline to the right and to the left, making prostration unto Allah, and they are lowly.
ولله يَسْجُدُ ما فى السَّمٰواتِ وَمَا فِى الأَرْض مِنْ دَابَّةٍ والمَلائِكَةُ وَهُمْ لا يَسْتَكْبِرون	**16-49** And unto Allah maketh prostration whatsoever is in the heavens and whatsoever is in the earth of living creatures, and the angels (also), and they are not proud.

يَخَافُونَ رَبَّهُم مِن فَوقِهِم وَيَفعَلُونَ مَا يُؤمَرُونَ	**16-50** They fear their Lord above them, and do what they are bidden.

2. **The specification** التمييز

It is expressed by an accusative and is resembling to Haal in having a finite verb but it is used to clarify what is less clear by the verb of the sentence. In English it may be translated sometimes by 'regard to' but is not true in all cases, e.g.

(طِبْ) نَفْساً be good in regard to soul (i.e. rejoice heartily).

In the Holy Qur'an:

لَنْ تَبْلُغَ الجِبَالَ طُولاً	**17-37** Nor canst thou reach the mountains in regard to height.

But most often it is used only to explain the verb as:

كَبُرَ مَقْتاً عِندَ اللهِ	**61-3** It is most hateful in the sight of Allah.
كَبُرَتْ كَلِمَةً تَخْرُجُ مِنْ أفواهِهِمْ	**18-5** Dreadful is the word that cometh out of their mouths.
لا تَمْلِكُ نَفسٌ لِنَفسٍ شَيئاً	**82-19** The day when no soul controls ought for another soul.
لا يُظْلَمون فتيلاً	**17-71** They will not be dealt with a whit unjustly.

يَدْخُلُونَ فِى دِينِ اللهِ أَفْوَاجا	**110-2** (and thou seest) men entering the religion of Allah in companies.

After كَمْ how much. how many. the noun will be singular accusative, e.g. كم أخا لَكَ ، وَكم أختا How many brothers you have and how many sisters. It (كَمْ) is also used to show that the object has a large number, in this case it is not used for questioning about the number and takes the following noun in genitive :

كَمْ مِن قَرْيَةٍ أهْلَكناها	**7-4** How many a township have we destroyed!
وَكَمْ قَصَمْنَا من قَرْيَةٍ	**21-11** How many a community that dealt unjustly have we shattered.

The Numarals take the following noun in 'tamiz'. Thus plurals of them are taken in genetive with idafa, e.g.

خَمْسَةُ كُتُبٍ five books, عَشَرَةُ أَقْلَامٍ ten pens.

The noun counted after numbers 13 to 99 are expressed in singular as accusative, e.g.

خَمْسَةَ عَشَرَ قلماً 15 pens تِسْعَةَ عَشَرَ كِتَاباً 19 books .

From hundred onwards the counted object (Tamiz) is treated as genetive singular, e.g. مائةُ حَبَّةٍ hundred pieces.

3. The Predicate of كان **and its sisters.**

e.g. from The Holy Qur'an :

كان مِزَاجُها كافوراً	**76-5** It was tempered with camphor.
كان شَرُّهُ مُسْتَطِيراً	**76-7** (A day) the evil of which is widespread.
ما كانَتْ أُمُّكِ بَغِيًّا	**19-28** Thy mother was not an unchaste woman.
كانَتِ امرَأَتى عاقِراً	**19-5** My wife is barren.
وَكانَ أمْرُ اللهِ مَفْعُولاً	**4-47** And the command of Allah is ever executed.
وكان الله غفوراً رَحِيماً	**4-96** And Allah is ever Forgiving, Merciful.

4. For the subject of إنَّ and its sisters, e.g. from The Holy Qur'an:

وَإِنَّ الدين لَوَاقِعٌ	**51-6** And the judgement will surely come to pass.
إنَّ الظَّنَّ لا يُغْنِى مِنَ الحق شيئاً	**10-36** Surely conjucture will not avail aught against the truth.
إِنَّ المُتَّقِينَ فى جنَّاتٍ ونهر	**54-54** Surely the God-fearers will be among garden and rivers.
لعلَّ الله يُحْدِثُ بَعْدَ ذلِكَ أمراً	**65-1** Allah may, after that, bring about an event.

كَأَنَّهُنَّ الياقوتُ والمَرْجَانُ	**55-58** As though they were rubies and pearls.
لَعَلَّهُ يَزَّكَّى	**80-3** He might purify himself.

5. In the construction of لا لنفى الجنس that is, after the لا which denies absolutely the class or species in the place or circumstances defined in the sentence. This accusative has no nonization, e.g. from The Holy Qur'an:

لا ريبَ فيه	**2-2** There is no doubt in it.
لا أصْغَرَ مِن ذلك ولا أكْبَرَ	**10-61** Nor anything less than that nor larger.
لا خلاق لهم فى الآخرة	**3-77** They have no portion in the Hereafter.

The negative ما is placed for the same purpose. They are termed as 'Negative Particles resembling in verb (ما و لا المشبه بليس) e.g. from The Holy Qur'an:

وَمَا هُمْ عَنها بغائبين	**82-16** And will not be absent form it.
وَمَا لهم من دونه من وَالٍ	**13-11** And besides Him they have no protection.
وَمَا أنتَ عليهم بجبَّار	**50-45** And there art not one to comple them.
وَمَا رَبُّكَ بِظَلَّامٍ لِلْعَبِيد	**41-46** And thy Lord is not in the least unjust to the servants.
ما هذا بَشَراً	**12-31** He is not a humanbeing.

6. When the Noun after the vocative particle حَرْفُ النِّداء is defined by a genitive, e.g.

يا عَبْدَ الله O' Abdullah. يا عَبْدَ الرحمان O' Abdur Rahman.

يا أميرَ المُؤمنين O' Calif of the believers.

7. Exception الإسْتِثْنَاء

The exception is expressed by the particle إِلَّا that generally takes the accusative in its following noun. A 'Sentence of an exception' has two parts, The Excepted and the Generality for example if we say: "The pilgrims came from all parts of the world apart from Muslims in occupied Palestin" "The Muslim of the world" is the generality, and 'Muslims in occupied palestine" is exeption.

كُلُّ شَىْءٍ هَالِكٌ إِلَّا وَجْهَهُ	**28-88** Every thing will perish save His countenance.

كل شَىْء هالِكٌ generality

إِلَّا Particle of exception

وَجْهَه excepted.

Most often the generality is not mentioned at all, e.g.

لا يَخْرُجُ إِلَّا نَكِدًا.	**7-58** Only evil cometh forth (from it)
ما يَعْلَمُ جُنُودَ رَبِّكَ إِلَّا هُوَ	**74-31** None noweth the hosts of thy Lord save Him.

The noun after إلَّا may occur in nominativ e

مَاتَعْبُدُونَ مِن دُونِهِ إلاَّ أسْماءً سَمَّيْتُمُوها	**12-40** Those whom ye worship besides him are but names which ye have named.
هَلْ جَزَاءُ الإحْسَانِ إلَّا الإحْسَانُ	**55-60** Is the reward of goodness aught save goodness.
ما يَعْلَمُهُم إلَّا قليلٌ	**18-22** None knoweth them save a few.
إنْ هُوَ إلَّا ذِكْرٌ لِلْعَالَمِينَ	**12-104** It is not else than a reminder unto the people.

8. For any adjective governing an accusative noun, or any noun in opposition to another accusative noun, e.g.

وَقُولُوا لَهُمْ قولاً مَعْرُوفاً	**4- 5** and speak kindly to them.
إنَّا أرسلناك شاهِداً ومُبَشِّراً	**33-45** (O' Prophet)Lo ! We have sent thee as a witness and a higher of good tidings.

9. In certain Exclamations the usual explanation being that there is a suppressed verb فعل محذوف e.g.

طُوبَىٰ لَهُمْ	**13-29** Joy is for them.
لا مَرْحَبا بِهِمْ	**38-59** no word of welcome for them.

The Genitive case has already been dealt with, in Chapters Three and Fourteen.

EXERCISE

1 Translate into Arabic :

I found Ahmad sleeping when I went to see him. Muslims were offering prayers in a straight row like a solid wall. They spent their nights reciting Holy Qur'an during the month of Ramadhan. He came back from the school in a jolly mood. He was caught by surpri se when saw the manner of sacrifice done by Muslims for the sake of their religion. It is most hateful in the sight of Allah to say much and do nothing. People entered in Islam in group after group. How much is the price of the book.

How many boys are in your class. So many townships .were destroyed by enemies. He got five books, ten pens, 15 pencils and one hundred pieces of paper sheets. His mother was a very noble lady and father was a minister of state but his companions were evil doers. Surely Islam is the rightest way of life.

Perhaps people may realize this fact in which there is no doubt.

Our Lord is not unjust to the human beings. All teachers have arrived except Mr. George. Indeed the reward of kindness is not but goodness.

2 Translate into English

بَيْنَمَا كَانَ الْخَلِيفَةُ عُمَرُ بْنُ الخَطَّابِ جالساً يَقْضِى بَيْنَ النَّاسِ وَكَانَ كِبَارُ الصَّحابَةِ جَالِسِينَ حولَه أقبلَ غلامٌ بَاكِياً صَائِحاً وَهُو يَقُولُ قُتِلَ وَالدى مَظْلُوماً ، قَتَله أحَدُ رُعاةِ الإبِلِ بِغَيْرِ الحَقِّ ، فَسَأَلَه سَيِّدُنا عُمَرُ كَيْفَ كَانَ ذٰلِكَ ، ومَنْ هُو القاتِل ؟ فقال الْغُلامُ إنِّى لاَ أعْرِفُ القَاتِلَ ، إنَّما وَجَدْتُ وَالدِى مَقْتولاً فِى بُسْتَانِهِ . وَبَيْنَمَا كانَ الغلامُ يَتَحَدَّثُ إلى الخَلِيفَةِ رَأى النَّاسُ فَتىً يَسْعىٰ إلى مَجْلس الْخَلِيفَةِ عُمَرَ ، وَالعَرَقُ يَتَصَبَّبُ مِن جَبِينِهِ فَقَالَ عُمَرُ مَا وَرَاءَك ؟ قالَ الفَتَى إنِّى ارْتَكَبْتُ جَرِيمَةً نكرَاءَ ، فَقَدْ قتلتُ شَيخاً كَان يحرسُ بُستَانه ، لأنَّهُ رَمىٰ ناقتى بحَجَر فَهَلَكَتْ ، فلَمْ أسْتَطِعْ الصَّبْرَ عَلَى هَلْكَةِ نَاقَتِى وَرَمَيْتُ بِالحَجَرِ إلى رأسِ الشَّيخ فأصْبَحَ جُثَّةً هَامِدَةً وجئتُ إليك لتُنَفِّذَ فِىَّ أمْرَ اللهِ وتُطَهِّرَنى مِنَ الإثْمِ فَإنِّى أخَافُ رَبِّى يَوماً عَسِيراً ، يَومَ لاَ يَنْفَعُ مَالٌ وَلاَ بَنُون إلَّا مَن أتى اللهَ بِقَلْبٍ سَلِيمٍ .

VOCABULARY

Sleeping	(يَنَامُ - نَامَ : verb) - نائِمًا
to offer	يُؤدِّى - أدَّى
straight	السَّوِىُّ
Row	الصَفُّ
solid	الْمُسْتَحْكَمُ (Passivepartx)
to recite	يَتلوا - تَلا
Jolly	فَرِحًا - مُنبَسِطًا
to get caught by surprise V	تَحَيَّرَ - يَتَحَيَّرُ
manner	الأسْلُوبُ - الطريقَةُ - الأدَبُ
sacrifice	التَضْحِيَةُ
hateful	مكْروه - بَغِيضٌ
How much- How many	كَمْ
Destroyed	يُخَرَّبُ - خَرَّبَ passive of II خُرِّبَ
Companion	صِحَابَةٌ صَحَابَة or أصْحَابٌ .PL صَاحِبٌ
unjust	ظَالِمٌ - غَيرَ عَادِلٍ

يَقضِي- قَضَى	to judge

أَقْبَلَ	came forward
غلام	a Lad
باكِيًا	Crying (from يَبْكِى - بَكَى to cry)
صائحًا	noising (from يَصِيحُ - صَاحَ to make noise)
رُعَاةً	Pl of راعِىٌ tender
الإبْل	camel
بِغَيْرِ الحَقِّ	without any legal right
فَتًى	a lad , a youth
يسعى	running (from يَسْعَى - سَعَى to run)
العَرَقُ	perspiration
يَتَصَبَّبُ	V/to perspire
مَجْلِسٌ	meeting place
مَا وَرَاءَكَ ؟	what do you want ? (Lit: What is behind you)
إرْتَكَبْتُ	VIII/I have comitted (a crime)
جَرِيمَةٌ	Crime
نكراء	very bad (lit. un usual)

يَحْرِس	protects (كان يحرس was protecting)
رَمٰى	he stoned (رَمٰى - يَرْمِى to throw)
نَاقَةٌ	She - camel
هُلِكَتْ	was killed (passive of هَلَكَ - يَهْلِكُ)
تُنَفِّذَ	to execute
فِيَّ	in me , on me
تُطَهِّر	to purify
عَسِير	tuff
يَنْفَعُ	profits (نَفَعَ - ينفع)

CHAPTER 26

CONDITIONAL SENTENCES

1. A conditional sentence is introduced by one of the following particles:

إِنْ if, e.g.

وَإِن تُبْدُوا مَا فِي أَنْفُسِكُمْ أَوْ تُخْفُوهُ يُحَاسِبْكُمْ بِهِ اللهُ	**2-284** And whether ye make known what is in your minds or hide it Allah will bring you to account for it.

مَنْ who, whom, whoever e.g.,

مَنْ يَعْمَلْ سُوءًا يُجْزَ بِهِ	**4-123** He who doeth wrong will have the recompense thereof.

مَهْمَا whatever, e.g.

وَقَالُوا : مَهْمَا تَأْتِنَا بِهِ مِنْ آيَةٍ لِتَسْحَرَنَا بِهَا فَمَا نَحْنُ لَكَ بِمُؤْمِنِينَ	**7-132** and they said: whatever portent thou bringest wherewith to bewitch us we shall not put faith in thee.

أَيٌّ which, whichsoever, e.g.

أَيًّا مَاتَدْعُوا . فَلَهُ الأَسْمَاءُ الحُسْنَىٰ	**17-110** unto which soever ye cry (it is the same) His are the most beautiful names.

لَو if. e.g.

وَلَو كُنْتُ أَعْلَمُ الغَيْبَ لَاسْتَكْثَرتُ مِنَ الخَيْر	**7-188** Had I knowledge there of unseen I should have much of good.

إذا when, e.g.

فَإذا ذَهَبَ الخوفُ سَلقوكم بألسِنَةٍ حِدَادٍ	**33-19** When the fear disparteth they scald you with sharp tongues.

لَئِن if, e.g.

لَئِن لَمْ يَفْعَلْ ما آمُرُه لَيُسْجَنَنَّ	**12-32** But if he do not what I bid him, he verily shall be imprisoned.
لَئِنْ شَكَرتُم لأَزِيدَنَّكُمْ	**14-7** If ye gives thanks. I will give you more

لَمَّا when, e.g.

وَلَمَّا دَخَلوا علىٰ يوسُفَ آوى إلَيْه أخاه	**12-69** And when they went in before Joseph. He took his brother into himself.

Some other conjunction followed by a negative particle لا as لولا "if not" or "had..... not", used for implied meaning, e.g.

وَلَوْلا إِذْ دَخَلْتَ جَنَّتَكَ قُلْتَ ما شاءَ اللهُ	**18-39** And wherefor didst thou not say, when thou entered the garden: It is as Allah pleased.
وَلَوْلا دَفْعُ اللهِ النّاسَ بعضَهُم بِبَعْضٍ لَفَسَدَتِ الأرضُ	**2-251** And were it not for Allah's repelling some men by others, the earth would be certainly in state of disorder.

Ther are some other conjunctions used in conditional sentences, though not occured in the Holy Qur'an but they are endorsed by Grammarians, for example:

متى whenever, e.g.

متىٰ تأتِهِ تَجِدْ عندَه خيراً	whenever you come to him will find what is good.

أيّان whenever

أيّان نؤمِنْكَ تأمَنْ غيرَنا	whenever we trust upon you, you will trust upon others than us.

2. A conditional sentence consists of two parts: شَرْط the condition (Protasis) and جَزَاءُ الشَّرْطِ or جَوابُ الشَّرطِ answer of the condition (i.e. Apodosis)

(a) In Arabic the condition, and its answer are used in a verbal sentences in Jussive, e.g.

وإن تَعُودُوا نَعُدْ	**8-19** If ye return we shall return.
إن يَثْقَفُوكم يَكُونوا لَكُم أعْداءً	**60-2** If they have upper hand of you they will be your foes.

(b) or in the perfect, with ف of conjunction prefixed to the verb of the "answer of the condition" (Apodosis), e.g.

فَإِذَا طَعِمْتُمْ فَانْتَشِرُوا	**33-53** When your meal is ended then disperse.
فَإِذَا فَرَغْتَ فَانْصَبْ	**94-7** So when thou art relieved, still toil.

(c) Without ف in the answer in case the perfect is used to indicate a habitual happening: e.g.,

فَإِذَا ذَهَبَ الخوفُ سَلَقوكُمْ بألسِنَةٍ حِدَادٍ	**33-19** When the fear disparteth they scald you with sharp tongue
وَإِذَا خَاطَبَهُمُ الجاهِلونَ قالوا سَلاماً	**25-63** and the foolish ones address them, answer: peace.

(d) The answer (Apodosis) of the لو may be introduced by the attached particle لَ to give stress on the nature of the sentence, e.g.

لَوْ شاءَ رَبُّكَ لَجَعَلَ الناسَ أُمَّةً واحِدَةً	**11-118** If thy Lord had wished, He would have made men one people.

لَوْ شَاءَ اللهُ لَأَعْنَتَكُمْ	**2-220** Had Allah willed He could have over-burdened you.

(e) The condition introduced by إِنْ may be used to express the impossibility of the condition, that is called in Arabic term as التَّعلِيقُ بِالمُحَالِ, 'to hang to the impossible', e.g.

قل إِنْ كَانَ للرَّحمٰنِ وَلَدٌ فَأنا أوَّلُ العَابِدِينَ	**43-81** Say (O' Mohammad), if the Beneficient hadeth a son I am the foremost worshippers.

Note: The Translaters of the Holy Qur'an took this إِنْ as a negative particle therefore, exact translation to them would be :

قُلْ إِنْ كَانَ لِلرَّحْمٰنِ وَلَدٌ فَأَنَا أَوَّلُ الْعَابِدِينَ	Say (O' Mohammad), The Beneficient one hath No son, I am first among the worshippers.

(f) إِن followed by إِلَّا is merely negative particle, e.g.

إن كُلُّ مَنْ فى السَّمٰوَاتِ والأرضِ إِلَّا آتِى الرَّحمٰنِ عَبْداً	**19-93** There is none in the heaven and the earth but cometh unto the Beneficient as a slave.

Sometimes without إِلَّا gives the same negative sense, e.g.

وإن أدرِى لَعَلَّهُ فِتْنَةٌ لكُم وَمتَاعٌ إلى حِين	**21-111** And I know Not if this may be a trial for you and a provision till a time.

EXERCISE

A. Translate into Arabic :

(1) If only (use لو أنّ) you had helped the Muslim soldiers they would not have fallen into the hands of that treacherous enemy.

(2) If you had seen what happened to the unbelievers who worshipped idols, you would have given up your false ideas and the teachings of the Holy Prophet (May peace and blessing be upon him) would have guided you to the right path.

(3) If you do the afternoon prayers earlier we can leave for Madina before sunset.

(4) When you open the door the sun comes in,

(5) If my friend had asked for a proof, I would have told him what was preached in th **Kh**utba on Friday.

(6) If what was on the table had not please him he takes what is in the cupboard also.

(7) If he acts (use عَمِلَ) according to the Islamic teachings he will gain the good rewards in this world and in the Hereafter.

(8) If you see a fire, call the fire brigade; they will come and put it out quickly.

(9) If he has faith in Allah he will not be afraid of the dangers.

(10) If you do not work hard you will certainly not succeed.

(11) Whatever (use مهما) the case may be the Muslims throughout the world will realize that their survival depends on their unity.

(12) If you do not find a boat on the river that is not my fault.

B. Translate into English :

لَو أَنَّكُم صَلَّيْتُمْ صلاةَ العَصْرِ مُبَكِّراً كانَ يُمكِنُنَا الخُرُوجُ قَبْلَ المَغْرِبِ ، لَو أَنَّكُم وافَقْتُمْ عَلَى المَشْرُوعِ قَبْل هٰذا العام لَكَانَتِ المَبَانى قَدِ اكْتَمَلَتْ حَتَى الآن ، إنِّى مُسَافِرٌ إلَى مَدِينَةِ الرَّسولِ صَلَّى اللهُ عَلَيه وسَلَّم بَعْدَ انْتِهَاءِ هٰذَا الأُسْبُوعِ ، إنْ كُنْتَ عاقِلاً عَمِلْتَ عَلَى نَصِيحَةِ وَالِدكَ وما ضَيَّعْتَ الفُرْصَةَ ،مَهْمَا كانَ بَلَدُكَ ولونَكَ أنتَ مسلمٌ وأخٌ لِكلِّ مسلمٍ ،لَو دَرَسْتَ الكُتُبَ الدِّينِيَّةَ لَعَرفْتَ أنَّ الإسْلَام دينٌ صَالِح لِكل زَمَانٍ وَمَكَان ، لَو قَرأتَ القرآنَ وحاوَلتَ أن تَفهَمْ مَعانِيَه لآمنتَ باللهِ ورسولِهِ لَئِن لَمْ تَفْعَل مَا أَمَركَ بِه دِينُكَ لَنْ تَجِدَ طريقَ الحَقِّ ، لو سَلَكْتَ طريقَ الهُدَى نِلْتَ الْخيرَ فِى الدُّنيا وَالآخِرَة .

VOCABULARY

حَرِيقٌ	Plural حرائق fire, conflagratron.
إنْطَفَأَ	VII / to get put out.
أَطْفَأَ	IV / to extinguish, put out.
فِرْقَةُ المَطافِئ	Fire brigade.
صَلَّىٰ	II / to pray.
صَنَم	Plural - أَصْنَام idol
عَبَدَ	to worship.
نَجَحَ	To succeed
الوَعْظُ	Preaching
الخُطْبَةُ	Lecture
دُولاب	Plural - دواليب Cupboard
وافَقَ	III / To approve
إكْتَمَلَ	To complete
تعالِيم	Teachings

Unbeliever	كُفَّارٌ Sing. كافِرٌ
Earlier	مُبكِّرًا

Sun	شَمْسٌ
Proof	الدَّلِيل
According to	وِفْقاً لـ
The Hereafter	الآخِرة
To be afraid	خاف (خاف – يَخَافُ)
Survival	البقَاء (بَقِي – يَبْقَى)
Unity	الوحْدَةُ
Fault	الخَطَأُ
Throughout the world. العالَمَ بأجْمَعِهِ	

CHAPTER 27

THE NOUN - DISTINCTION AND PATTERNS

1. Distinction

The Noun is distinguished from that of verbs and particles by :

I It can be modified by vowels and governed by preceeding elements, e.g. (Nom) ذلك الكتابُ This book, (Acc) قَرأتُ الكتابَ I read the book, (ejer) وَجَدْتُ فى الكتابِ I found in the book.

II Its gender can be changed from singular to dual and plurals, e.g.

	sing	Dual	Plu
(Nom)	كتابٌ	كتَابَانِ	كُتُبٌ
(Acc an gen)		كتَابَيْنِ	

III It accepts أل of the definite article, e.g. كتابٌ Kitaabun الكِتَابُ alkitaabu.

2. Patterns

There are three main patterns of a noun:

I. Simple nouns.

II. The nouns derived from verbs or from other nouns.

III. The verbal nouns.

I. Simple nouns are formed by the root-form of a word by slight changes in the vowelling, e.g. دارٌ house, أُذُنٌ ear, عينٌ eye, أرضٌ earth, سَمَاءٌ heaven, جَنَّةٌ garden نارٌ fire . etc. . .

II-A. Derived nouns from the verbs are formed by vowels infixed and letters prefixed or by both, e.g.:

(a) a long vowel infixed after the first radical to form a pattern for an active participle as:

عامِلٌ doer from عَمَلٌ to do
عَالِمٌ learned (one) from عِلْمٌ to know
شَاعِرٌ poet from شَعَرٌ to feel.

(b) a long vowel infixed after the second radical forms a pattern, denotes the meaning of a passive participle from a root which has no measure of فاعِلٌ for act. Part. as وَزِيرٌ from وَزَرَ to support because وازر waazir is not heard.

- or though the pattern of فاعِلٌ is found but used in a different meaning as شاهِدٌ observer but شَهِيدٌ martyer.

- or describes an adjective possessed by someone as a natural feature, i.e. not gained by himself as beautiful, جميلٌ ugly. قَبِيْحٌ

- or derived from the roots of which the third person

singular, perfect has damma in its second radical as كَرُمَ - شَرُفَ - عَظُمَ thus the act. participle is كريمٌ - شَرِيفٌ - عَظِيمٌ respectively, the plural is usually of the measure فَعْلَى and فِعَالٌ e.g. جَرِيحٌ plural جَرْحى wounded, from جُرْحٌ قَتِيلٌ murdered, plural قَتْلَى from قَتْلٌ مريضٌ plural مرضى from مَرَضٌ

Examples from The Holy Qur'an:

عَلِمَ أَنْ سَيَكُونُ مِنْكُمْ مَرْضَى	**73-20** He knoweth that there are sick folk among you.

and كِرَامٌ pl. of كَرِيمٌ ، عِظَامٌ pl. of عَظِيمٌ e.g. كِرَامٍ بَرَرَةٍ nables poius nes.

(c) Pattern for the passive participle is formed by prefixing a 'mim' and infixing a long (و) vowel after the second radical, e.g. مَفْعُولٌ done from فعل to do
مَقْبُولٌ accepted from قَبِلَ to accept.

(d) Patterns denoting place and times إسمُ الزَّمانِ والمكان The noun of Place and Times expresses the place where the action of a verb is committed, as the time or occassion of that verb. Such nouns are measured on pattern.

مَفْعَلٌ Maf ع alun or مَفْعِلٌ maf ع ilun

Examples from The Holy Qur'an:

مَشْرِقٌ East from شَرَقَ to rise.

مغربٌ West from غربَ to set

وللهِ الْمَشْرِقُ والْمَغْرِبُ	**2-115** For Allah is the East and the West.

مَسْجِدٌ Mosque from سجد

شَطْرَ الْمسْجِدِ الْحَرامِ	**2-144** Towards the Sacred Mosque.

مرعى Pasture from رعى to tend cattles

وَالَّذِى أخْرَجَ الْمَرَعى	**87-4** And who brought forth herbage

مَلْجَأً Refuge from لُجُوءٌ to take refuge

لا مَلْجَأَ مِنَ اللهِ إِلَّا إِلَيه	**9-118** There was no refuge from Allah but in Him.

ماوى abode from أولى إلى to resort to

فإن الْجَنَّةَ هى الْمَأوَى	**79-41** The garden is surely the abode.

مَوْعِدٌ The place or the of meeting from وَعْدٌ to promise

إنَّ مَوْعِدَهُم الصُّبْح	**11-81** Their appointed time is the morning.

Note: Words on this and all above given patterns are frequently used in the Holy Qur'an.

(e) Patterns expressing names of instruments اسم الآلة are formed by prefixing a 'mim' and infixing a long (الف) vowel after the second radical on the measure:

مِفْعَلَةٌ mif ع alatun as مِرْوَحَةٌ mirwahatun, (Fan) from رَوْحٌ to blow.

مِفْعَلٌ mif ع alun as مِبْرَدٌ mibradun (a file) from برد to file

مفعالٌ mif ع aalun as مفتاحٌ miftaahun (key) from فَتْحٌ to open.

Examples from The Holy Qur'an:

مِفْعَلَةٌ مِنْسَأَةٌ from نَسَأَ to make late

تَأْكُلُ مِنْسَأَتَه	**34-14** Eats his stuff.

مِفْعالٌ = مِثْقَالٌ from ثقل heavy , to weight

مِثْقَالَ ذَرَّةٍ	**99-7** atom's weight.

مِفْعَالٌ = مِيزانٌ from وَزَنَ to weigh.

وَوَضَعَ الْمِيزَانَ	**55- 7** and He hath set the measure

مفتاح Plural مفاتيح from فتح to open

وعِنْدَه مَفَاتِحُ الغَيْبِ	6 - 59 and with Him are the keys of the invisible.

II-B. Derived nouns from the nouns as حَمِيَّةٌ zealotry from الحمى enthusiasm , جاهِلِيَّةٌ age of ignorance from الجَهْلُ ignorance.

Both of these two words occured in one verse of the Holy Qur'an :

إذْ جَعَلَ الَّذِينَ كَفَرُوا فى قُلُوبِهِمُ الْحَمِيَّةَ حَمِيَّةَ الْجَاهِلِيَّةِ	48 - 26 When those who disbelieve had set up in their hearts zealotry , zealotry of the age of ignorance.

EXERCISE

1. Name the patterns of the following words:

يَدٌ ، أَنْمُلَةٌ ، رَأسٌ ، مِرْجَلٌ ، أَرْجُلٌ ، مَسَانِدُ ، مِقْبَضَةٌ، منْقَلَةٌ،
مِرْصَادٌ ، الوطنيةُ ، مجوسٌ ، راضيَةٌ ، مَنْظورَةٌ .

2. **Translate into Arabic :**

Muslims say their prayers inside the mosques , sometimes they offer prayers in their home , in fields , trains and everywhere because Allah is every where. The East and the West belong to Him.

The appointed time for all of us is the day of judgement.

Mecca is a meeting place for Muslims from every country.

Allah is only God who created blacks , whites , reds and people of all colours. Every human being has an equal right of living.

Arabic is the key to the treasures of knowledge. Muslims love their homeland and offer all kind of sacrifices for their land but , however , they do not worship it. Non-Muslims have a very distorted conception of Islamic Religion. Islam commands you : think only of what is good for all humanbeing , consider not the wrong that has been done to you , pardon others and do good to all.

3. Translate into English :

أمر المغفورُ لهُ جَلالَةُ الْـمَلِكِ عَبْدُ الْعَزيز بتَوسِعَةِ **المَسْجِدِ** النّبوى الشَّريفِ وَكانَ هٰذا الأَمْرُ نُقْطَةَ البَدْءِ فى التّنْفيذِ الفِعْلى . وَقَد تَضَافَرتِ القُوى عَلى إنجازِ المَشْروعِ العَظيمِ بأَسرَعِ مَا يُمْكِنُ ، وَلم تَمْضِ **إلا سَنَواتٌ** قَليلَةٌ حَتّى اسْتَوى البِنَاءُ قائِمًا ، يَبْهرُ **الأَنْظارَ** وَيسُرُّ القُلُوبَ بمَا احْتَوى مِنْ آياتِ الفَنِّ وَالجَلالِ ، **مِمَّا** يَليقُ بقُدْسيَّةِ المَسْجِدِ النَّبوى الشَريفِ ، وَمَكانتهِ السَّامِيَةِ فى قُلُوبِ الْمُسلِمينَ ، وَفى حَفْلٍ **عَظيمٍ** حَضَرتْهُ **وفُودٌ** شَتّى مِنَ جَميعِ أنحاءِ العَالَمِ الإسلامى افتَتَحَ جَلالَةُ المَلِكُ التَّوسِعَةَ الحَديثَةَ بيْنَ التَّهليلِ وَالتَّكْبيرِ .

VOCABULARY

To say prayer أدّى الصَّلاةَ	impef Perf. يؤدّى أدّى تأديةٌ
Inside the Mosque	داخِل المسجد
Everywhere	كُلَّ مكان
Appointed time	الموعد
The day of Judgement	يومَ الدين
Creater	الخَالِق
Sacrifice	التضحية ضحّى ـ يُضَحّى التَّضحية

distorted	البَتْر بَتَر – يبتر للبتُور
conception	النَّظرِيَّة
command	الأمْر
wrong	الظُّلم

مِئذنة	The minaret from which call to the prayers is made. Plural مآذن
مِدخَنَةٌ	Chimney
مَعمَلٌ	Factory
مَصْدَرٌ	Source
النداء	Calls from نَادى ، يُنادى ، النداء
الصُّفُوف . الفُصُول	Classes
الشَّرُّ	The Evil
كُلٌّ	All
السّهل	Easy
المُلْتَبَس	Confused
المجهول	Unknown
الحفظ	to keep
التقوية	to strengthen

المَغْفور له	forgived one
جَلالة الملك	his Majesty
توسِعة	Extension
نُقطة	Point
البَدْء	Commencing
التنفيذ	Executing
الفِعْلى	Practical
تَضَافَرتْ ، تَضافر ، يتَضَافَرُ	got together
المَشْرُوع	Project , Plan.
أسْرَعَ ما يُمكن	As soon as possible
سَنَواتٍ	Years
استوى	stood (constructed)
يَبْهَر	To wander
الأنظارَ	sights
يَسرُّ	to make happy
إحتوى	contains
آيات	signs. Pl of آيَةٌ
الفنَّى	The artistic

وُفُود	deligates.
شَتَّى	different
أَنْحاء	corners
إفْتَتَحَ	inaugurated
الجَلَال	Mighty

CHAPTER 28

THE VERBAL NOUN

1. The Arabic root-form is called " مَصْدَر source" that can be seen most clearly in the third person masculine of the perfect of a simple verb. Whereas the root-form or مَصْدَر not infrequently includes a letter of increase. For example دُخُول is a 'Masdar' as دَخَلَ to enter but the latter is used to be the first entry in an Arabic dictionary while the former is seemed to be a derived form from دَخَلَ
Therefore, Grammarians differentiate between مَصْدَر that expresses the verbal idea and إِسْمُ الْمَصْدَر verbal noun which always stands as a noun

2. The verbal forms are not governed by a certain rule, as all of them are "سَمَاعِى heard ones" According to **Seebawaih** and **Suyuti** there are 30 permanent measures for the verbal nouns. Most of them are frequently used in the Holy Qur'an. Here Only one example from each measure is being mentioned:

Verbal Nouns

فَعْلٌ : قَتْلٌ　　فَطَوَّعَتْ لَه نَفْسُه قَتْلَ أخيه	5-30 His mind made it easy for him killing his brother.

شِرْكٌ : فِعْلٌ	إنَّ الشِّرْكَ لَظُلْمٌ عظيم	31-13 Surely scribing partners to Him is a grivous inquity.
غُلْفٌ : فُعْلٌ	وقالوا قُلُوبُنَا غُلْفٌ	2-88 They said : our hearts are repositories.
كَبَدٌ : فَعَلٌ	لَقَدْ خَلَقْنا الإنسانَ في كَبَدٍ	90-4 We have certainly created man to face difficulties.
فَرِحٌ : فَعِلٌ	إنه لَفَرِحٌ فَخُورٌ	11-10 He is exultant boastful.
كُبَرٌ : فُعَلٌ	إنها لَإحْدى الكُبَرِ	74-35 Surely it is one of the gravest (misfortune).
قُبُلٌ : فُعُلٌ	إن كان قَمِيصُهُ قُدَّ مِنْ قُبُلٍ	12-26 If his shirt is rent in front.
رَحْمَةٌ : فَعْلَةٌ	ذِكْرُ رَحْمَةِ رَبِّكَ	19-2 A mention of the mercy of thy Lord.
قِسْمَةٌ : فِعْلَةٌ	تِلْكَ إذاً قِسْمَةٌ ضِيزَى	53-22 This indeed is an unjust division.
عُدْوَةٌ : فُعْلَةٌ	إذ أنتُمْ بِالعُدْوَةِ الدُّنيا	8-42 When you were in the nearer side (of the valley)
صَدَقَةٌ : فَعَلَةٌ	فَفِدْيَةٌ مِنْ صِيامٍ أو صَدَقَةٍ	2-196 so a compensation by fasting or alms.
كَلِمَةٌ : فَعِلَةٌ	وتَمَّتْ كَلِمَةُ رَبِّكَ	6-115 And the word of thy Lord has been accomplished.
ذِكْرى : فِعْلَى	إن هُوَ إلا ذِكْرَى	6-90 It is not but a **reminder.**

فَمَا زَالَتْ تِلْكَ دَعْوَاهُم دَعْوَى : فَعْلَى	**21-15** And this cry of theirs ceased not.
يَا بُشْرَىٰ ! هٰذَا غُلَامٌ بُشْرَىٰ : فُعْلَى	**12-19** O' good news! This is a youth.
غَضْبَانَ أَسِفًا غَضْبَان : فَعْلَان	**7-150** Wrathful, grieved.
غُفْرَانَكَ رَبَّنَا غُفْرَان : فُعْلَان	**2-285** Thy forgiveness our Lord!
وَالفُسُوقَ وَالعِصْيَانَ عِصْيَان : فِعْلَان	**49-7** and transgression and disobedience.
وَإِنَّا عَلَى ذَهَابٍ بِهِ لَقَادِرُونَ ذَهَابٌ : فَعَالٌ	**23-18** and we are indeed able to **carry it away.**
وَهُوَ أَلَدُّ الخِصَامِ خِصَامٌ : فِعَالٌ	**2-204** and he is the most violent **of adverseries.**
ظَلَمَكَ بِسُؤَالِ نَعْجَتِكَ سُؤَال : فُعَال	**38-24** Surely he has wronged thee in **demanding** thy ewe.
بَرَاءَةٌ مِنَ اللهِ بَرَاءَةٌ : فَعَالَةٌ	**9-1** A declaration of **immunity** from Allah.
أَجَعَلْتُم سِقَايَةَ الحَاجِّ سِقَايَةٌ : فِعَالَةٌ	**9-19** Do you hold the **giving of water** to the pilgrims.
وَقَبْلَ الغُرُوبِ غُرُوبٌ : فُعُولٌ	**50-39** And before the setting
فَتَقَبَّلَهَا رَبُّهَا بِقَبُولٍ حَسَنٍ قَبُولٌ : فَعُولٌ	**3-37** so her Lord accepted her with a goodly acceptance.

لَقَد جِئْتِ شَيْئًا فَرِيًا　فَرِيٌّ : فَعِيلٌ	19-27 O' Mary thou has indeed brought a strange thing.
حَمُولَةً وَفَرْشًا　حمولَةٌ : فَعُولَةٌ	6-142 And of the cattle (He has created) some for burden some for slaughter.

3. The verbal noun on measure of فَعَلان denotes meaning of something continously flowing and moving without stop as جَرَيان to flow the water. سَرَيانٌ to infitate - but not used in The Holy Book.

4. There is a kind of مصدر called المَصْدَر الميمى in which a 'mim' (م) is prefixed. Its measure is same as مَفْعِل ، مَفْعَل of the إسمُ الزَّمانِ والمكان also مُفْعَل . Few Examples from The Holy Qur'an are as following:

رَبِّ أَدْخِلْنِى مُدْخَلَ صِدْقٍ　مُدْخَل : مُفعَل	17-80 My Lord! make me enter a truthful entering.
وَأَخْرِجْنِى مُخْرَجَ صِدْقٍ　مُخْرَجَ	17-80 and make me go forth a truthful going.
حَسُنَتْ مُسْتَقَرًا وَمُقَامًا　مُقَام	25-76 Goodly is the abode and the rest.

5. Another measure of the verbal nour فِعْلَةٌ is used to express the kind or type of an act. e.g. يَمشى مِشْيَةَ الجُنْدى He walks like a soldier (like the walking of the soldier).

6. There is a measure فَعْلَةٌ among the measures of the verbal noun called اسم المَرَّةِ to specify the number of time to act is committed. e.g.

قَبَضْتُ قَبْضَةً مِنْ أَثَرِ الرَّسُولِ	20-96 I took a handful from the footprints of the Messenger.

The measure فَعْلَةٌ as قَبْضَةٌ is used for the single act and it takes the dual قبضتانِ the sound feminine plurals as قَبَضَاتٍ.

7. **The Diminitive** اسم التصغير is formed from a noun of three consonants according to the measures. فعيلٌ as فُلَيْسٌ from فَلْسٌ money.

From a noun that has more than three consonants, four or five the measures of the diminitive would be

فُعَيْعِلٌ as دُرَيْهِم from درهم

فُعَيْعِيل as عُصَيْفِير from عصفورة

8. **The Comparative and Superlative of adjectives** اسم التفضيل, is formed from the three radicals and its measure is same as that of colours and defects. Thus from حبيبٌ beloved, is formed أَحَبُّ more beloved, dearer. From كبير great is formed أكبر greater . e.g

وَإِثْمُهُمَا أَكْبَرُ مِن نَفْعِهِمَا	2-219 and their sin is **greater** than their advantage.

The feminine of أفْعَل as أكبر is فُعلى as كبرى but the form أفعل is used for feminine comparative adjective, e.g.

إِلَّا هِيَ أَكْبَرُ من أختها	43-48 But she is greater than her sisters.

Though أَفْعَل has a dual and plural forms: أفعلان as أكبران and أفاعل as أكابر but, also the feminine form فُعْلَى as كُبْرَى has its plural form فعليات as كُبْرَيَات but only أفعل is used in all cases. e.g for dual:

إِذْ قَالُوا لَيُوسُفُ وأخوه **أَحَبُّ** إلى أَبِينَا مِنَّا	**12-8** When they said: certainly Yusuf (Joseph) and his **brother** are dearer. to our father.

Students may note the form أحب singular has been used instead of أحَبَّانِ of dual.

For Plural:

قل : إنْ كانَ آبَاؤُكُم وَأَبْنَاؤُكُم وَإِخوَانُكُم وَأَزْوَاجُكُمْ وَعَشِيرَتُكُمْ وَأموالٌ اقْتَرفْتُمُوهَا وَتِجارَةٌ تَخشَوْنَ كَسَادَهَا ومَسَاكِنُ تَرضَونَها **أَحَبَّ** إِلَيكُم مِنَ اللهِ وَرَسُولِهِ	**9-24** If your father and your sons, and your brothers and your wives and your kinsfolk and the wealth you have acquired and trades whose dullness you fear and dwelling you love are **dearer** for you **than** Allah and His Messenger.

But if this type of noun is used in the meaning of Elative the gender and the number will be preserved accordingly, e.g. الله أكبر Allah is great.

يومَ نَبْطِشُ البَطْشَةَ الكُبْرى	**44-16** On the day when We seize (them) with the most violent seizing.

وَكَذٰلِكَ جَعَلْنَا فِى كُلِّ قَرْيَةٍ أَكَابِرَ مُجْرِمِيهَا	**6-123** And thus have We made in every town the greaters of its guilty.

The comparative and superlative measure is derived from three radicals. Thus from كبير is formed أكبر from صَغير is formed أصغر In case of participles of the derived forms. words with more than three consonants, and words of the pattern أفعل the comparative is formed either by أكثر or أشدُّ followed by a noun in the accusative (a verbal noun, as a rule), e.g. أبيض white; أشَدُّ بَيَاضاً whiter, e.g.

والَّذين آمنوا **أشَدُّ** **حُبًّا** لله	**2-165** And those who believe are stronger in (their) love for Allah.
أنا **أكثرُ** مِنْكَ مالاً **وَأعَزُّ** نَفَرًا	**18-34** I have **greater** Wealth than thou, and am **mighter** in followers

EXERCISE

A. Translate into Arabic:

In all systems of education, Language is the medium containing the culture as well as the store - house of knowledge. But as far as Islamic culture is concerned, the Arabic Language stands for more than that since it is the medium of the Qur'an which is the source of Islamic culture, its spirit as well as the core of Islamic science, injunctions Lawas, Laws, principles and ethics. It is, therefore, impossible to speak of Islam, its culture and science separately and away from the Arabic Language. This does not mean that Islam has imposed one language on all Muslims since difference of language and speech is a universal law of human nature.

But this does not mean that the language of the Quran is the language of knowledge for all those who believe in the religion of Islam. Every Muslim knows this fact whatever his race, nationality and dialect among Muslims does not prevent the language of the Quran from being the first and the foremost of the Islamic languages. ∘

∘ Dr. Tawifiq Mohammad alshai - " The Arabic Language and Islamic Education ", a paper submitted to First World Congress on Muslim Education.

B. Translate into English:

طَلَعْتُ جَبَلَ النور وَوَقَفتُ عَلى غارِ حِراء وقلتُ لنفسى : هُنا أكْرَمَ اللهُ بالرِّسالة محمداً صلى الله عليه وسلم ونزل عليه الوَحْيُ الأوَلُ . فمِنْ هنا طلعت الشمس التى أفاضَتْ على العالَم نوراً جديدا وما أكْثَرَ ما استَقْبَلَ العالَمُ صَباحاً لا جِدةَ فيه ولا طَرافَةَ ولا خيرَ فيه ولا سَعَادة . وما أكْثَرَ ما استَقْبَلَ العالَمِ صباحًا استيقظ فيه الإنسانُ ولم تَستَيقِظِ الإنسانيةُ وَاستَيْقَظتْ فيه الأجْسَامُ وَلَم تَستَيْقِظ فيه القلوب والأرْواحُ ، وما أكثَرَ النَهار المُظْلمُ والصبح الكاذِبُ فى تاريخ العالم ،ولكن من هنا طلع الصُبحُ الصادقِ الَذى أشْرَق نُوره عَلَى كلٍّ شيء وَاستَيْقَظَ فيه الكونُ وتَغَيَّر مَجْرى التاريخ .*

VOCABULARY

System	مَنْهَجْ Plural مَنَاهج
Education	التَّعليم (V) (N) II
Medium	واسطة Plural وَسَائط
Culture	الحضارة Plural الحضَارات
Store-House	المَخْزَن Plural المَخَازِن
Stand for	يقوم لِـ
Sprit	رُوحٌ Plural أرْوَاح

- Prof. Sayyid Abal Hasan Ali Nadwi الطريق إلى المدنية P. P 48. Dar el qalam Cairo 1974.

Core	لبٌّ Plural ألْبَاب
Injunction	الإرْشاد IV
Principles	المَبادِئ Plural of المَبدأ
Impossible	مُسْتَحِيل Act. Part. X
Ethics (Adj. N.)	الآداب Plural of الأدَب
Separately	مُنْفَصِلاً Act. Part انفصل VII (Use in accusative)
Impose	فرَض ـ على
Since	لِمَا؛ منذ ـ مَا دَام (use any suitable particle)
Universal	العالمي
Nature	الطبيعة
Race	النَّسْلُ
Nationality	الجِنْسية - الوطنية
Dialect	اللَّهْجَة
Prevent	منَعَ ـ يمنع
Foremost	قبل كل شئ ـ أهم شئ

طَلَعْتُ	1 st Pers. Sing Perf. طلع – يَطْلع to climb. to accend
وَقَفْتُ	1st pers. Sing. Perf. وَقَفَ – يَقِفُ to stop. to stand
غار	cave
اكْرَمَ	3rd Pers. Sing. IV. to give honour.
الرِّسالَةُ	Prophethood (Lit. communication)
نَزَلَ	come down
الوَحْي	revelation
طَلَعَتْ	3rd Pers. Sing. Fem. Perf. Arose.
أَفَاضَتْ	3rd Pers. Sing. Fem. Perf. Bestowed.
يستَقْبل	3rd Pers. Imperfect. Sing. Masc. Receives
ما أكثرما ...	So Many times
جِدَّة	Newlyness
طَرَافة	Uniqueness
اسْتَيقَظَ	3rd Pers. Sing. Masc. X. awoke up
الأَجْسَام	bodies, plural of body
النَّهارُ	day

الْمُظْلِمْ	dark (Act. Part. IV)
الكَاذِبْ	liar
الصَّادِقُ	The true
أشْرَقَ	delighted IV
الكَوْن	universe
تَغَيَّر	changed V
مَجَرَى	current

CHAPTER 29

CONJUNCTION & INTROJECTION

1. The Particles used as conjunctions are:

(a) و Waw, "and" - to link a sentence to anohter one or a noun to another noun, e.g. (From Holy Qur'an):

وَإِذْ يَرْفَعُ إبراهيمُ القواعِدَ من الْبَيتِ وَإسْمَاعِيلُ	**2-127 And** when Ibrahim (Abraham) **and** Ismayil (Ishmel) Raised the foundation of The House.
إذا زُلْزِلَتِ الأرْضُ زِلْزَالَها وَأَخْرَجَتِ الأرضُ أثقالَهَا وقَال الإنسانُ مالَها ؟	**99-1/3** When the earth is shaken with her shaking **and** earth brings forth her burdens **and** man says: what has befallen her?

و between two sentences, of which the second is a Nominal Sentence, often means "while", that forms a sentence of Haal, and this و is called واو الحَال e.g.

ودخل جنّتَهُ وَهُوَ ظالِمٌ لنَفْسِهِ	**18-35** And he went into his garden **while** he was unjust to himself.

أَأَلِدُ وَأَنَا عَجُوزٌ	11-72 Shall I bear a child **while** I am an old woman?

The و is usually dropped when a verbal Haal Sentence follows:

وجَاءَ مِنْ أَقْصَا المَدِينَةِ رَجُلٌ يَسْعَى	**36-20** And from the remote part of the city there came a man **running.**

(b) ف "fa, then" expresses sequence as well as it joins the sentences e.g.

فَتَلَقَّى آدَمُ من ربه كلمات فَتَابَ عَلَيهِ	**2-37** And Adam received words from his Lord and He turned to him.
الَّذِى خَلَقَ فَسَوَّى ، والَّذِى قَدَّرَ فَهدَى والَّذِى أَخْرَجَ الْمَرْعَى فَجَعَلَه غُثَاءً أَحْوَى .	**87-2/5** Who created **then** made complete and Who measured **then** guided and who brought forth herbage **then** made it dried up dust-coloured.

(c) أَوْ ow, "or" for one of two or more than two things; to express doubt or give choice of one among few mentioned deeds. e.g.

لَبِثْنَا يَوْماً أَوْ بَعْضَ يَوْمٍ	**23-113** We tarried a day **or** part of day

فكفَّارتُه إطعامُ عَشَرَةِ مَسَاكِينَ - مِنْ أَوْسَطِ ما تُطْعِمُونَ أَهْلِيكُمْ - أو كِسْوَتُهُمأو تَحرِيرُ رَقَبَةٍ	**5-89** So its expiation is the feeding of ten poor men (with average (food) you feed your families with) or their clothings, or the freeing of a neek.

(d) " أَمْ ءam, whether" for determination of one among few objects. In this case a Hamza (ء) is put before one of two equivalents, e.g.

أَأَنْذَرْتَهُمْ **أَمْ** لَمْ تُنْذِرْهُمْ	**2-6** Alike to them whether thou warn them or warn them not.

(e) " إِذْ since, when, after, because" is used with Nominal or verbal sentences such as:

إِذْ يَرْفَعُ إبراهيمُ القواعِدَ	**2-127 When** Ibrahim used to raise the foundation.
إِذْ قال رَبُّكَ لِلْمَلائِكَةِ	**2-30** (Remember) when thy Lord said to the angels....

(f) " إِذا when, if", originally used of times

وَ**إِذَا** قِيلَ لَهُم آمِنوا ..	**2-13** and when it is said to them believe!
وَإِذَا لَقُوا الَّذِينَ آمَنُوا قَالُوا : آمَنَّا	**2-14** And when met those who believe they said we believe.

The difference between إذ and إذا is that the former refers to something happened in past while the latter indicates to a time related to the present or future, thus a sentence such as " إِذْ قَالَ رَبُّكَ.. when thy Lord said" reminds a happening of past; but " إِذا جَاءَ نَصْرُ اللهِ when Allah's help has come"(has appeared) denotes the then situation of the Islamic call and response of people, and the sentence " إِذا زُلْزِلَتِ الأَرْضُ زِلْزَالَها when the earth is shaken its shaking" informs about a situation relating to the future.

(g) ثُمَّ **thumma** · after that, then, thereupon", e.g.

وَلَقَدْ خَلَقْنَاكُمْ ثُمَّ صَوَّرْنَاكُمْ ، ثُمَّ قُلْنَا لِلْمَلائِكَةِ ..	**7-11** And We indeed created you then We fashioned you, then We said to the Angels....

(h) " حَتَّى hatta, until, even, up to" to indicate the termination of an object, e.g. أَكَلْتُ السَّمَكَةَ حَتَى رَأْسَها I have eaten the fish up to its head (or even its head).

Example from The Holy Qur'an:

حَتَّى مَطْلَعِ الفَجْرِ	**97-5** It is till the rising of the morning.

(i) " لٰكِنْ and لٰكِنَّ laakin and Laakinna, "but" the former being followed by a verb, the latter by a noun in the accusative, or pronominal suffixes:

لكِنَّكُم ، لكِنِّي ، لكنَّها ، لكنه etc.

Examples from The Holy Qur'an:

ما كان مُحَمَّدٌ أبا أحَدٍ مِن رِجالِكم ولكن رَسولَ اللهِ وخاتَمَ النَّبيينَ	**33-40** Muhammad is not the father of any man among you, **but** he is the messenger of Allah and the last one among the prophets.
فلم تَقتُلوهُم وَلَكِنَّ الله قَتَلَهُم وما رميتَ – إذ رميتَ – وَلَكِنَّ الله رَمى	**8-17** Ye (Muslims) Slew them not, but Allah slew them. And (O' Mohammad) thou threwest not when thou dist throw but Allah threw.

(j) " إمّا imma, either", followed by أو or (إنمّا) self, e.g.

فإمّا منًّا بَعْدُ وإمّا فِداءً	**47-4** and afterwards either grace or ransom.

(k) " أمّا amma, "as for", with a following Nominative, the predicate always being strengthened with a ف e.g.

أمّا السَّفينَةُ فَكانَتْ لِمَساكِينَ	**18-79** As for the ship it belonged to poor people.
وَأمّا الغُلامُ فكان أبَواه مُؤمِنَيْنِ	**18-80** and as for the lad, his parents were believers.

These particles إمّا and أمّا are not endorsed by authentic grammarians like **Ibn ع Aquil** and **Ibn Hisham al Ansari,** among conjunction particles.

2. **Interjection حُرُوفُ النِّدَاء**

It is expressed by the particle يا followed by a noun in the Nominative without article and without Nunation in the singular, e.g. يا وَلَدُ ، يا فلانُ . يا الله etc.

If the person addressed is absent or the noun is determined by some word or words after it, then the noun is put in the accusative, e.g. يا غافِلاً O' careless, يا داعياً إلى الخير O' caller to the good....

Likewise in case of Idafa (Possessative case) the mudaaf (the possessed one) will be put in the Accusative:

يا عَبْدَ اللهِ O' Abdullah, يا أميرَ المؤمنين O'chief of Believers.

Sometimes pronominals are omitted and replaced by a Kasra showing the omission or a تِ to denote emotional feelings towards the addressed one, e.g.

يا رَبِّ O' my Lord - Note: ى of 1st person is ommitted.

يا أبتِ O' my father - here a ت is replacing the ommitted ى e.g.

يا أبتِ افْعَلْ مَا تُؤمَرُ	**37-102** O' my father do as thou art commanded.

(a) Often the vocative يا is omitted along with the pronoun; only a kasra which replaces ى indicates at the type of phrase, e.g.

قال : رَبِّ إنِّي دَعوتُ قومي	**71-5** He said O'my Lord! I have called my people.

(b) أيُّها and يا أيُّها are followed by the noun in the Nominative with the article, When addressing a gathering أيُّها is used as أيُّها الإخوة O' brothern! otherwise most often it will be preceded by يا to become يا أيُّهَا e.g.

يا أيُّهَا الناس	O' people
يا أيُّها الكافِرون	O' disbelievers.

(c) To express feelings or affections towards someone or something يا followed by a verbal noun or a nominal sentence is used, e.g.

يا بُشْرَى هٰذا غلامٌ	**12-19** Good luck! here is a youth.
يا أسفَى على يوسف	**12-84** Alas, my grief for Yusuf (Joseph)

Sometimes an alif replaces the 1st person pronoun (ى) to denote deep sorrow, e.g. واأسَفَا O' sorrow! واحَسْرَتا O' grief!

(d) To express hard or anguished feelings towards someone the particle وَيْلٌ always followed by a لِ is used in an indirect speech, e.g.

وَيْلٌ لِلْكَافِرين	**14-2** Woe unto disbelievers.
ويلٌ لِكُلِّ هُمَزَةٍ لُمَزَةٍ	**104-1** Woe unto every slanderer defomen.

In direct speech , the pronouns take place of ل as وَيْلَكَ woe to you , وَيْلِى woe to me , وَيْلَنَا woe to us , e. g. وَيْلَكَ ! أمِن woe to thee ! Believers !

Also وَيْكَ is used for the same purpose , e. g.

وَيْكَ أنَّ اللهَ يَبْسُطُ الرِّزْقَ	**28- 82** Ah ! Welladay ! Allah enlargeth the provision.
وَيْكَ أنَّه لا يُفْلِحِ الْكَافِرُونَ	**28-82** Ah , Welladay ! The disbelievers never prosper.

Besides the above ones , يَاوَيْلَتَىٰ (with fem. ending ة) and with' alif maqsura instead of ى of 1st person pronoun , is used for the same type of expressions e. g.

يَاوَيْلَتَىٰ ءَأَلِدُ وأنا عَجُوزٌ	**11 - 72** She said , Oh , Woe is me ! Shall I bear a child when I am an old woman.

Compassionate	الْمَرْحَمَةُ
Gift	هَدِيَّةٌ . عَطَاءٌ . عَطِيَّةٌ
Fallen - state	النُّزُولُ
Inspiration	إِلْهَام
Turned towards (man)	تَابَ على ...
OPt returning	التَّوَّابُ
Expulsion	الخُرُوج
Vicegrent	الخَلِيفَةَ
distinctive	المُمَيَّز
get down	النُّزُولُ
Guidance	الهُدَى - الهِدَايَةُ
Fear	الخَوف
To Grieve	الحُزْنُ

CHAPTER 30

SOME DIFFERENT TYPES OF THE VERB

1. **The verb** لَيْسَ **not to be** - Only perfect tense of this verb is heard. The conjugation would be as following:

Sing.		Dual	Plural
3rd Pers. Masc.	لَيْسَ	لَيسا	ليسوا
3rd Pers. Fem.	لَيْسَتْ	لَيْسَتَا	لَسْنَ
2nd Pers. Masc.	لَسْتَ	لَسْتُمَا	لستم
2nd Pers. Fem.	لَسْتِ		لَسْتُنَّ
1st Pers. Masc. & fem.	لَسْتُ		لَسْنَا

This verb takes its predicate in the accusative (مَنْصُوبٌ) e.g.

وَيَقُولُ الَّذِينَ كَفَرُوا : لَسْتَ مُرْسَلاً	**13-43** And those who disbelieve say: Thou art not a Messenger.

It is frequently used with بِ :

أَلَيسَ اللهُ بِأَحْكَمِ الحَاكِمِينَ	**95-8** Is not Allah the Best of the judges.

2. **The verb of praise and blaim** أفعال المدح والذَّمْ are represented by نِعْمَ and بِئْسَ . They are also like

ليس occur in the perfect, and have the meaning of imperfect. Moreover the only existing forms of this verb are of the 3rd person, as mase نِعْمَ fem. نِعْمَتْ e.g.

نعم زَيْدٌ	Zaid is good.
نعم زيدٌ مُعَلّماً	Zaid is good as a teacher.
نِعْمَتْ فاطِمةُ	Fatima is good.
نِعْمَتْ فاطمَةُ زَوْجَةً	Fatima is good as a wife.
بِئْسَ الْكَلْبُ هذا	The bad dog is this are. (this is a bad
بِئْسَتِ القِطَّةُ هذه	The bad cat is this are dog -cat etc.).

If second person is meant to be addressed by one of these verbs it will be used as:

نِعْمَ الصديقُ أنت	Really you are a good friend.
نِعْمتِ الأمُّ أنتِ	Really a good mother you are.

Examples from The Holy Qur'an:

نِعْمَ المولى ونِعْمَ النَّصير	**8-40** (He is) The best guardian and the best Helper.
ونِعْمَ أجْرُ العاملين	**3-136** the good reward of the workers.
لبئس المولى ولبئسَ العَشِير	**22-13** Certainly an evil guardian and an evil associate!

3. **The Verb ع asaa عَسىٰ**

This verb, which has no imperfect or any form except some of the perfect tense is used as a supporting verb and means: It may be, perhaps, It is very likely to be, or it is well hoped to. Therefore, it is followed by a sentence in the subjunctive introduction by أنْ the subject of which is also the subject of عسى :

عَسى أن يَبْعَثَكَ رَبُّكَ مقاما محموداً	**17-79** It may be, thy Lord will raise thee to a position of great glory.
عَسَىٰ أَلَّا أَكُونَ بِدُعَاءِ رَبِّى شَقِيًّا	**19-48** Maybe I shall not remain unblessed in calling upon my Lord.

This verb gives the sense of 'nearness', and in the rare instances in which it occurs in 1st or 2nd person it means: nearly as عَسَيْتُم أن تقولوا ذلك You are nearly saying that ....

4. **The verb of Wonder افعال التَعجُّب**

It is formed on the Measure of dervied form IV (i.e. with a prefixed Hamza) from an adjective:

From حَسَنٌ good أَحْسَنَ

طَيِّبٌ good أَطْيَبَ

كَرِيمٌ noble أَكْرَمُ

and used with a preceding ما , while the noun is put in accusative:

ما أحْسَنَ زيدًا	How good is Zaid	Note that the same pattern is used for Masc. Fem, Singular and Plural.
ما أحْسَنَ فاطِمَةَ	How good is Fatima	
ما أكْرَمَ الرجالَ	How noble are the men	
ما أطْيَبَ الْمعلّمَاتِ	How good are the teachers	

Examples from the Holy Qur'an:

قُتِلَ الإِنْسَانُ ، مَا أَكْفَرَهُ	**80-17** Man is (self) destroyed; how ungrateful!
فَمَا أَصْبَرَهُمْ على النَّارِ	**2-175** How constant are they in their strife to reach the fire!

A most beautiful form found in the Holy Qur'an is of Singular Masculine Imperative of Form IV, prefixed ب to be object (thing or person)

Examples from The Holy Qur'an:

أَبْصِرْ بِهِ وَأَسْمِعْ	**18-26** How clear of sight is He and keen of hearing!
أَسْمِعْ بِهِمْ وَأَبْصِرْ يَوْمَ يَأْتُونَنَا	**19-38** How clearly will they hear and see on the day when they come to me.

5. **The Verb ما زالَ and its sisters:**

Perfect	Imperfect Indicative	Accusative	Jussive
ما زَالَ or لا زَالَ	لا يزالُ	لن يَزَلَ	لم يزل
ما بَرِحَ	لا يَبْرَحُ	لن يَبْرَحَ	لَمْ يَبْرَحْ
ما فَتِئَ or فَتِئَ	لا يَفتَأُ يَفتَأُ	لن يفتأَ	لَمْ يفتأ

in the aut negative particle

These verbs mean that the action is still continuing, e.g.

مازال حَسَنٌ ذَاهِباً لم يزل يَذْهَبُ	Hasan is still going (Lit. did not cease to go)
ما بَرِحَ على عاملا لم يَبْرَحْ يَعْمَلُ	Ali still working
ما فَتِئَ حامدٌ ذاكراً يَفتَأُ - لا يَفتَأُ يَذْكُرُ	Hamid still remembers

Examples from The Holy Qur'an

فَمَا زَالَتْ تِلكَ دَعْوَاهُم حَتَّى جَعَلْنَاهُم حصيدًا خامِدِين	**21-15** And this cry of theirs ceased not till We made them cut off extinct.
فَلَنْ أَبْرَحَ الأرضَ حتى يأذنَ لى أبى	**12-80** So I shall not leave this land until my father permits me.

قالوا : تَاللهِ تَفتَؤُا تذكُرُ يُوسُفَ .	**12-85** They said: By Allah! Thou wilt not cease remembering Yusuf (Joseph)

6. The Verb كَادَ means: to be one the point of, but it is used to mean 'nearly' or 'almost' followed by the Imperfect indicative or occasionally, by أن plus the subjunctive:

كاد أن يَقتُلَ عَدُوَّهُ	He was nearly to kill his enemy
كِدْتُ أَقتُلُهُ	I was nearly to kill him.

when used in the negative, it means 'scarcely':

ما كاد يَنْظُرُ إليَّ	he scarcely looked at me.
لم يَكَدِ العَربُ يَعْرِفُونَ عَدُوَّهُمْ	The Arabs scarcely knew their enemy.

Examples from The Holy Qur'an:

وَإن كَادوا لَيَستَفِزُّونَكَ مِن الأرْضِ	**17-76** Surely they proposed to unsettle thee from the land.
لَقَد كِدتَّ تَركَنُ إليهِمْ	**17-74** Thou rightest have indeed inclined to them.
تكاد تَميَّزُ من الغيظِ	**67-8** Almost bursting for fury.
يَكَادُ زَيتُها يُضِيءُ ولو لَم تَمسَسْهُ نَارٌ	**24-35** The oil whereof gives light, though fire touches it not.
تَكَادُ السَّمَوَاتُ يَتَفطَّرْن منه	**19-90** The heavens may alomst be rent thereat.
وَلَا يَكَادُ يُسيغُهُ	**14-17** And he is not able to swallow it.

7. **The verb كان and its sisters**

As already dealt with in Chapters 5 & 9 the verb كَانَ to be takes a predicate in the accusative, e.g.

كان النّاسُ أُمّةً واحِدةً Men used to be one nation.

Certain other verbs termed its sisters كان وأخواتها do the same as لَيسَ not to be.

The following are the principle verbs of this group:

بَقَى	to remain
دامَ	to last
زَالَ	to cease
صَارَ	to become
IV أَصْبَحَ	to become
IV أَمْسَى	to become
باتَ ـ يَبِيت	to become

e.g. بَقَى الإسْلاَم دِينًا لِلْعَالمِينَ Islam remained as a religion for all the worlds.

وأصْبَحَ فؤادُ أُمِّ موسٰى فارغاً	**28-10** And the heart of Mother of Musaa (Moses) became free

8. **The Verb** صار to become أخذ to take, جَعَلَ to make or do or put also mean to begin if followed by a verb in the Imperfect.

صارَ الْمُسْلِمون يدخلون ...	Muslims begin to enter ..
أخذوا يُنَفِّذُونَ كتابَ اللهِ وَسنَّةَ رَسُولِهِ .	They started executing a Book of Allah and the tradition of His prophet.
جعلوا يَرْجِعُونَ إلى الدينِ ...	They started turning to the religion.
أخَذْنا نَتَعَلَّم لُغَةَ الْقرآن الكريم	we began to learn the language of the Holy Qur'an.

EXERCISE

A. Translate into Arabic:

" Muslims are brothers in religion ; and they must not oppress one another , nor abandon assisting each other , nor hold one another in contempt. The seat of righteousness is the heart ; therefore , that heart , which is righteous , does not hold a Muslim in contempt ; and it is wicked to hold a Muslim in contempt : and the things that are unlawful for a muslim res ar dinf to another : his blood , property and reputation ; he must not act or speak that by which the blood of a Muslim might be split , and his property destroyed ; and his reputation lost. The people for Paradise are three ; the first , a Just King , a doer of good to his people , endowed with virtue ; the second , an affectionate man , of a tender heart to relations and others ; the third , a virtuous man."

"The duties of Muslims to each other are six. " It was asked :

What are they, O Prophet? He said, " When you meet a Muslim salam to him; and when he invites you to dinner, accept it; and when he asks for advice, give it to him; and when he is sick visit him; and when he dies, follow his bier ".

B. Translate into English

١ ـ كُتِبَ عليكم القتال وَهُوَ كُرْهٌ لكم وَعَسَىٰ أن تَكْرَهُوا شيئاً وَهُوَ خيرٌ لكم وَعَسَىٰ أن تُحِبُّوا شَيئاً وَهُوَ شَرٌّ لَكمُ والله يَعْلَمُ وَأنتم لَا تَعْلَمُونَ

٢ ـ كُتِبَ عليكم القِصاصُ فى القتلى الحُرُّ بالحُرِّ والعَبْدُ بالْعَبْدِ والأُنثى بالأُنْثَى . فَمَنْ عُفِىَ له من أخيه شَىْءٌ فاتباع بالمعروف وأداءٌ إليه بإحسان . ذلك تخفيف من رَبِّكم وَرَحْمَة فَمَنِ اعْتَدى بعدَ ذلك فَلَهَ عَذابٌ أليم . وَلكم فى القِصاص حَيَاةٌ يا أولى الأَلْبَاب .

٣ ـ كُتِب عليكم ـ إذا حَضَرَ أحدكم الموتُ ـ (إن ترك خيراً) الوصِيةُ للوالدين ، وَالأَقْرَبِينَ بالمعروف . حقًّا على المتقين .

٤ ـ وَقَالَتِ اليَهُودُ ليستِ النصارى على شَىْءٍ وقالت النصارى ليست اليَهُودُ على شَىْءٍ وَهُمْ يَتْلُونَ الْكِتَاب .

٥ ـ كُتِبَ عَلَيكُمُ الصِّيَامُ . كَمَا كُتِبَ عَلَى الَّذِينَ مِنْ قَبْلِكُمْ . لَعَلَّكُم تَتَّقُونَ ..

C. State the measures of the following words:

القصاص ، القتلى ، الأنثى ، الإحسان ، تخفيف ، الوصيّة .

D. In the verse given in Chapter No. 4 for translation, state in وَهُمْ يتلون الكتاب what the (و) stands for.

E. Turn the following phrases from Plural to the singular and Vice versa

كتب عليكم . ليست النصارى على شَىْءٍ . ليست اليهودُ على شَىْءٍ .

وَهُم يتلون الكتاب . ولكم فى القصاص حياة .

F. It is assumed that by this stage a laborious student can start understanding the meaning of the Holy Qur'an. Now at the end of this book you are invited to examine your Arabic knowledge by yourself through rendering first 10 verses from the Surah 12, namely "Yousuf" (Joseph)

VOCABULARY

Brotherly	الأخَوِىُّ
Love	الحُبُّ الأخَوِىُّ – الحب Brotherly Love
Mutual Assistance	التعاون
Inculcate	يطبع ، يغرس فى الذهن
Emphatic	المُؤكَّد
Oppress	يظلم

One another	بعضهم بعضاً
Wicked	فظيع . شرٌّ
Contempt	الازدراء . التحقير
Righteous men	الصادقون
Unlawful	الْحَرَامُ
Blood	الدَّمُ pl. دِمَاء
Property	الأحوال
Endowed with the Virtue	مُلْتَزِم العِفَّة / المتَّصف بالفَضِيلة
Virtuous man	العَفِيفُ
Invite	يَدْعو
Dinner	عَشَاء (المأْدُبة)
Advice	يخبر / ينصح
Sick	المريض
Dies	يَموت
Bier	الجَنَازَةُ

كُتِبَ	has been written (Passive of كَتَبَ)
القِتَال	Fighting

كَرِهَ ـ يَكْرَهُ	To dislike
حَضَرَ	To arrive, to approach
خَيْرًا	(Acc.) Lit. good-but here is meant wealth.
الصِّيَام	Fasting
nom الوالدان	Acc gen الوالدين The Parents
الأَقْرَبِين	Relatives
المَعْرُوف	According to the tradition
حَقًّا	(Acc) duty bound
المُتَّقِين	God fearing people, Plural of مُتَّقِي duplicated radical Verb VII
القِصَاصُ	Retaliation
الحُرُّ	Free
الأُنْثَىٰ	Female
عُفِيَ لَهُ	Forgiven
اتِّبَاع	To follow
إحْسَان	Good manners
تَخْفِيف	Alleviation
أَلْبَاب	Plural of لُب Ethics

إيضاحات حول هذا الكتاب

١ ـ الآيات القرآنية التى استشهد بها لتطبيق القواعد فهى مرقمة برقمى السور والآيات حيث الرقم الأول لرقم السورة والثانى لرقم الآية .

٢ ـ لم يلتزم المؤلف بنقل الآية بكاملها فى كل مكان . بل أحيانًا يأتى بفقرة أو جملة تفيد الغرض . وهو « الشاهد » للقاعدة النحوية أو الصرفية .

٣ ـ عندما ذكرت الشواهد عن القرآن الكريم يذكر بوضوح «مثال من القرآن الكريم» .

Example from The Holy Qur'an:

٤ ـ فى التمارين تختلط الآيات بغيرها من الجمل المختارة ، وتفصلها الفواصل والأرقام حيث لم يلتزم فى التمارين أن تكون كلها من القرآن الكريم .

٥ ـ ترجمة الآيات القرآنية نقية صافية «روعيت فيها الصحة والدقة ومطابقة بما حواه تفسير الطبرى» .

كلمة شكر وتقدير

يطيب لى أن أذكر بالشكر والتقدير والاعتراف بالجميل اسم معالى الشيخ محمد صالح القزاز الأمين العام لرابطة العالم الإسلامى (سابقا) حيث عهد إلى فى رمضان عام ١٣٩٤ هـ أن أتولى اصدار مجلة رابطة العالم الإسلامى باللغة الانجليزية ، وكان من بين الأبواب الثابتة التى اخترتها للمجلة «تعلم لغة القرآن» Learn the language of the Holy Qur'an عنوانا لباب كنت أكتبه متواليا لاعدادها ، إلى ان انصرفت من الرابطة وانتظمت فى هيئة أعضاء التدريس بجامعة الملك عبد العزيز بمكة المكرمة ، ثم بدا لى أن أتناول هذه الدروس بالزيادة فى الإيضاح وجمع الشواهد من القرآن الكريم وأن أضيف إليها فصولا جديدة فكان هذا الكتاب .

ويسعدنى أن أشكر دار الشروق بالقاهرة لجهودها فى طبع هذا الكتاب والاهتمام الشخصى لصاحبها الأستاذ محمد المعلم فقد لقيت منه ومن الجهاز العامل فى مؤسسته كل عون وترحاب ، وإنى مدين بفضل أخى فى الله الأستاذ نذر الحفيظ الندوى لسهره على تصحيح البروفات ومتابعته المتواصلة لمراحل الطبع .

ويسرنى أن أتشكر الاخوة الذين ساعدونى فى التبييض ومراجعة المسودات وهم الاخوة الأساتذة : محمد أنس الندوى وأحمد الله خالد وأحمد ذى الشان ، تقبل الله منا ومنهم صالح الأعمال .

د . عبد الله عباس الندوى

نفسك (Teach yourself) ويرى أن اللغة كائن نام حي لا يمكن تلقيها إلا من كائن حي فالمدرس الخبير بالعربية لغة ونحواً وطريقة تعليم يستطيع وحده أن يرشد الطالب ويأخذ بيده إلى هدفه .

ومما يجدر بالذكر أن هذا النهج الذى اتبعته ليس من ابتداعى ، بل سبقنى إليه أستاذى فى تاريخ الحديث النبوى الشريف ، الأستاذ عبد السلام القدوائى مدير التعليم لجامعة ندوة العلماء بالهند ، فقد أجرى التجربة على عدد كبير من المثقفين من المشتغلين بالتجارة والوظائف الحكومية فثبت نجاح هذا المبدأ وشوهد الطلبة وقد قطعوا مسافات سنوات فى شهور .

أما الأمر الذى قمت به وهو أنى وَسَّعْتُ هذا المنهج ليشمل على أكثر القواعد النحوية المحتاجة إليها فى تلقى العربية ، واللغة التى اخترتها للتأليف هى الانجليزية لأن أغلبية من يريد تعلم العربية من غير العرب هم ممن ينطقون هذه اللغة أو تثقفوا بها فأصبحت الانجليزية لغة علم وفهم لديهم .

ويرجع الفضل فى إخراج هذا الكتاب إلى المربى الكبير الأستاذ محسن أحمد باروم مدير عام دار الشروق بجدة الذى تولى مشكوراً طبع هذا الكتاب ، مشكوراً فله منى أصدق الامتنان والعرفان بالجميل ، كما أنى مدين بالشكر للأستاذ محمد المعلم مدير عام دار الشروق بالقاهرة على ما بذله من جهد فى إتقان الطبع والصحة فى إخراج هذا الكتاب بالجودة والاتقان .

يسر الله أمورنا وهدانا السبيل وآخر دعوانا أن الحمد لله رب العالمين .

د . عبد الله عباس الندوى

مدرس بجامعة الملك عبد العزيز

مكة المكرمة

أى أن هذا الاستعمال قديم مهجور يوجد فى الشعر والقرآن ولا يقترح على الطالب اتباعه للاستعمال العام.

ومن الفقرات التى أتى بها المؤلفان لتطبيق القواعد كشواهد نجد على صفحة ٣٩٢ (طبع لندن عام ١٩٦٥).

«حسبت محمداً كذاباً»

«أخبرت حسناً محمداً كاذباً»

وإنى لم أعثر على كتاب ألفه أحد هؤلاء «الأعلام» إلا وفيه أمثال هذه الضغائن تجسدت فى كتاباتهم.

ومن المؤسف أن المثقفين من المسلمين ممن تعلموا الانجليزية لأنها كانت لغة المستعمرين فى بلدانهم إذا أرادوا تعلم العربية لم يجدوا أمامهم إلا ما كتبه هؤلاء الأساتذة المتحيزون، مما ترك وما يزال ـ فراغا يحتاج إلى أن يملأ من قِبَل المسلمين أنفسهم فكان هذا الشعور دافعاً إلى وضع هذا الكتاب الذى توخيت فيه:

١ ـ الاعتماد على شواهد من القرآن الكريم ليكون الطالب المسلم الذى يريد تعلم العربية لأجل الإسلام والقرآن منسجماً مع لغة القرآن الكريم منذ أول خطوة يخطوها نحو تلقى العربية، وللأمثال تأثير فى الفكر أقره علماء التربية ولا يختلف فيه اثنان!

٢ ـ تبسيط القواعد واختصار الطريقة حتى يستطيع كل من يتفرغ لساعة أو ساعتين من النهار أو الليل أن يدرس العربية فى مدة وجيزة.

٣ ـ جعل القرآن الكريم أداة لتعليم العربية وفتح المجال له للتوسع فى دراستها وإتقانها إلى أقصى حد ممكن.

ومما يجدر الإشارة إليه أن الكاتب لا يؤمن بالطريقة التى تدعو لتعلّم

القرآن الكريم مباشرة بدون وسائط الترجمات ـ سهل قولاً ، وصعب عملاً . فإن المسلمين منتشرون فى شرق الأرض وغربها . ولهم ما لغيرهم من مشاكل الحياة ومشاغل الكسب ومعالجة شئونهم المحلية فأنّى لهم أن يتفرغوا لتعليم العربية وقضاء عدة سنوات لدراسة هذه اللغة وقواعدها النحوية .

ومن أجل ذلك اتجه تفكيرى إلى وضع منهج يراعى فيه التبسيط والتيسير ويمكن تلقى العربية عن طريقه فى مدة وجيزة والبحث عن مثل هذا المنهج الذى يلائم عقول الطلاب الأجانب والمثقفين بثقافة انجليزية جعل الكاتب إلى أن يلقى نظرة على المناهج الموضوعة باللغة الانجليزية لتعليم العربية فوجد أصنافا من الكتب وضعت باللغة الانجليزية لهذا الغرض واطّلع على عدد كبير منها فوجد أن الأمر الذى يشترك فيه جميع المؤلفين هو أنهم يهدفون إلى تعليم أبناء بلادهم اللغة العربية لأغراض دبلوماسية سياسية وتجارية فكان تركيزهم على أساليب الصحف السيارة ولغات الأفلام والروايات كما لاحظ أن هؤلاء مع مقدرتهم العلمية لم ينجحوا فى إخفاء ما فى صدورهم من غل وحقد وكراهية للعرب والإسلام ، ففى ثنايا إيضاحهم القواعد وشرحهم لأصل من أصول اللغة يستعملون لغة تقنع الطالب أن اللغة العربية لغة عويصة معقدة تعتمد على الشذوذ أكثر من اعتمادها على الأصول . وإذا صادف أن ذكروا قاعدة تخص اللغة العربية الفصحى فقط نبهوا طلبتهم إلى عدم جدواها ومثال ذلك أن كتاب النحو العربى الجديد الذى ألفه هيود وناهمد (Hm nahmad و Ahay wood) عندما يذكر المفعول معه ويأتى بمثال له «سافر زيد وأخاه» يقول :

This usage is rather antique. it is found in poetry and the Quran. and is **not** recommended to the student for general use.

مقدمة

الحمد لله ولى النعم وسلام الله عى نبى خير الأمم سيدنا محمد وآله وصحبه أولى المكارم ومحاسن الشيم وبعد :

فقد عكف كاتب هذه السطور ردحاً من الزمن على دراسة ترجمات لمعانى القرآن الكريم إلى اللغة الانجليزية ومقارنة بعضها ببعض ، وقد انتهت به هذه الدراسة إلى أن الترجمات ـ مهما تحرّى أصحابها الدقة والإجادة ـ عاجزة عجزاً كلياً عن استيفاء المدلولات الكاملة لآى الذكر الحكيم فضلاً عن نقل ما فى كتاب الله من الروعة والجمال وما فيه من قوة التأثير فى القلوب والنفوذ إلى العقول كما تبين له أن القاصد إلى فهم كتاب الله العظيم من خلال ترجمة من الترجمات فى خطر ، فقد تعمّد المترجمون من غير المسلمين إلى تشويه جمال القرآن وتقويض دعائم الإسلام والتشفى لأحقادهم على المسلمين عن طريق ترجماتهم كما أن آخرين منهم أرادوا من القرآن الكريم أن يجعلوه مطيّة لبيان عقائدهم الشاذة وآرائهم التى ينفردون بها معارضين مما كان عليه السلف الصالح وما عليه جمهور المسلمين من أهل السنة والجماعة .

وليس مما يحل هذه المشكلة أن تضاف ترجمة أخرى إلى مجموعة ترجمات موجودة فإن طبيعة الترجمة تأبى أن تكون أمينة ومستوفية حيث أن كل لغة تمتاز فى صياغة ألفاظها وتراكيبها النحوية التى تلبس الكلمات حللاً فى المعانى والأساليب البيانية مما لا يمكن نقله إلى أية لغة أخرى على الإطلاق

فكان الحل الوحيد أن يُدعى المسلمون إلى تعليم هذه اللغة التى خصّها الله للوحى الصادق وهذا المطلب ـ أن يتعلم المسلمون العربية حتى يفهموا

بسم الله الرحمن الرحيم

ٱلْحَمْدُ لِلَّهِ ٱلَّذِى هَدَىٰنَا لِهَٰذَا وَمَا

كُنَّا لِنَهْتَدِىَ لَوْلَآ أَنْ هَدَىٰنَا ٱللَّهُ

[صدق الله العظيم]

تعلّم لغة القرآن الكريم

دكتور عبد الله عبّاس الندوي

كتاب بهون
١٧٨٤ - كلاں محل ، دریا گنج ، نئی دہلی ۱۱۰۰۰۲ (الهند)